CRISIS IN THE ACADEMY

Also by Christopher J. Lucas

American Higher Education: A History

CRISIS IN THE ACADEMY

RETHINKING HIGHER EDUCATION IN AMERICA

Christopher J. Lucas

St. Martin's Press
New York

CRISIS IN THE ACADEMY
Copyright © 1996 by Christopher J. Lucas

All rights reserved. Printed in the United States of America. No part of this book may be used or reproduced in any manner whatsoever without written permission except in the case of brief quotations embodied in critical articles or reviews. For information, address St. Martin's Press, Scholarly and Reference Division, 175 Fifth Avenue, New York, N.Y. 10010

ISBN 0-312-12936-X

Library of Congress Cataloging-in-Publication Data

Lucas, Christopher J.
    Crisis in the academy : rethinking American higher education / Christopher J. Lucas.
        p.   cm.
    Includes bibliographical references and index.
    ISBN 0-312-12936-X
    1. Education, Higher—United States—Aims and objectives.
    2. Education, Higher—Social aspects—United States.
    3. Universities and colleges—United States—Administration.
    I. Title.
LA227.4.L83 1996
378.73—dc20   95-33674
                                                      CIP

Book design by Acme Art, Inc.
First edition: August 1996
10 9 8 7 6 5 4 3 2 1

CONTENTS

Acknowledgements

Special thanks are owed to Clyde Iglinsky and John Murry for their comments, criticisms, suggestions, and help with source materials; to Martin Schoppmeyer and Karen Stauffacher who kindly consented to review and critique preliminary manuscripts drafts; to Sonja Bennett and Leanne Hoofnagle for clerical support; to Gary Shepard for technical assistance; and to Jennifer Farthing and Maura Burnett of St. Martin's Press. A special debt of gratitude is owed to Tim Brooker, without whose collaboration this project could not have been completed.

PREFACE

Public disillusionment with American education seems to have increased markedly in recent decades. Escalating costs and reports of declining academic achievement, together with the near collapse of anything resembling viable public schooling in the inner cities, have become staples of political debate, editorial commentary, and citizen protest.[1] Laments over the general decay of the nation's school system come laced with indictments of bloated and ineffectual educational bureaucracies out of touch with children's needs, of ill-prepared teachers, students who refuse to learn, decaying facilities and support resources, inadequate or inequitable funding—the list goes on.

The curriculum, it is claimed, is in shambles, the inevitable result (depending on a critic's ideological predilections) of too much or too little community oversight and control; of resistance to reform from obstructive teachers' unions or a puerile teacher-education establishment; of timorous or purblind textbook publishers; and of the centrifugal forces of a society increasingly splintered and divided against itself. Unable to sustain a consensus on what it wants from its educational system, so it is argued, the public remains locked in paralysis. All the while, children give birth to children, youngsters show up at school toting handguns, drug dealers ply their trade at recess, and gangs of pre-adolescent thugs terrorize the playgrounds. Out in suburbia and rural America, things are reportedly quieter, but it is a placidity born of nonachievement and intellectual drift. The litany of allegations in the last few years has been practically endless. Prescriptions for school reform vary, though they all tend to reflect a broad conviction that the present system shows unmistakable signs of decay.[2]

Yet until quite recently, with the exception of complaints over escalating tuition costs, higher education was spared the barrage of criticism directed at lower schools. No matter how harsh the accusations heard elsewhere, colleges and universities seemed almost immune from the cacophony of popular protest. There appeared no counterpart, for example, to *A Nation at Risk* leveled at colleges and universities, no searing indictment of higher education as a cataclysmic failure. Hence the presumption went unchallenged that all was well in academe. The United States could take pride in its world-class system of higher learning, the envy of the rest of the world.

Beginning in the mid-1980s, that comfortable assumption began to come under assault. Suddenly and quite unexpectedly, there erupted a whole succession of government reports, best-selling books, and articles critical of the nation's colleges and universities. Heated media debates ensued. At first, the near-hysterical hyperbole of the more intemperate critics was dismissed as exaggerated and overblown. As harsh exposés multiplied, however, it grew more and more difficult to resist the impression that higher education had indeed fallen into a state of "crisis."

Ever since college- and university-bashing seem to have become a favorite indoor sport, the modern equivalent of the anticlericalism so fashionable in the late eighteenth century.[3] It also has grown into something of a cottage industry, marked by the release of books and articles whose titles variously proclaim the "demise" of higher education; a "killing of the spirit" of higher learning; the political "corruption" of the academic enterprise by "tenured radicals"; the "moral collapse" of the university; a professorial "scam" perpetrated upon the American public by lazy and irresponsible college teachers; the "closing of the American mind" and a "betrayal" of democracy by an entrenched academic establishment; the elevation of "illiberal education" by assorted multiculturalists, radical feminists, and militant minorities; the "impoverishment" of the souls of today's college students; and so on. One book follows another with depressing regularity, each more strident and alarmist than its predecessor.

Quite unlike most of the staid analyses authored from time to time by academics, written chiefly for the benefit of peers within the community of scholars, the new apocalyptic manifestos rely heavily on shock value for effect. The fairest judgment seems to be that what they lack in balance or evenhandedness of treatment, they more than compensate for with rhetorical fervor and strength of conviction. And to a far greater extent than has been the case with the measured prose of university presidents and other academic leaders served up in the past, books critical of higher education since the 1980s have received a hearing far beyond the precincts of college campuses. The new literature of iconoclasm and dissent, it may be observed, is quite unlike anything seen since the heyday of campus protest and turmoil a third of a century or more ago.

Recent books and articles assailing American academe for its foibles betray no consistent ideological orientation or perspective. If anything, they operate from mutually exclusive presuppositions and assumptions. What these various jeremiads do share is a common belief, first, that things have gone seriously wrong within the groves of academe, and, second, that drastic measures are called for to redress matters. Above all, a sense of urgency about the need for reform is apparent. Whether the focus is on "political correctness," academic standards, minority access and affirmative action, equity issues related to gender or ethnicity, gay rights, escalating costs, sexual harassment, collegiate athletic scandals, disputes over tenure, funding problems, claims of curricular fragmentation and overspecialization, or internal governance, ax-grinding tends to proceed apace, accompanied by growing bewilderment, anger, and confusion, on the part of the general public.

Contemporary higher education probably is nowhere near the full-blown state of "crisis" some critics profess to have uncovered. Nevertheless, as the twentieth century draws to a close, most informed observers will concede that institutions of higher learning are in trouble. Behind the appearance of business-as-usual, deep divisions of opinion beset the academy. The main issues of contention are at once real and substantial. They range the gamut from questions about the alleged politicization of campus discourse and intellectual freedom, to controversies about external accreditation, cultural diversity, curricular reform, student admissions, professorial hiring and promotion practices, institutional accountability, and a host of other divisive issues.

Some of the problems that plague collegiate halls of ivy are genuinely new. But many are not. Most of the controversy, in fact, stems from features of the academic enterprise forever open to disagreement and disputation. What is novel, or at least feels new, is the degree of urgency forcing the professional community and the public in general to reappraise the academic system as a whole.

The academy's inveterate conservatism is at once a liability and a force for stability. Colleges and universities as institutions respond to external pressures only slowly, and usually only in ad hoc fashion. Academics tend to be a cautious lot, especially when changes called for by outsiders seem to strike at the center of things, as in matters of curricula. The story is told of Oxford dons in the nineteenth century who, when faced with demands for innovation, responded with stout opposition. "I can but fear the worst," reported a faculty member, "a majority of fourteen in convocation voted in favor of . . . modern history. We did indeed by a large majority reject the details of this novelty, but the principle has been admitted. . . . We have fallen into the weakness of yielding to the spirit of the age."[4]

Reluctance to accept "novelty" encourages institutions of higher learning to be adroit at co-opting critics, defusing controversy with bland reassurances that problems are under control, and otherwise trying to ride out the storm however best they can. The tacit goal always is to preserve the status quo, or, failing that, to modify it as little as possible. Rarely is the need for truly fundamental change of any sort acknowledged. The advantage, of course, is that to some extent colleges and universities are able to insulate themselves from dangerous trendiness. In deflecting the less well considered but importunate demands placed upon them by their diverse constituencies, they are better able to protect the integrity of what they are about and the ways in which they work to fulfill institutional goals and objectives.

Inverting the argument, some critics would claim that the more common response from institutions of higher learning has not been one of intransigence in the face of change but precisely the opposite: that nowadays at least they demonstrate all too clearly their willingness to yield to "the spirit of the age." What recent history shows is nothing so much as a record of their having embraced popular pressures with alacrity, however ill-considered or unprincipled. Lacking any coherent vision of their own identities as academic institutions, colleges and universities hasten to become and to do whatever the public professes to want from them. From this perspective, the real problem is not lack of responsiveness to the imperatives for change. Quite the opposite, it is one of too much responsiveness and of too many changes made that, in the final analysis, do violence to fundamental academic principles and values.

On balance, until one descends to specifics, it is virtually impossible to assess in any meaningful way the allegation that the overall condition of American higher education at the end of the twentieth century is crisis-ridden. That *some* parts or aspects of the contemporary college or university show signs of crisis is undoubted—the state of undergraduate learning in the modern multiversity affords a major case in point. Whether *all* the constitutive elements or components of all, or even of most, institutions of higher learning in America are so afflicted is quite another matter.

Academe, such as it is, with all of its serious defects and shortcomings, exhibits remarkable resilience and flexibility where it matters. Millions of young people have enrolled in the nation's colleges and universities in decades past, and they continue to do so in record numbers today. By and large, most—though not nearly enough—of today's collegians are well served by the education they receive. For good or for ill, preparatory training for a range of specialized occupations unimaginable a scant few years ago is currently offered, and at a level of sophistication and complexity that is virtually without historical precedent. The work of scholarship continues on a grand scale; and in the laboratories and clinics of leading institutions across the country, cutting-edge research in dozens of different disciplines advances on a scale never before attempted.

Whether all this energy and dynamism can be maintained indefinitely remains to be seen. Probably it cannot. But to imply, as a handful of zealous critics have done in recent years, that the nation's entire system of higher learning is so irremediably flawed that it totters on the verge of disintegration and must inevitably collapse of its own weight seems at once woefully unrealistic and unduly pessimistic. More likely by far is the short-range prospect that higher education will continue on in future much as it has done in years past, albeit (thanks in part to emerging new technologies) perhaps assuming forms one can now only dimly imagine.

At the approach of a new millennium, it seems an opportune time to take stock, to reassess the general condition of American colleges and universities in light of the recent past. The present work represents one modest effort to contribute to this task of thinking things through afresh. Some of the issues treated are philosophical, at least in the rough-and-ready sense that they extend well beyond matters of empirical fact to encompass normative judgment and critical analysis. A necessarily cursory overview, a bird's-eye view of the higher education landscape, serves to open the discussion. Succeeding chapters address questions having to do with basic institutional purposes and aims, access to colleges and universities, the shape or structure of the undergraduate curriculum, faculty priorities, and, finally, imperatives arising from a rising tide of demands for greater accountability in academe.

Briefly, it is argued, first, that American higher education is so diverse and varied in character that most sweeping generalizations about its overall condition are practically meaningless. At the risk of reiterating what should be obvious, it still needs to be observed that current circumstances differ from institution to institution and by type. What may hold true of private liberal arts colleges does not necessarily apply to graduate, research-focused universities, and vice versa. Two-year community colleges are very different academic institutions from most four-year schools. Conditions obtaining in Ivy League schools do not always much resemble those within large public state universities, and so on. Localism plays a part as well. What might be true of West Coast public institutions might not apply to midwestern state universities, and still less to schools ranged along the Atlantic seaboard. This is not to claim that no general conclusions whatsoever may be drawn, but, simply, that rethinking what is happening on the nation's campuses today requires, at a minimum, that the analysis take into account the specific sort of institutions under scrutiny.

Second, if there is a true crisis in American higher education today, it is chiefly a crisis of purpose within the university. The hegemony of the multiversity as a regulative idea is well-nigh complete, but its preeminence does not seem to have come about as the outcome of principled decisions or any discernible process of rational choice. On the contrary, it appears to have been the inevitable result of an academic system seeking to garner popular support by attempting in most times and places to be all things to all people. In the process, a single model of the university as a multipurpose institution dedicated simultaneously to teaching, research, and service has gained the ascendancy. Its predicament at this historic juncture, it must be observed, is not unlike the juggler balancing too many objects in midair. The spectacle is awe-inspiring, vastly entertaining even. But whether and for how long it can be sustained seem open to serious question.

Third, a brief attempt is made to present the case for a quite unfashionable view, namely, that the United States in recent decades has overbuilt and overinvested in higher education. Oversubscription occurred in the early nineteenth century, and in the second half of the twentieth century it has happened again. Quite bluntly, the American effort to construct a system of mass postsecondary education unlike anything found elsewhere in the world must be reckoned a mixed success at best. Though many will deny it vehemently, near-universal access to what passes today for higher learning has contributed to a real and tangible decline in both academic expectations and scholastic attainment. Program offerings on most campuses have degenerated to the point where they amount to little more than vehicles for professional credentialing, serving purposes largely extraneous to the academic enterprise itself.

Fourth, it is argued that whatever else they may be, institutions of higher learning first and foremost must once again become agencies of student instruction. Universities in particular must honor undergraduate teaching as a major responsibility, after the fashion of most of the nation's better colleges. Whatever other involvements they may pursue, no matter how far-flung their ancillary enterprises (ranging from research to public service to mass entertainment), colleges and universities alike have an obligation to put teaching first. Failing this, sooner or later they must inevitably lose whatever measure of popular support they currently enjoy. To dismiss complaints over the neglect of teaching as "sophomoric—and intended to play out at about that level," as some critics have done, is to court disaster.

Fifth, today's professoriate has a professional obligation to struggle anew with the age-old problem of restoring greater coherence and intelligibility within a common undergraduate curriculum. Never before has the challenge been so difficult—or so urgent. In an era marked by proliferating information—sometimes dubbed quite incorrectly a "knowledge explosion"—the task of framing a contemporary response to Herbert Spencer's query about what knowledge is of greatest worth is still worth engaging. Different institutions may settle upon different answers and employ differing means to achieve the goal. But the principle that students should share some knowledge in common, and that underlying an almost infinite array of alternatives something akin to "core learning" can be preserved, is a prospect still deserving intense reconsideration. Unfortunately, faculty priorities today do not much encourage the careful thinking and arduous effort that must go into restoring an integrative undergraduate curriculum. Some of the factors responsible are briefly explored.

Finally, institutions of higher learning must learn how best to respond to public demands for accountability. Simplistic formulas and cookbook recipes (what critics contemptuously and rightly refer to as "bean-counting") will not suffice. Today's accountability movement is not apt to disappear conveniently any time soon. But only when institutions are clear as to what they are about can they frame meaningful responses about their performance, *and only at whatever level of precision and exactitude the questions posed allow.* At root, issues of accountability speak not only to matters of procedure or technique, but to basic intellectual purposes and goals.

The following interpretation is aimed at a rather broad audience: academic administrators and college trustees, public policymakers and other stake-holders, state legislators with an interest in higher education, members of the professoriate concerned about the larger context in which they work, students of higher education as a field of inquiry in its own right, parents and families of students attending college, the literate public at large. Given the scope of higher education in America as a general topic, the coverage of issues is neither compendious nor exhaustive. The aim instead is to focus on a select few of the major dimensions of colleges and universities as institutions and the policy framework within which they function.

The exposition throughout does not purport to offer a purely "objective" or neutral analysis of its subject matter. It is inevitably written from a particular point of view; and every effort has been made to make that view explicit. The ultimate test of any particular analysis or interpretation set forth is whether it is constructive and adequate to its aim, that is, whether it serves to provoke critical reflection and further analysis on the part of others. Here as always, the final verdict in this respect must rest with the hearts and minds of readers.

I.

AMERICAN ACADEME: AN OVERVIEW

PATTERNS IN THE MOSAIC

The American system of higher education is not, strictly speaking, a true "system" in the usual sense of the term. That is, higher learning in the United States as a whole exhibits little of the structural logic, integration, or rational articulation of parts characteristic of a formal social system. Rather, the appearance it presents is one of a vast, untidy array of academic institutions, of widely different types and sizes, engaged in the pursuit of what often seem to be quite disparate goals. No succinct characterization can thus do full justice to the scope and breadth of postsecondary education throughout the nation. Seemingly chaotic, often bewildering in its variety and diversity, the country's institutionalized higher learning lends itself neither to sweeping generalizations nor to simple description. In the final analysis, it is a complex, multifaceted, and profoundly paradoxical phenomenon. To resort to a somewhat hackneyed metaphor, higher education in America suggests an elaborate mosaic, though one whose pieces reveal few predominating patterns.

Institutional aims or objectives and basic priorities are apt to differ tremendously from one American college or university to another. As observers are prone to remark, collegiate goals and functions often appear to overlap or even to stand in contradiction to one another. Linkages or connections between institutions, where they exist at all, seem fragmentary and incomplete. What colleges and universities offer by way of instruction and courses of study, the ways in which their curricula are organized, the particular constituencies they seek to serve, and the specific purposes and values to which they bend their efforts vary markedly from institution to institution. In "ecological" terms, it might be observed, each seeks to identify its own separate "niche" in the larger scheme of things and thereby thrive within it.

Some two-year schools sponsor an associate arts degree within a fairly specific range of academic specialties or applied fields. Examples of the latter might include accounting, business practices and office machines, optometric technology, dental hygienics, paramedical or paralegal training, restaurant management, and so on. Many community colleges define themselves as so-called terminal institutions catering to the needs of students who do not aspire to earn four-year academic credentials. Their emphasis is heavily vocational or professional; and they measure success by the degree to which their graduates secure employment. Other two-year schools regard themselves primarily as "feeder" institutions providing an academic foundation for subsequent study pursued elsewhere toward a bachelor's degree. Still other community colleges try to fulfill both functions simultaneously, though the balance between them differs, depending on the individual institution.[1]

Again, many colleges confer a four-year baccalaureate degree in one or another of the traditional liberal arts disciplines—in history, literature, foreign languages, psychology, geography, biology, and so on. Others also offer graduate-level professional training in a broad array of fields up through the master's level. Still others sponsor a comprehensive array of degree programs, ranging from a two-year certificate up to and including the doctorate in multiple specializations. Some colleges attract applicants on the basis of a particular specialization or field of study for which they have become especially well known. (Alfred University in New York, for instance, has long enjoyed repute as a center for the study of ceramic engineering. The University of Missouri and Columbia University, respectively, both have well-known journalism programs.) A school's reputation may come to depend chiefly on the excellence of the one or two programs to which it gives particular emphasis.

Special-purpose colleges or schools catering to a particular ethnic clientele are by no means unknown. But neither are they common. Historically, for example, in the United States there have been few Hispanic or Latino institutions of higher learning. In recent years, however, a handful have attracted enrollments consisting predominantly of Hispanics. Tribal colleges catering to the unique needs of Native

Americans similarly have been few in number. Black colleges are more numerous. For decades they have played a prominent role in offering minority students opportunities for higher learning. By 1990, for instance, the nation's three dozen or so public Black colleges claimed a total enrollment of over 140,000, or roughly one-fifth of all African Americans attending college, and about 60 percent of all those attending all predominantly Black institutions, public and private combined.

Certain institutions deliberately articulate their curricula with marketplace career opportunities, perhaps in medical administration or hotel management or the tourism industry. Others minimize the importance of occupational relevance and implicitly dismiss their more vocationally oriented competitors as "mere trade schools." Among the more prestigious universities, grantsmanship and research activity characteristically rank as compelling institutional priorities. For others, attention paid to undergraduate instruction and individualized student mentoring are of paramount concern, sometimes to the virtual exclusion of all else.

A growing number of colleges and universities pride themselves on their open admission policies. Basically, they accept virtually anyone who applies. Others in varying degree impose selective admission policies, restricting their enrollments according to whatever particular criteria they regard as appropriate. Some—a very few—employ highly competitive admission standards. In effect, they withhold admittance to all but the best and brightest applicants. Certain colleges and universities can thus be said to have assumed a "populist" or egalitarian stance with respect to admission. Practically anyone minimally qualified is afforded at least an opportunity to succeed. Some go farther in deliberately recruiting "high-risk" students, those handicapped by inferior preparation yet who are presumed to have the potential to succeed in college. Still others schools, for reasons they deem cogent, intentionally limit the number of those accepted for enrollment. They are unabashedly "elitist" in determining who shall even be considered. In the case of public institutions, some are mandated by legislative fiat or a state regulatory agency to keep admissions as open as possible. Contrariwise, the faculties or governing boards of curators, regents, or trustees at certain private colleges impose stringent admission criteria in the interest of safeguarding high academic quality.

Something of the increasing popularity of open admission policies, especially within the public sector, is suggested by the fact that throughout the 1930s and early 1940s, most students accepted into college had placed in the upper third to upper fourth of their high school graduating classes. By the late 1980s, it was variously estimated that perhaps almost half of all students accepted for admission into a college or university ranked well below the top third, with an ever-increasing percentage drawn from the bottom half of their respective high school rankings. Of course, the typical student's options in choosing a college to attend still depend largely on ability to pay. Despite occasional claims to the contrary, lack of financial means as an impediment to college choice remains an economic fact of life for many. Regardless of tuition waivers, scholarships, low-interest loans, or other forms of aid to those meeting certain eligibility criteria, prospective applicants are apt to find they are limited almost as much by financial considerations as they are by any shortcoming in prior academic achievement or scholastic aptitude.

Public institutions tend to be least costly. Some private schools, the more prestigious among them at any rate, have been obliged to price themselves far beyond the means of a majority of potential applicants. Throughout the 1990s, in fact, as college tuition rose faster than the rate of inflation, and with tuition increases routinely ranging from 7 to 15 percent or higher annually, more and more students were compelled to turn to public colleges and universities as the only affordable alternatives.

Economic considerations undoubtedly have had much to do with another common pattern of the 1990s: the increasing length of time needed to satisfy the requirements for the baccalaureate degree. Whereas at the century's midpoint the overwhelming majority of all collegians who were candidates for a bachelor's degree completed their programs within the traditional four-year span, the completion rate dropped precipitously during the last two decades of the twentieth century. Rising costs associated with the pursuit of the degree, expanded degree requirements themselves, and college students' need to hold down part-time or even full-time jobs while pursuing their studies were undoubtedly all factors contributing to the lengthening of the time required for completion. The presence on campus of more and more part-time students with families and careers already underway has helped accentuate the trend toward longer college careers. It used to be said of the bachelor's degree that there was little agreement as to its structure, content, or purpose, but unanimity of opinion that completing it ought to require about four years. Now even that truism seems outdated.

Certain venerable institutions of higher learning in America are well established, with histories extending back almost three centuries.

Others are brash newcomers, raw and as yet unformed, still struggling to find their own place and identity in a competitive academic world. A handful or so, chiefly Ivy League colleges and universities (Harvard, Princeton, Yale, and Dartmouth, along with other distinguished institutions such as Stanford, Brown, and William and Mary), command worldwide prestige and respect for their traditions of academic excellence. Dozens of others (mostly large, public-assisted state universities) in recent decades have achieved almost the same level of eminence at the national level.

At the opposite end of the spectrum are found those few schools hard-pressed to meet even minimal accreditation standards, institutions whose reputations for scholastic integrity are—to put it kindly—suspect at best. The most notorious among them amount to little more than diploma mills. Their chief stock-in-trade is a credential of dubious academic legitimacy, readily bartered for cash, with little regard paid to actual scholastic achievement. And in the broad pecking order between the two extremes stand the vast majority of American colleges and universities, each of them vying with one other for students, resources, status, and competitive advantage or market position.

American colleges and universities range in size from gargantuan to minuscule. Some academic institutions are huge as gauged by enrollments and facilities. Their great sprawling campuses extend for hundreds of acres; and they are apt to be thronged with students numbering in the thousands. Operating budgets of the leading multiversities run into the millions annually. Other colleges, more than a handful, are comparatively small. Dwarfed by the giants that dominate the academic landscape, many of these little schools operate on little more than a shoestring, and their student enrollments typically amount to no more than a few hundred at a time. Given their dependence on tuition revenues, even a slight decline in enrollment can spell the difference between solvency and acute financial exigency. To all intents and purposes, they operate at the periphery or margins of the academic mainstream.

Mention also must be made of those small institutions with impeccable credentials, colleges whose endowments are quite substantial despite the modest size of their faculty body and student enrollment. They have deliberately chosen to preserve their academic quality by remaining small and cohesive. Yet for all their limitations and restrictions, they do offer their students a first-rate academic experience. At one extreme are to be found such institutions as Trinity

College in Vermont or Ursuline College of Ohio, whose respective enrollments fall under 700, less than the student population typically found in a large suburban or metropolitan high school. At the other end of the spectrum loom the true mega-universities: the University of Texas at Austin, with a student enrollment of about 50,000; two-year Miami-Dade Community College in Florida, with almost 52,000 students in attendance; Ohio State University, whose main campus alone accommodates upward of 53,000 collegians; or the University of Minnesota–Twin Cities, which currently lists a student enrollment total exceeding 54,000. Complicating matters still further are those institutions with identifiable main campuses, but around which are clustered satellite campuses and extension or continuing education centers, each with its own separate student enrollment. Off-campus centers and "colleges without walls" operating so-called external degree programs serve to complicate the pattern even further.

Institutions of advanced learning are categorized either as agencies of the state or as private corporations. Even academic institutions classified as public, however, tend to depend heavily on private endowments to sustain their operations. Likewise, institutions ostensibly free of public oversight and lacking state assistance are classified as private, notwithstanding the fact that many of their students receive scholarships, grants-in-aid, or loans funded wholly or in part through the public treasury, without which many schools could not survive. Oversimplifying somewhat, it seems fair to observe that in "real-world" terms most institutions rely on an indeterminate combination of public and private funding. Some types of support are received directly (in the form of tuition, gifts, endowments, research and development grants). Other monies are garnered indirectly (through supplementary funding, grants-in-aid, scholarships, student loan programs, and so on).[2]

More than a few public institutions originated strictly as local or regional enterprises but were later assimilated within a coordinated statewide administrative system. Many of them began life as normal academies devoted to teacher training and subsequently evolved into teachers' colleges under public auspices. From the 1950s onward, most such colleges strove to downplay their specialized identification with teacher preparation. The preferred and more prestigious strategy was for a teachers' college to claim identity as a multipurpose institution; to divest itself of its regional character as much as possible; and, finally, to seek authorization to transform itself from a college into a university, in name if not always in substance. Parenthetically, to be branded a "teacher training" institution today practically amounts to an epithet of disapprobation in higher education. Institutions that have sought to retain their identity as teacher-preparation institutions first and foremost, and continue to take pride in their historic mission, probably can be counted on the fingers of a single hand. George Peabody in Tennessee, Ball State in Ohio, and Teachers College, Columbia University, immediately come to mind as examples.

Virtually all public colleges and universities are avowedly secular in character. That is, their implicit posture is one of neutrality and nonpartisanship in matters of spirituality, personal morality, and religious conviction—or the lack thereof. Many private institutions are secular as well. Others were founded as agencies of sectarian groups, pledged to safeguard the purity of faith and discipline of the sponsoring denomination. In some cases a school's linkage with a particular founding body over the years has grown purely nominal. In other instances the association still remains intimate, controlling, and authoritative.

The contrast between denominational and nonsectarian institutions is apt to be striking. Secular institutions hold to strict neutrality and noninvolvement in matters of religious conviction. Their posture toward students' personal beliefs and extra-academic conduct is, for want of a better phrase, one of principled noninterference. Some church-related schools, on the other hand, are true bastions of sectarian orthodoxy; and they seek to buttress their authority with compulsory chapel attendance, close supervision of students' extracurricular activities, and mandatory codes of conduct regulating life outside the classroom. Hence, at one pole are institutions of higher learning for which religiously inspired concerns and interests are seemingly peripheral or nonexistent. At the other repose schools whose very *raison d'être* is religious and spiritual through and through.[3]

American colleges and universities differ from one another in countless other ways, with endless permutations and combinations the rule rather than the exception. Some schools are heavily invested in intercollegiate athletics and owe their reputations more to gridiron prowess or success on the basketball court than to any particular academic distinction. Others support only a modest program of intercollegiate athletics, if at all. Some are situated in the heart of an urban center. City colleges by and large depend almost completely on commuter students to fill their programs. Many of the nation's residential liberal arts colleges, on the other hand, are tucked away in bucolic rural settings far removed from the city's bright lights and presumed distractions.

CLASSIFYING TYPES OF INSTITUTIONS

The American Association of University Professors (AAUP) currently utilizes a five-category system to classify different types of colleges and universities. Category I (doctoral-level institutions) includes schools marked by a "significant" level and breadth of activity involving doctoral-level education, as measured by the number of doctorate recipients and diversity in doctoral-level program offerings. Included in this category are those institutions that grant a minimum of thirty doctoral-level degrees annually. It is stipulated that these degrees must be granted in three or more unrelated disciplines.

To Category IIA (comprehensive institutions) are assigned schools offering postbaccalaureate programs but granting fewer than thirty doctoral-level degrees annually. Schools in this category offer an interdisciplinary postbaccalaureate degree program or grant a minimum of thirty postbaccalaureate degrees yearly.

Category IIB (general baccalaureate) institutions, according to the AAUP system, are grouped on the basis of their primary emphasis on general undergraduate baccalaureate-level education. These institutions are not significantly involved in postbaccalaureate instruction (fewer than thirty graduate-level degrees granted annually) and offer postbachelor's degrees in three or fewer program areas.

Category III (two-year institutions without academic ranks) is reserved for schools conferring three-quarters or more of their degrees below the baccalaureate level.

Category IV (institutions without academic ranks) supplies a rubric mostly for two-year colleges lacking academic ranks, though it may include a few general baccalaureate institutions as well.

The most recent revision of the classification system put forth by the Carnegie Foundation for the Advancement of Teaching, on the other hand, utilizes nine separate categories for classifying postsecondary institutions. "Research universities" are assigned to one of two categories, depending on the amount of federal support they receive annually. Otherwise both groupings consist of research-oriented institutions offering a full range of degrees up through the doctorate (awarding fifty or more doctoral degrees each year).

The "Doctoral Universities I" category is reserved for institutions awarding at least forty doctorates annually in five or more disciplines. Schools assigned to the category of "Doctoral Universities II" award annually at least ten doctoral degrees in three or more disciplines or twenty or more doctoral degrees in one or more disciplines.

The fifth and sixth categories in the Carnegie classification system are designated "Master's (Comprehensive) Universities and Colleges" I and II, respectively. The first group consists of schools awarding 40 or more master's degrees annually in three or more disciplines. Assignment to the latter category requires that a member institution award twenty or more master's degrees annually in one or more disciplines.

"Baccalaureate (Liberal Arts) Colleges" I and II identify primarily undergraduate colleges with a major emphasis on baccalaureate degree programs. Category I schools are selective in admissions and award forty percent or more of their bachelor's degrees in liberal arts fields. Category II colleges are less selective in their admissions or award less than 40 percent of their baccalaureate degrees in liberal arts fields.

"Associates of Arts Colleges" consist of those institutions offering associate-of-arts certificates or degree programs and, with few exceptions, no baccalaureate degrees. A final category, "Professional Schools and Specialized Institutions," serves as a catchall for theological seminaries; Bible colleges emphasizing training of the clergy; free-standing health profession schools; separate schools of engineering and technology; schools of business and management; independent schools of art, music, design, or law; teachers' colleges; maritime academies; military institutes; tribal colleges; and other institutions that do not fit any other classification category.

EXPLOSIVE GROWTH

At its inception, higher learning in America was an exceedingly modest affair. During the colonial era, only a handful of institutions of higher learning existed, none of whose enrollments exceeded a few hundred students at any given time. They very much resembled one another in character and function, each struck off the same original English model, and all catered to men only. Their numbers included tiny Harvard (founded in 1636); Yale (chartered in 1701 as the Collegiate School at New Haven); William and Mary (founded in 1693); the College of Philadelphia (founded in 1740 and later renamed the University of Pennsylvania); the College of New Jersey (founded in 1746 and subsequently christened Princeton College); King's College (founded in 1754 and later renamed Columbia University); the College of Rhode Island (founded in 1764 and later renamed Brown); Queen's College (founded in 1766 and renamed Rutgers College); and Dartmouth College (founded in 1769). Each was an independent entity governed by its own supervisory board.

Over the course of the whole seventeenth century, less than 600 men attended Harvard, of whom no more than 465 were graduated. Similar trends prevailed elsewhere. Yale had a total of 36 students in 1710; enrollment reached a peak of 338 in the year 1770. Harvard had 170 students attending in 1710 and 413 in 1770. Its largest pre-Revolutionary graduating class (1771) numbered no more than 63 matriculants. Overall, probably no more than one in every thousand male colonists attended any of the colleges in operation prior to 1776, and fewer still graduated with academic degrees.

Nor did the percentage of the population attending college begin to increase significantly until well into the antebellum period of the nineteenth century. No fewer than nineteen new colleges were established between 1782 and 1802, more than twice as many as had been chartered in the preceding century and a half. Most were sectarian denominational institutions. Almost as many were semipublic enterprises born of local pride and boosterism. On the eve of the Civil War, the total had jumped to 250. Many of these schools proved to be short-lived, however, and of those that managed to survive and remain viable, very few were ever able to attract large number of applicants. The typical American college of the 1800s tended to number its students by the dozens, not in the hundreds. As one measure of the scale involved, it is estimated that even at the close of the nineteenth century, fewer than 3 percent of the nation's population had ever attended college, much less earned a bachelor's degree.

Nevertheless, near-exponential growth in the numbers of students attending college *has* been the dominant and continuing overall trend throughout the last century or so, as has the increase in the percentage of the total population, men and women alike, attending an institution of postsecondary learning.[4] In the 130 years between 1840 and 1970, for example, college enrollments rose 417 times, as compared with a population increase of 12 times. Most of that growth took place after 1900. From 1872 to 1898, the largest increase relative to population was in graduate enrollment, which increased 14 times, compared with a gain of little more than one time for undergraduates.[5] Fewer than 1.5 million students were enrolled in college during the academic year 1939-40. Sixty years later, enrollments exceeded 14 million and were still rising.

Coincident with monumental growth in student enrollments, of course, have been equally dramatic increases in financial expenditures, both public and private, in support of American higher learning. While reliable figures are difficult to obtain for some earlier periods, current-fund expenditures in institutions of higher education have doubled several times over in the past half century. Between 1977-78 and 1989-90, to cite a case in point, expenditures rose 44 percent: 38 percent in public institutions and 58 percent in private schools, reaching $92 billion and $53 billion respectively. A further 47 percent increase was projected for the period from 1989-90 to 2002-2003.[6] Judged by almost any measure or standard, higher education has grown to the point where it constitutes a fiscal enterprise of considerable proportions. When the regular operating revenues of thousands of colleges and universities are added to local, state, and federal revenues allocated for university-based research and development, student aid, and capital expansion, the total amount of monies currently expended on behalf of higher learning becomes even more impressive, exceeding an estimated $150 to $175 billion, depending on how costs are assigned.

A rise in the number of academic degrees conferred at various points in the past likewise helps illustrate higher education's record of expansion and growth over time. At the end of the 1899-1900 academic year, institutions of higher education collectively awarded a total of about 29,000 degrees; for the 1949-50 academic year, the comparable figure had risen to nearly half a million. Between 1977-78 and 1990-91, the number of bachelor's degrees awarded increased from 921,000 to about 1.1 million yearly; and the total was projected to exceed 1.3 million by the year 2003.[7]

The number of master's degrees granted showed an equally dramatic rise, from 284,000 conferred in 1983-84 to 352,838 in 1993-94, with a projected yearly total of 365,000 by 2003. Similarly, whereas 32,000 doctoral degrees were granted in 1977-78, the number had risen to 40,659 by 1994; and the total was expected to increase to almost 42,000 shortly after the turn of the century.[8] In 1986, all schools combined were awarding annually about three and a half times the number of degrees conferred in the late 1940s.

Throughout the first half of the twentieth century, numbers of students in higher education roughly doubled every fifteen years or so, as did the number of faculty employed in colleges and universities. Graduate education grew even faster, with the number of earned doctoral degrees doubling every eleven years.[9] More specifically, combined student enrollments increased 49 percent between 1900 and 1910; 68 percent between 1910 and 1920; 84 percent between 1920 and 1930; 36 percent between 1930 and 1940; 78 percent between 1940 and 1950; 31 percent between the century's midpoint and 1960; 120 percent during the "baby boom" years of the 1970s; 45 percent between 1970 and 1980; 17 percent between 1980 and 1990; and a projected 13 percent between 1990 and the end of the century.[10]

Enrollment increases could hardly have occurred to the extent they did from the mid-1800s onward had there not been correspondingly massive growth in the number of colleges and universities established. Something of the scale of that growth is highlighted by the fact that in 1875 or thereabouts, there were no more than about 300 institutions of higher learning in the entire country, most of them quite small as judged by today's norms. Their numbers were augmented rather quickly in the opening years of the century following, reaching a total of no less than 1,600 on the eve of America's entry into World War II. Since then the total number of postsecondary institutions has more than doubled. Hence, within scarcely more than two generations, the nation has witnessed a proliferation of two-year community colleges, four-year colleges, and universities virtually without historical precedent anywhere else in the world. Slightly over half of the American colleges and universities operating in the 1990s did not even exist fifty or sixty years earlier—which is to say, about 2,000 new collegiate institutions have appeared on the scene since 1945.

According to census tallies offered in the last decade of the twentieth century, there were no fewer than 3,638 accredited American colleges and universities operating in the mid-1990s. The total included 1,024 two-year public colleges, about 510 public-sector four-year schools, and 94 public universities, or some 1,628 in all. Likewise contributing to the total were 445 two-year private community colleges, 1,507 private four-year colleges, and 62 private universities, for a subtotal of 2,014 institutions. As of 1996, there were 6.2 million students enrolled in four-year public institutions and roughly 2.9 million in private four-year schools, making for a combined enrollment of just over 9.2 million.

Two-year public institutions in 1996 claimed a combined student enrollment of just over 5.5 million, and private two-year schools a student population of between 237,732 and 277,000, for a shared total of just over 5.5 million. By way of contrast, in 1940-41 no more than 100,000 students were attending junior or community colleges, which numbered a few hundred at most. By the early 1970s, more than a thousand such colleges had opened their doors. Enrollment thereafter grew fivefold within a single decade. By almost any measure, a projected total of almost 6 million students attending over 1,450 two-year schools by the end of the century is especially noteworthy.

About 10.2 million undergraduates were attending public colleges and universities at the midpoint of the 1990s, whereas 2.8 million were in private institutions, a combined total of over 13 million. Out of a total of 1.8 million graduate students, 650,000 were reported enrolled in private schools, while those remaining, just under 1.2 million, were in public universities. An estimated 8.2 million students in 1996 were enrolled full time; and their numbers were expected to increase to 8.9 million by the year 2000. Some 6.5 million were part-time students; and their ranks were projected to increase to a total of over 6.7 million by the turn of the century.

DEMOGRAPHIC SHIFTS

Whereas schools hosting a few hundred or so students were the norm in the 1930s, and institutions with upward of 10,000 collegians enrolled were considered rarities, by the mid-1980s several campuses were already hosting more than 50,000 students at a time. Universities with student bodies exceeding 9,500 enrolled less than a fifth of all students attending college in the years immediately preceding World War II. Before the end of the decade of the 1980s, at least 80 percent of all those enrolled in college were attending a school with more than 10,000 students enrolled.

Much of the student enrollment growth throughout the twentieth century was a function of rising levels of educational persistence at all levels: a steady increase in the proportion of the population completing high school, the expanding proportion of high school graduates entering college, more women enrolled in colleges and universities, and a rise in the percentage of college graduates who extended their studies at the postbaccalaureate level.[11] With respect to the percentage of high school graduates entering college, for example, in 1960 around 40 percent of all seniors were applying to college; by 1970 the percentage had risen to 52 percent. The percentage had increased only slightly by 1980, but by 1990 almost 61.5 percent of graduating seniors—almost two-thirds of all graduating high school students—were preparing to enroll for further study in a college or university.

Likewise contributing to mounting college enrollments throughout the latter half of the century was a rise in both the relative and absolute numbers of the traditional college-age population cohort, those between the ages of eighteen and twenty-one. Those born in the 1940s, the so-called postwar baby boomers, came of college age in the late 1960s and early 1970s, thereby helping to stimulate burgeoning enrollments. A second demographic surge in the late 1950s and early 1960s produced another enrollment burst in the late 1970s, peaking in the early 1980s.

Public academic institutions from the 1960s and 1970s onward absorbed a disproportionate share of student enrollment growth at the expense of private colleges. Toward the close of the nineteenth century, a little more than an estimated 80 percent of all students attending a college were enrolled in private colleges or universities. By 1947, two years after the end of World War II, some 2.3 million students were enrolled in over 1,800 four-year and two-year institutions; and near the century's midpoint enrollments were almost evenly divided between public and private colleges or universities.[12] By 1960 public institutions of higher learning accounted for fully 59 percent of all student enrollments, and by 1963, public enrollments had reached 64 percent of the total enrollment.[13]

This enrollment shift from private to public institutions grew even more pronounced in succeeding decades. Collegiate enrollments stood at 8.5 million in 1970, 6.2 million of which were in four-year institutions and 2.3 million in two-year colleges. Whereas 2.1 million were attending private schools, fully 6.4 million out of the 8.5 million total, or about 75 percent of all students attending college, were registered in public institutions of advanced learning. Total student enrollment amounted to 9.5 million in 1980, of which 7.5 million were in four-year schools and 2 million in two-year colleges. Public school enrollment had increased 3 million over the decade, while private school enrollments had increased by about a half million. By 1986 enrollments were running at 12.3 million, with fully 77 percent of all students in public institutions. Out of an estimated 12.5 to 12.6 million students enrolled in higher education four years later, in 1990, fully 10.5 million were in public colleges or universities, accounting for slightly over 80 percent of all enrollments combined. Private school enrollments in 1980 stood at 2.5 million and had grown to 2.8 million a decade later, but still accounted for no more than a 20 percent share of total enrollment. Projections for the year 2000 placed public enrollments at 12.1 million, compared with 3.4 million in private colleges and universities.[14]

The specific combination of factors responsible for student enrollment increases throughout the last third of the twentieth century itself changed over time. From the mid-1970s on, an increase in the number of women attending college contributed substantially to growth. So too did the increasing percentage of African Americans and other minorities seeking postsecondary education. The balance between undergraduate and graduate education shifted also. More important still was the marked increase in the numbers of part-time students. Most dramatic of all was the change in the age composition of the college student population, with ever increasing numbers of older, so-called nontraditional students attending as compared with previous decades.

Estimates for the academic year 1995-96 calculated the college-attending total at 14.9 million, with a projected increase to between 15.4 and 15.6 million by the year 2000. Of the 1995-96 total, 11.4 million were enrolled in public institutions of higher learning and 3.2 million were attending private schools. There reportedly were 4.6 million part-time students attending college in 1978. That total rose to 6.1 million in 1991, making for a 34 percent increase in only 13 years. By 1995 fully 56 percent of all students in college were enrolled part time. In particular, among those attending two-year colleges, undergraduate enrollments were dominated increasingly by part-time students. Whereas the percentage of all part-time undergraduates increased at an annual average rate of 2.3 percent throughout the 1980s, including those registered at both two-year and four-year institutions, expanding numbers of part-time graduate students fueled an even greater share of the increases in graduate enrollments typical of the 1980s and 1990s. About 8.2 million of the 15.5 or so million undergraduate and graduate students enrolled in 1995-96 were identified as regular, full-time students; the remainder (about 6.5 million) were attending school on a part-time basis.

Since 1978 graduate enrollment has gone up at a slightly faster rate than undergraduate enrollment. The latter went from 9.7 million in the late 1970s to about 12.2 million by 1991, an increase of 26 percent; while graduate enrollments for the same span of time rose from 1.3 million to 1.7 million, marking a 30 percent increase. By the year 2000 the United States Department of Education projected graduate enrollments at 1.8 million, while undergraduate enrollment was expected to top out at 13.3 million.[15]

Extending a trend that had begun long before 1950, women began to outnumber men among those attending colleges and universities. There were an estimated 5.6 million women on campus in 1978;

by 1991 their numbers had increased to an estimated 7.8 million, growing at a yearly rate of 2.5 percent, or by 38 percent over the thirteen-year period. Between 1970 and 1991 the number of women attending college had actually more than doubled, with the largest increases in attendance registered by White females (followed by the next highest percentage increase among African Americans of both sexes).[16] In 1990 women comprised fully 54 percent of all college students enrolled in a college or university. Likewise, undergraduate women in 1989 had received almost 53 percent of all the bachelor's degrees awarded that year. By 1995, 55 percent of all collegians were female. In 1973, according to figures compiled by the National Research Council, women were awarded around 18 percent of all doctorates conferred. A decade later the total had risen to around 21 percent; ten years later it stood at 23 percent. By 1996 some 8.1 million women were in college; and it was projected that their numbers would grow to between 8.3 and 8.7 million by 2000.[17]

Practically all assessments and projections of the mid-1990s anticipated significant shifts in the age distribution of college students continuing into the twenty-first century. Students between the ages of eighteen and twenty-one had increased from 7.2 million in 1983 to an estimated 7.8 million by 1991, representing an increase of 8 percent. That number was expected to rise to 9.2 million by 2003, up 19 percent. Consequently, the proportion of students age eighteen to twenty-four, which declined from 57.4 percent in 1983 to 54.8 percent in 1991, was expected to increase again to about 57.2 percent at the end of the 1990s. On the other hand, students twenty-five years of age and older had increased from 5.1 million in 1983 to an estimated 6.2 million in 1991, an increase of 23 percent. The number was expected to reach 6.7 million or so by 2002, an increase of about 7 percent. The percentage of females age thirty-five or older between 1972 and 1991 had gone up from 3.4 percent to 6.3 percent; and indications were that the numbers of older students joining the ranks of their younger peers on campus were destined to climb still higher before the century's end.

Minority enrollments were expected to expand, in both absolute and relative terms, faster than any other segment of the college population. Gains registered by African Americans have been particularly significant. In 1964 there were an estimated 15,000 Black students enrolled in predominantly White colleges in the South, representing a fourfold increase since 1957. Meanwhile, African American undergraduate enrollments in northern colleges had increased from about 45,000 in 1954 to almost 95,000 in 1967-68.[18] The number of African Americans attending predominantly White colleges in the South during the first half of the decade of the 1960s rose from 3,000 in 1960 to 24,000 in 1965, and to 98,000 by 1970. Between 1965 and 1970 African American enrollments more than tripled, and the total enrolled as a percentage of all students attending college nationwide mounted steadily thereafter.[19] By 1971 the figure stood at 8.4 percent; by 1977 it had risen to 10.8 percent of total college enrollment. By 1980 minority enrollments (chiefly accounted for by African Americans) stood at 17 percent. A decade later the same figure had risen to 18.4 percent; and at least one-quarter of all African Americans between the ages of twenty and twenty-one were enrolled in college, albeit disproportionately in two-year institutions or at historically black four-year colleges.[20] Estimates from 1994 placed the percentage of minorities enrolled at 22.5 percent of the total college population.

Figures for the 1990-91 year released by the United States Department of Education yielded a mixed picture overall. The number of minority students enrolled in colleges had climbed 9.1 percent from 1990 to 1991, with minority enrollments standing at an all-time high of 2.9 million, representing 20.6 percent of the total college population. The number of American Indian and Alaska native students had climbed 10.7 percent to 114,000; the enrollment of Asians and Pacific Islanders rose 11.2 percent, to 637,000; Hispanic enrollment had grown 10.7 percent to 867,000; and the number of Black, non-Hispanic students had increased 7.1 percent, to an estimated total of 1.3 million. The enrollment of White, non-Hispanic students had gone up 2.4 percent, to 10.9 million. Despite these impressive gains, members of minority groups continued to be proportionately underrepresented on campuses, and some states were reporting actual declines in minority-group enrollments compared with previous years.[21]

Summarizing, major contrasts between America's collegiate population shortly before the midpoint of the twentieth century and at its end may be said to include the following:

- Prewar undergraduate students were predominantly male (about 60 percent); today the "typical" collegian is more likely to be female (over 55 percent).
- A collegian of 1940 or thereabouts was likely to be White (97 percent); today more than one in five is a member of a racial or ethnic minority.

- Students attending college toward the close of the Depression years and into the 1940s were likely to be drawn from the upper third of their high school graduating classes. Similar high standing is less likely to characterize an ever-expanding portion of today's college students.
- In 1950 most colleges numbered their enrollments in the hundreds. Few universities had more than 10,000 enrolled. A student of the 1940s or 1950s typically attended a school with fewer than 9,000 enrolled; today eight out of every ten collegians attend a school with 10,000 or more students enrolled.
- Fifty years ago the modal age of undergraduates fell between eighteen and twenty-one. An increasing percentage of today's baccalaureate candidates are likely to be in their mid-twenties or slightly older.
- Enrollments in private and public institutions of higher learning were about evenly divided immediately prior to 1950. By 1995 more than eight out of every ten were attending a public college or university.
- The overwhelming majority of students going to college in the postwar years were single, attended school full time, lived on a residential campus, and pursued a liberal-arts degree program bounded by extensive common course requirements. Most completed their degrees within four years. Few went on for an advanced degree. Contemporary college students are more apt to divide their time between working and attending school part time, to commute to campus instead of residing in a dormitory or fraternity or sorority house, and to require more than the usual four years to finish their degrees. Many of them are married. A higher percentage are candidates for professional degrees. Proportionately more than their counterparts of fifty years ago intend to go on for a postbaccalaureate degree.

Collectively, demographic changes occurring over the past half century or so have served to transform the character of higher learning in America, conferring upon campus life a peculiar coloration quite unlike anything formerly prevailing. What that transformation portends for the future of colleges and universities in the United States still awaits further analysis and clarification.

THE AMERICAN PROFESSORIATE

As the mixture of students attending institutions of higher learning has changed markedly over time, so too has the composition of the American professoriate. The stereotype of the college teacher of yesteryear is a stock character of popular culture: the White, male professor as an absentminded and bemused figure, somewhat eccentric perhaps, marked by an abstracted air, garbed perhaps in a threadbare tweed jacket adorned with leather patches. Variations on the theme preserve images of the professor as a benevolent mentor and exemplar (someone on the order of Mr. Chips) or, alternatively, as a stern and unforgiving classroom tyrant. Those stereotypical images probably bear no closer correspondence with reality than the equivalent stereotypes of undergraduate collegians, from the days of raccoon coats and goldfish-swallowing contests, to the long-haired revolutionaries of the late 1960s, to the more sedate if less colorful images purveyed by television or the movies today. In any case, it seems safe to claim that as the size of the American professoriate has grown, so too has its heterogeneity. Today popular stereotypes are even less adequate for doing justice to the diversity of those who teach or otherwise are employed in colleges and universities, their mix is so diverse. In short, if ever professors truly were a uniform type, that era has long since passed.

A 1988 survey conducted by the United States Department of Education of 11,013 faculty members at 480 colleges and universities indicated that there were an estimated 489,000 professors employed full time in American higher education.[22] Almost 73 percent were men; 27 percent were women.[23] Fully 89 percent were White; the remainder was accounted for mostly by Asians (4.2 percent), Hispanics (2.3 percent), and African Americans (3.2 percent). The age distribution of those surveyed ranged from thirty (1.6 percent) to sixty and older (12.7 percent), with over three-quarters of the population falling between the ages of thirty to fifty-nine. Well over half held doctorate degrees. Full professors made up about a third of the total, followed by associate professors (23.7 percent), and assistant professors (22.8 percent); the rest held lesser ranks.

Viewed by gender, 34 percent of male faculty were full professors. Roughly 36 percent of all White male faculty members had achieved that rank, 27 percent of Asian faculty, 23 percent of Native Americans, 22 percent of Latinos, and 18 percent of African Americans. Only 12 percent of all women faculty were full professors, with more than 30 percent at the assistant professor level. About 13 percent of White female faculty were full professors, 10 percent of Asian women, and 9 percent of women of color. Women comprised a small percentage of American doctorates in traditional, male-dominated fields such as the physical and biological sciences. African American, Hispanic, or Latino, Asian and Native American females were disproportionately underrepresented in terms of holding doctorate degrees.

Approximately 96,000 professors were employed in public re-search-oriented universities; 39,000 in private research universities; another 36,000 in public doctoral institutions; and 15,000 in private doctoral universities. Public comprehensive institutions reportedly employed 93,000 faculty members, while private comprehensive schools employed 35,000. All liberal arts colleges combined accounted for another 39,000 faculty. Public and private two-year schools combined reported employing no fewer than 95,000 academic teachers. Another 40,000 were working in medical schools or other miscellaneous types of academic institutions.

Whereas in 1980 there were an estimated 685,000 full-time and part-time faculty combined working in colleges or universities, by 1990 their numbers had swollen to 726,000. According to a 1993-94 survey sponsored by the American Association of University Professors, the total number of full-time faculty was 377,496, with 146,118 working in Category I (doctoral) institutions, 159,000 in Category II (comprehensive or general baccalaureate) institutions, 28,811 in Category III (two-year) schools, and 43,131 in Category IV (unranked) colleges.[24] Once again, about 36.3 percent of those surveyed held the rank of full professor, 27.8 percent were identified as associate professors, 26.5 percent were assistant professors, and about 9.5 percent held lower rank.

A profile supplied by the National Center for Education Statistics as reported in 1995 yielded a similar picture.[25] Since the 1970s, it was observed, there had been a substantial increase in the actual number of professors on American campuses. But whereas full-time faculty accounted for 77 percent of all faculty at that time, a quarter century later fewer than two-thirds could claim that status. In over two decades or so, the percentage of full-time teachers at four-year colleges had dropped from 80 to 71 percent.

Education Department data showed that 34 percent of faculty positions were to be found in the health and natural sciences. Humanities accounted for about 13 percent of the academic labor market; the social sciences made up 17 percent; business, education, and the fine arts contributed seven percent each; and agriculture-related positions comprised 3 percent.

AAUP data from 1993-94 indicated that almost two-thirds of faculty (63.7 percent) in all institutions combined were tenured, ranging from 96.7 percent of all full professors, to 83.7 percent for associate professors, 16 percent for assistant professors, and about 28 percent for instructors, lecturers, and those without formal academic rank.

MULTIPLE ACADEMIC WORLDS

Just as college teachers of both sexes differ greatly in terms of age, socioeconomic background, ethnicity or race, career position and rank, status, salary, and assignments, so, too, do the ways in which members of the professorate experience academic life. Much depends on the institutional settings in which they work: large or small, public or private, two year or four year, undergraduate or graduate, college or university, denominational or secular, and so on. Teaching in a public two-year vocational school, clearly, is a different proposition from serving on the faculty in a private four-year liberal arts college. Working in a major graduate research university offers yet another sort of experience. In short, precisely because American higher education is neither monolithic nor uniform, its diversity creates multiple "worlds" or environments for faculty to inhabit.

At the risk of stating the obvious, to cite one example, smaller schools may be said to offer greater possibilities for sustaining a sense of "community" that embraces the whole. Faculty are more apt to know one another personally; they interact with one another more regularly; and their affinity or affiliation is linked to the institution itself. Larger institutions offer fewer (or perhaps different) opportunities for fostering some feeling of shared identity. The environment tends to be less cohesive. The bigger and more complex the institution, the greater is the likelihood that people's allegiances are to sub-units of the whole: to separate colleges, particular departments, and even to smaller subdivisions thereof. The circle of one's acquaintances and professional colleagues typically is more limited, perhaps circumscribed almost entirely by those with whom one works on a daily basis.

In large schools especially, the tendency of academics is to identify themselves first with their respective professional disciplines and academic specialties. Only secondarily do they identify with the institution where they happen to be employed. The distinction sometimes drawn is between faculty "cosmopolitans"—those whose professional orientation is to a discipline or profession—and "locals"—those whose professional identity and sense of loyalty derive from their role within a particular institution.

Community is not solely a matter of size. Residential campuses where most of the students live in residence halls are more likely to nurture a sense of shared identification or affiliation among all parties. Schools with a high percentage of commuting students find it more difficult to achieve that feeling of interrelatedness. In the latter case, the campus—if there is one—is unlikely to be perceived by students as much more than a temporary habitat, a place to visit only briefly while attending classes.

Professors in liberal arts colleges and smaller public regional institutions tend to have extensive teaching and student-advisement responsibilities. They are not necessarily expected to conduct research, make scholarly presentations, or publish their findings in professional journals, though they increasingly find it advantageous to do so. For many such teachers, monitoring and nurturing students is their chief source of job satisfaction; and how well they perform in the classroom is the major criterion by which their overall performance is assessed. Academics in larger, more research-focused universities, on the other hand, are expected to be productive scholars as much as they are good teachers. "Productivity," of course, is measured by the frequency with which they secure research grants and service contracts, author books and articles, or deliver papers at professional convocations.

Job differentiation and specialization are more common features of the work environment in a large university. Some few researchers rarely venture outside a clinical or laboratory setting. Their instructional duties, if any, are limited. Especially distinguished scholars of senior rank (semifacetiously dubbed luminaries or superstars) may have no assigned classes at all. Or they may teaching nothing other than a graduate-level seminar or two each year. Only infrequently do they have responsibilities involving undergraduate students. Student advisement is assigned to full-time advisors employed for that exclusive purpose.

Meanwhile, those of lower rank or lesser experience are expected to teach between three and five courses each academic term. In addition, they are not absolved of responsibility for establishing and maintaining themselves as scholars and researchers in their own right.

Also, if they are employed at an institution offering graduate degree programs, they will be expected to serve as advisors for master's and doctoral candidates. Almost everyone is obliged to share responsibility for the institution's multiple service and outreach functions, not to mention the internal committee work that seems a ubiquitous feature of academic life.

For two-thirds or so of the professoriate, holding an academic position amounts to a full-fledged career. Circumstances differ for the remaining third. Some work part time by choice, and teach or otherwise offer their services as a strictly supplemental enterprise. Others are seeking full-time academic employment, but perhaps so far have been unsuccessful in securing a regular position. Bolstered by the hope of eventually obtaining a full-time appointment, they accept whatever more limited opportunities are available. In effect, they labor on the academic equivalent of a piecework basis, teaching particular courses as needed.

One popular impression of professorial life is that it offers those privileged to work within an institution of higher learning almost unlimited opportunities for leisured contemplation and study. Insulated from the cutthroat pressures of the commercial world, it is said, professors are free to enjoy the life of mind, of ideas valued for their own sake, of scholarly exchange and open-ended discussion. According to this view, the groves of academe are isolated havens, protected enclaves where disinterested inquiry and learning proceed unhindered by external interference.

Any such view rather quickly lends itself to overstatement. Curiously enough, though, it does embody a partial truth. The ivory tower, in the final analysis, is not entirely a fiction. The fact of the matter is, working in a collegiate environment for many *can* be somewhat less stressful, less constrained by the "bottom line" imperatives of the economic marketplace, less harried in comparison with the workplace routines prevailing in corporate business and industry. As those suited by ability and temperament to scholastic pursuits will attest, academic life answers a profound need for personal autonomy, for individual control over one's professional time and creative effort.

The professor's job is unique: It yields the economic security of a salaried employee as well as most of the privileges and flexibility enjoyed by the self-employed. Because experience rather strongly indicates that faculty members function best when they are left to their own devices, professors are usually allowed (within certain broad limits) to define their own work roles. At the very least, once well established in their careers, academics are free to strike a balance among those professional activities to which they most prefer to dedicate themselves.

"Once established in their careers" is the critical qualifier. Academic life as it is lived and experienced by a tenured senior faculty member with full-professor rank is characteristically different from that of an untenured instructor or assistant professor just beginning. A newly minted Ph.D. fresh out of graduate school and now employed in a tenure-track position, for instance, is likely to see things from a rather different perspective from that of a more experienced senior colleague. The proximate goal for junior faculty, of course, is to secure tenure. But, typically, job expectations and performance standards are at once diffuse and ill-defined. Pressures on the individual are multiple; and the new faculty member feels pulled in many directions simultaneously during those first few years on the job.

There are classes to prepare for: The new faculty member knows he or she must do a good job of teaching—or at least must avoid conspicuous incompetence in the classroom. Then there are the inevitable committee assignments that present themselves, not to mention other service demands on one's energies. All the while, time needs to be set aside for scholarship and writing. The message in research-focused institutions especially is unmistakable: One must publish if there is to be any hope of eventually attaining tenured status. Yet the fledgling scholar also wants to be regarded as a "good citizen" of the academic community. Certain relationships with colleagues must be cultivated, and these can require a significant investment of time and effort. As a newcomer, there are hidden pitfalls to be avoided in one's dealings with others; and treacherous psychological terrain (both real and imagined) must be negotiated with care. Consequently, the first few years of an academic career are apt to be stressful, even frenetic. It is a far cry from the secure world of the established faculty member for whom such imperatives are less pressing and immediate.

Graduate teaching assistants face a still different situation. Their association with a given institution is clearly temporary, lasting in most cases only until they have completed all the requirements of a graduate degree. Time is divided between study and teaching (or research). Most find it a delicate balancing act. Ironically, graduate students who are least experienced are most often assigned to teach the largest introductory-level courses, presumably on the theory that so-called entry-level courses demand the least pedagogical skill or expertise. Graduate assistants share many of the responsibilities of regular faculty. Yet as academic apprentices, they are precluded from claiming even the most basic faculty prerogatives and privileges. The potential for abuse is real. Exploitation occurs. Nevertheless, few major universities could afford to dispense with their services. Needless to add, without the modest stipend an assistantship supplies, many students would find it impossible to continue their studies at all.

Outsiders' perceptions of academic life understandably fall short of doing justice to its complexity. The popular impression that professors are a pampered lot without enough to do affords a case in point. The truth of the matter is that on-the-job effort is most likely distributed about as it is within any other work force. There are members of the faculty who drive themselves to work long hours. These contented "workaholics," as they are fond of characterizing themselves, invest in their careers unstintingly. And contrary to some allegations, not all of them are younger faculty bent on proving themselves before the next tenure or promotion review. Some are senior members who keep up the pace over the course of an entire career. Then there are the time-servers whose performance is, to put it charitably, minimal. They surface to teach their classes or to observe mandated office hours. Then they disappear. Most professors, of course, fall somewhere in between the two extremes.

In actuality, college and university teachers as a group do tend to work long hours—if not upward of the fifty-five or more hours weekly that faculty surveys regularly allege, then certainly more on average than a standard forty-hour work week. They teach, counsel students, conduct experiments and otherwise do research, delve into the library's archives, sit on committees, write grants, engage in consulting activities off-campus, supervise student interns in field sites, read books and articles to keep current in their fields, participate in campus activities, prepare class notes, and attend professional conferences and meetings. The list is lengthy. Part of the problem of trying to quantify the number of hours professors work has to do with the nature of the job itself. Academic life lacks limits or boundaries; it can encompass almost everything to which the individual faculty member devotes his or her energies.

The public's estimation of academe as a tranquil retreat from the "real" world therefore demands serious qualification. Among other things, the campus is not the idyllic haven it sometimes appears from the outside looking in. More typically, the halls of ivy are highly charged places, where everything is politicized and even the smallest event or incident assumes grossly exaggerated importance. It has been observed that academic politics is harsh and petty precisely because there is so little at stake. Evidence to confirm that assessment is not hard to find. An offhand remark by the institution's chief executive officer at a luncheon, a memo distributed by the dean, an informal exchange as two colleagues pass in the hallway all become grist for the rumor mill. Even the most casual comment or remark may be held up to scrutiny and examined for whatever covert significance it presumably contains. Hidden agendas are suspected everywhere. Jockeying for position, status, and influence goes on constantly. Gossip dominates conversations in the faculty lounge or commons. Even those who assiduously try to avoid office politics cannot escape it entirely.

The specific issues or concerns that animate academics are not significantly different from those that occupy people's attention in the corporate workplace. Who enjoys the department head's confidence and who has fallen into disfavor? Who is covertly seeking a job elsewhere? Who is slated for promotion and who will be turned down? Is the latest curriculum proposal a grab for power on someone's part? Are some departments growing at the expense of others? Why did a particular colleague get assigned a corner office with a large window? Are teaching loads equitable? Are the favored few pulling their fair share of the load? Do committee assignments suggest favoritism on someone's part? What has the administration been up to lately? Have resources been equitably divided? Will a replacement be authorized for someone slated for retirement? Is a faculty member carrying on an illicit relationship with a student? Why did the latest faculty member hired in the department receive a brand-new computer system, while others did not? Who will be recommended for tenure? Who is "in trouble" and probably will be encouraged to leave? Almost anything is grist for the gossip mill.

Another abiding source of tension in the academic workplace stems from the dichotomy—some would call it a yawning chasm—between faculty and administration. Steeped in tradition, hallowed by ancient precedent, a certain tension between those who lead, manage, and administer, on the one hand, and those who teach or do research or counsel students, on the other, helps define a rift or breach never fully bridged. (At the risk of some oversimplification, it might be noted that in institutions where the faculty are unionized or collective bargaining is the norm, the polarization between administrators and faculty is apt to be even more pronounced. Faculty prerogatives are possibly more secure, but that security is purchased at the cost of reinforcing the "us" versus "them" mentality.) Happily, in some institutions tension between the two is mitigated by the canons of decorum, collegiality, and compromise. Yet not always are the conflicts so well concealed. They can erupt at the surface of campus life quite unexpectedly, at any time.

The demonology on both sides is well developed. Oftentimes faculty members view administrators with deep and abiding distrust. Their commitment to intellectual values and standards is suspect. Some are condemned as crass philistines obsessed more with the bottom line than with considerations of academic quality. Or the administrators are said to be rigid, authoritarian, power-hungry. Some academic factotums (or so faculty will claim privately among themselves) are at heart political autocrats who all too frequently have forgotten their academic origins (if they had any) and now, attempting to justify their own existence, conspire to occupy the faculty's time with meaningless trivia, bureaucratic red tape, and "make-work." At best the administrative hierarchy is a necessary evil to be tolerated, albeit reluctantly. At worst, it serves as an obstruction hindering the "real" work of the department, college, or university.

Administrators—some at least—harbor similar attitudes. The more arrogant among them look upon the faculty as little better than "hired hands" within the institutional structure of power and authority. The faculty as a whole is judged to be naive in supposing that it can manage affairs with any degree of efficiency. Academics, it is said, should stick to teaching and research. The running of the institution itself is best left to the full-time professionals. Faculty are seen as indecisive and vacillating. So far as provosts or chancellors or deans are concerned, the faculty in its endless disputations and deliberations regularly demonstrates the paralysis that must necessarily ensue when governance by consensus prevails and direct democracy runs riot.

Academics, it is further alleged, are prone to avoiding the hard choices; and they are all too willing to abdicate responsibility when the going gets tough. In fact, the most common professorial reflex, administrators are fond of saying, is for faculty to appoint a committee to study any matter at hand—as a means of postponing effectively the need to reach a decision. Worst of all, faculty are alleged to have little sensitivity or appreciation for fiscal constraints and resource limits. Their constant refrain is a plaintive demand for more of everything. Faculty are akin to egomaniacal children who must be cajoled or "managed."

The regulative formula or principle that supposedly adjudicates faculty-administration conflict is not always helpful. In theory, faculty governance over purely academic matters is supposed to hold sway. The faculty establishes broad policies. It decides on matters of curricula and degree program requirements. It sets admissions policies and determines who shall be admitted to particular programs. Faculty determine the content of individual courses and how they are to be taught. Academic freedom therefore requires that administrators assume a strict "hands-off" posture when it comes to the specifics of academic content and instruction. All else—the minutiae of budgets and planning, of student services, academic record keeping, physical maintenance and upkeep, public relations, alumni affairs, and fund-raising—repose in the hands of the institution's administrative managers. Alternatively, the argument goes, governance structures should be devised that encourage genuine collaboration and shared decision making between administrators and faculty—hence the endless proliferation of committees that professors claim is the bane of their existence.

Theory, however, is difficult to apply in specific situations, mainly because there are so many constituencies to satisfy and so many diverse players involved. State legislatures regularly and incessantly impose demands on public colleges and universities, not all of them well considered. So, too, do state departments of higher education. The federal government weighs in with its own voluminous rules and regulations affecting the institution. The school's governing board may not rest content to serve as a body rubber-stamping proposals brought before it; its members may want to implement decisions of their own. Alumni expect to have their say in certain matters. So do students if they feel their welfare or special interests are threatened. External accrediting agencies and their mandates cannot be ignored either.

Meanwhile, administrative heads are persuaded that effective leadership demands that they help the institution "articulate its mission," or "bring the faculty into line" on some particular issue, or "identify priorities." Bureaucrats allocate resources and in so doing make choices that impact profoundly on the health and well-being (or lack thereof) of specific departments and academic programs. They likewise establish policies, rules, and procedures; commission studies and reports; and issue demands of their own. As a result, the line between purely academic matters and administrative considerations becomes hopelessly blurred.

The most common outcome is a precarious and uneasy set of compromises. Faculty in most situations lack the power to bend administrators to their will. Administrators for their part cannot always dictate directly to the faculty either, however much some might wish to do so.

Students cannot safely be ignored altogether, nor can vital outside interests. Hence governance within an academic institution entails a process of constant negotiation and accommodation among various competing protagonists or interest groups. Whenever possible, some judicious balancing of interests tolerable to all is sought. Overt confrontation between administration and faculty is assiduously avoided or papered over. In sum, there are few decisive victories on anyone's part. Faculty who are part of the process come to accept it as an accustomed feature of academic life. But the bafflement and bemusement of outside observers over how the system works—or fails to work—is perhaps quite understandable.

ENDURING QUESTIONS

Campus controversies ebb and flow; and the specific issues most likely to animate impassioned debate at any given historical moment change over time. In the 1940s and into the 1950s, the predominant issues were those involving faculty loyalty oaths and the right of certified, card-carrying Communists to teach or even speak on campus. In the early 1960s, conflict over free speech—the right of faculty and students to speak out on matters of public policy and to criticize authority—convulsed scores of institutions of higher learning across the nation. In some cases the entire academic enterprise was brought to a temporary halt. The remainder of that decade and into the next marked an especially tumultuous era in American higher education. Students marched and staged protests: over military adventurism, civil rights, academe's involvement in war-related research and development, the imperatives of shared governance and participatory democracy. Successive debates ensued in the 1970s over feminism, ethnic studies programs, women's studies, affirmative action mandates, and university investments in countries marked by repressive regimes, among other issues.

Over the past decade and a half or so, new topics coming to the fore have included the disputed legitimacy of enacting (or proscribing) "hate speech" codes on campus, gay and lesbian rights, multiculturalism and cultural diversity, questions about the so-called curricular canon ("Is culturally legitimated knowledge dominated by the achievements of Dead White European Males?"), sexual harassment, "political correctness," professorial ethics, the continuing viability of the hallowed institution of faculty tenure, adapting new technologies

in education, and soaring costs. The litany of recent causes and
concerns is extensive.

Even as debate focused on such specific topics continues, however, it is important to underscore that there occurs within American
higher education and, indeed, throughout society at large a kind of
contrapuntal accompaniment, another level of discussion and debate
entirely. This more abstract or generic debate is not conducted entirely
separate and apart from that focused upon any of the particular issues
that happen to capture public attention. But philosophically it is more
fundamental or basic in character. What it amounts to is an ongoing
conversation addressed to policy issues that are perennial to higher
learning, those questions that must of necessity be posed and responded
to anew by each succeeding generation. The total number of such
enduring inquiries is relatively small. But each in turn encapsulates a
host of subsidiary questions, few of which admit of easy answers.

Furnishing a logical starting point are questions having to do with
the role and mission of the college or university in contemporary society.
If, as seems readily apparent, colleges and universities simultaneously
fulfill multiple functions, which priorities ought to control their institutional goals and objectives? Should teaching be deemed more important
than research and scholarship? Are there appropriate limits to the service
obligations and responsibilities academic institutions assume? Should
four-year colleges and universities serve primarily in an ancillary capacity to business, government, and industry, providing a well-trained and
obedient work force? Or do they have a still more important mission to
fulfill? And no matter what purposes institutions of higher learning
serve, there is a further question: Who should bear the costs involved?

Asking questions about the basic purposes of institutions of higher
learning opens up the possibility that different types of schools have—
and by right ought to have—different missions within the social order.
The tasks performed by two-year community colleges are not precisely
the same as those undertaken by four-year colleges and universities,
even allowing for some overlapping of functions. Certain private institutions (sectarian or denominational schools in particular) have agendas
inappropriate for public, state-assisted schools to pursue. The converse
holds true also. Technical schools exist to fulfill needs and goals quite
unlike those inspiring liberal arts colleges. Conversely, colleges and
universities devoted to providing a solid foundation in the liberal disciplines possibly can afford to focus their efforts differently than institutions engaged in preparing people directly for the world of

occupations. Comprehensive universities, public or private, are apt to place greater emphasis on undergraduate teaching. Graduate universities with a strong research focus, in contrast, may more appropriately emphasize professional training, particularly at the postbaccalaureate level. Land grant institutions have a historic service function to perform quite unlike the imperatives driving other types of universities.

If higher learning serves multiple aims, which are most import-ant, and why? Students, obviously enough, embark upon an under-graduate career for many different reasons. For some, it may be scarcely more than a pleasant interlude between adolescence and adulthood, a hiatus of sorts, a way of effecting a transition from childhood dependence to adult autonomy. For others, perhaps no more than a minority percentage, college is more than a simple rite of passage. It can be, rather, a time of intense self-exploration and discovery—emotional, social, intellectual, and spiritual. For still others, college means little more than the pursuit of a paper credential and the opportunities thereby represented for achieving (or preserving) a certain level of socioeconomic status within the marketplace. Indi-vidual motivations for acquiring the bachelor's degree aside, what is its most defensible social value? What, if anything, defines the edu-cated person? What attributes, sensibilities, forms of consciousness, abilities, or characteristics ought to be exhibited by someone who by common consent is said to be well educated?

Questions about what it means to be an educated person tend to link up with queries about who should be admitted to college and who denied admission. Should prior academic achievement serve as the deciding factor? What if not everyone has enjoyed equal opportunities to succeed previously? Is it fair to deny admission to those whose life circumstances or background may have limited their chances of doing well in school? Furthermore, does past academic success serve as the single best predictor of future success? (What about those proverbial "late bloomers" and those who, for whatever specific reasons, simply have not lived up to their potential?) Might it not be fairer to allow anyone in who gives evidence of a sincere commitment to scholarship?

Alternatively, let it be supposed that ability, not actual academic achievement, ought to be the controlling consideration. How is "ability" to be identified? What if the standard measures of academic potential are themselves somehow contaminated? Can any formal test be "cul-ture-free" or otherwise free of bias that works unfairly to the disadvan-tage (or advantage) of certain applicants?

Further suppose that certain minority populations within society have suffered from a history of discrimination, prejudice, and exclusion at the hands of a dominant majority. Should minority applicants therefore now receive special consideration when applying to college? Can past injustice be redressed and the scales of justice righted by offering special incentives and support to members of groups historically denied equality of opportunity? Or do affirmative action practices amount to "reverse discrimination" and simply serve to perpetuate injustice?

Assume for the sake of argument that anyone seeking entry to a college or university ought by right to be granted admission. What has been gained if those of inferior ability or inadequate preparation are allowed on campus in large numbers? Will academic standards plummet, to everyone's detriment? Must scarce resources be diverted to offer poor students the remedial training they require? Or should the institution simply allow the overall student attrition rate to skyrocket, in which case admission becomes simply a "revolving door" through which incompetent applicants pass, only to be summarily ejected once they fail? Does a system of true open admission, in other words, amount to a cruel hoax perpetrated in the name of equity?

Against the background of different institutions performing functions that are not fundamentally isomorphic to one another, questions having to do with who should pursue higher education take on even greater complexity. It might turn out, for instance, that considerations guiding who attends a four-year, baccalaureate degree granting college or university should differ greatly from factors weighed in decisions about who attends a two-year school. Some private colleges might adopt selective admissions standards that are wholly inappropriate for certain other state universities. Possibly, or so it might be argued, the academic standards honored at some institutions would serve no comparable purpose within other types of postsecondary institutions. Whatever the truth of the matter, and despite the differences among them, virtually all colleges and universities must grapple in some way with questions of admission standards and achievement criteria, adopting applicable policies best suited to their respective needs and overall objectives.

One set of policy questions leads logically enough to others. Once admitted, what should college students be required (or strongly encouraged) to study? More particularly, what sort of accommodation is viable between studies intended to lead to proficiency in a specific field and those thought to be conducive to intellectual breadth and a widening of intellectual and cultural interests? Some have argued that students should be allowed to vote with their feet or, rather, with their course selections. Those who wish to specialize in a given discipline or tailor their programs to narrow career goals should be allowed, as tuition-paying customers, to do precisely that if they so choose.

Others argue passionately that an academic institution through its policies and requirements has an obligation, in effect, to "save" such students from themselves. Its task is to afford students opportunities to explore a broad range of subject fields, not all of which necessarily relate to any specific occupation or prospective vocation. If necessary, coercive measures may be imposed to preclude the possibility of premature or excessive specialization.

The case for imposing certain basic requirements is sometimes advanced on the grounds that students whose career goals are not yet formulated need guidance and direction. Bereft of focus, they deserve guidance in exploring the multiple universes of discourse and inquiry represented by many different disciplines, with a view toward selecting at least one of them eventually for fuller, in-depth familiarization. The institution cannot fairly leave undecided students to their own devices indefinitely, or allow them to wander about intellectually unassisted and without direction. Nor should the overall curriculum be treated by students as a gigantic smorgasbord, where offerings can be picked or rejected at will. Any institution that allows its students to do so, it is said, ultimately does them a grave disservice.

The most enduring question so far as the curriculum is concerned is the type of balance to be struck between those studies that lead naturally to competence in a given discipline or field and those intended to service purposes and values unrelated to vocations and the various professions. In an age where specialization has become the norm, where external accreditation standards increasingly control program standards and requirements, and where various occupational groups have a vested interest in expanding preparatory training, the encroachment of professional training upon what used to be referred to as liberal or general learning of a broader, less specific nature is already well advanced. Meanwhile, structurally and otherwise, powerful pressures operate to divide faculties within an institution according to their respective discipline-based interests and programs. Forging any set of general education requirements in such an environment oftentimes more nearly resembles bartering for credit hours than it does the reasoned and disinterested deliberations of academics united by common purposes and goals.

Framed purely in the abstract, inquiry about the proper content of higher education might appear almost incomprehensible. Taking into consideration the breadth and complexity of human knowledge today, it may no longer make sense even to pose, for example, a question about whether there is anything educated persons can or should come to know or to be able to do in common. Perhaps the imperatives of specialization must supersede any traditional concern for commonalities, as many people now allege. Yet the basic issue is not at all nonsensical when it comes down to asking specific questions about whether there should there be some framework, an armature for a common curriculum to which all undergraduates at a given institution are exposed. What, in other words, remains of general or liberal learning in the modern university? What is the appropriate trade-off between professional preparation engaged in chiefly with a view toward certain extrinsic considerations and a liberal arts education pursued first and foremost for its own intrinsic value?

Subsumed within any consideration of the role of the professorate in academe is a whole nexus of difficult questions touching on teaching, research, service, and related matters. Managing curricula and instruction, for example, does not begin to exhaust the functions and professional activities professors engage in. Within larger universities especially, faculty members are involved in research and service wholly unrelated to undergraduate teaching. Here, at the heart of the academic enterprise, questions of priorities and choices have to be decided. Teaching may be held to be of paramount importance, but the imperatives of scholarship and research also exercise their claims upon professors' time and energies. Recent years have brought allegations that teaching as an activity is seriously undervalued at some institutions, that undergraduate instruction is neglected as a priority or consigned to the hands of graduate students to an unwarranted extent, and that professors have forsaken their classroom obligations for other pursuits, namely research and published scholarship.

Research conducted by academics similarly has come under fire for a variety of reasons, ranging from charges of triviality or irrelevance to claims about the inappropriateness of proprietary research and academic entrepreneurship in certain fields. Equally problematic has been the nature and extent of the university's service mission in contemporary society, with some critics arguing that academe as a whole has grown too insular and removed from the actual circumstances and exigencies of modern life. Overall, some of the most fundamental issues that can be raised about conditions in higher education are framed by questions pertaining to the multiple, controversial, and sometimes conflicting roles of the American professoriate. In these and other matters, academic life has come under closer scrutiny than ever before, with every indication that public interest in faculty behavior will continue unabated for years to come.

Part of the public's concern over higher education finds expression in demands for greater accountability on the part of colleges and universities. In today's climate of opinion, it is difficult to argue against the concept of academic accountability, at least when it is posed as an issue in general or abstract terms. It is less clear *who* is to be accountable, to *whom,* for *what,* and in which specific ways. Students and parents want value received for tuition paid and expect a return on their investment. Legislators demand evidence that the institutional recipients of their largesse are carefully husbanding resources and putting them to good use. Corporate and individual donors impose the same demands. Academic authorities similarly expect faculty to be accountable for their time and efforts. Thus, in any given context, it turns out that *everyone* at every level is caught up in a web of reciprocal obligations and responsibilities.

At its most basic level, accountability in academe reduces perhaps to a question of stewardship, of how well available resources are managed in the service of activities which, unfortunately, are not always susceptible or amenable to precise measurement or quantification. Unfortunately, much nonsense is perpetrated in this regard. The silliness assumes many forms, (the most egregious of which probably ought to prompt both derision and despair, in about equal measure). At a macrocosmic level, initiatives aimed at reforming state funding formulae for publicly-assisted colleges and universities sometimes are advanced out of a professed desire to improve accountability. A traditional stratagem is to tie allocations to student full-time–equivalent enrollments—which carries the virtue of stabilizing per capita expenditures while simultaneously rewarding growing institutions. (Whether bigger is better remains an unanswered question.) Less often is adequate provision made for the differential costs entailed in graduate versus undergraduate education, which thereby tends to work to the disadvantage of institutions with specialized and more costly advanced-level programs.

Another approach is to weight a whole complex of factors beside enrollments, including admission scores, student attrition rates, performance on academic achievement tests administered immediately prior to graduation, and so on. The chief advantage from the viewpoint of those who guard the public treasury is that multiple measures purport to allow more control over how resources are allocated. The chief disadvantage for recipient institutions is, for example, that if they do not control their own admission standards, their ability to improve attrition rates may turn out to be negligible, and so on. Similarly, answers to questions about the validity and reliability of achievement tests relative to curricula have proven more than a little ambiguous. Some few institutions have experimented with so-called "value-added" approaches, in essence comparing differences in successive academic achievement measures taken immediately subsequent to admission and immediately prior to graduation. (A well-publicized experiment at Northeast Missouri State University dating back to the early 1980s affords one conspicuous illustration.) Sponsoring institutions, of course, gladly claim credit for whatever performance gains are registered—though they may lack ways of controlling for the influence of extraneous intervening variables.

At a microcosmic level, accountability demands at some institutions have encroached upon virtually every aspect of academic life. Students' numerical ratings of individual courses and instructors—sometimes carried out several decimal places on a multiple-point scale—dominate estimations and comparisons of teaching prowess. Numbers of articles published or papers presented serve to measure scholarship—refined in some instances by consulting lists bearing the paid circulation totals of the journals involved! Faculty are enjoined to maintain annual lists of everything they do with scrupulous care, to document each and every committee assignment, to record the numbers of their advisees, their course enrollments, and so forth.

Meanwhile, a crude sort of positivism predominates, a mind-set that holds that only what can be counted—literally—counts. This impulse toward quantification, once entrenched, recognizes few boundaries or limits. Hence, before long entire cadres of administrative personnel are set to work tracking such things as student-income ratios, per-unit costs of semester credit-hours generated, programmatic overhead, and the like, *ad infinitum*. Enthusiasts claim hard data are needed as the basis for sound decision-making and therefore provide a measure of accountability otherwise lacking. To critics, it is mathematical madness. But either way, the imperative of providing some coherent measure of accountability to vested constituencies remains, and it is a challenge likely to extend debate both within academe and outside of it for years to come.

Ultimately, achieving anything approaching total consensus on which issues—from admissions to accountability—are *most* fundamental in contemporary American higher education is probably impossible. But it is likely that the questions already cited having to do with basic institutional purposes and goals, policy issues pertinent to admissions and academic standards, controversy over undergraduate curricula, questions about academic culture, and accountability concerns would be cited by most analysts as likely candidates for inclusion.

What follows in succeeding chapters are attempts to explore some of these enduring controversies in greater detail. The effort throughout is to delineate and characterize the "shape" of the debates in such a way as to throw the issues involved into bold relief so they are more recognizable and more easily dealt with. Finally, in some instances, the intent is to offer up provisional judgments as foils for possible consideration and further sustained debate.

II.

MISSIONS AND GOALS:
WHAT ARE COLLEGES
AND UNIVERSITIES FOR?

AIMS AND PURPOSES

Pondering the "aims" of education in the sense of purposes or objectives is commonplace. The term itself has its literal application in the context of activities such as shooting or throwing, where "aiming" is associated with the concentration of attention needed to fulfill an intention to hit or pierce something. Used more figuratively, it carries the same suggestion of concentrated effort to fulfill an intention, the nature of which, however, may be sometimes unclear. For example, one is most likely to ask a person what he or she aims to do precisely when that individual seems to be confused or is thrashing about in an "aimless" way. Querying someone about what he or she is aiming at, in other words, is a way of helping to clarify the person's intent or purpose. It is obvious enough, therefore, why the term "aim" is used in the context of discussion about education. As R. S. Peters has observed, this is "a sphere where people engage with great seriousness in activities without always being very clear about what they are trying to achieve. To ask questions about the aims of education is therefore a way of getting people to get clear about and focus their attention on what is worthwhile achieving."[1]

The same point applies inter alia to debate over the aims of colleges and universities. Diverse and even contradictory claims about the purposes of any given type of institution of higher learning often are advanced. But one need not be misled by this variety of views to conclude that there is nothing for it but to give up talking about what a college or university is for and talk only about what it actually does. In other words, the discussion need not confine itself to simple description or empirical analysis alone. Debate may take up normative questions about what the institution *ought* to be doing—what its aims should be as well as what purposes it now tries to fulfill.[2] The very act of raising questions about aims can have the salutary effect of encouraging clarification of what institutional goals and objectives are most worth pursuing. In short, building a reasoned case for prescribing, not merely observing or describing, certain institutional aims or priorities is a valid element in any overall assessment of higher education.

Higher learning in the United States, of course, occurs within many different institutional settings and is intended to serve many ends. Not surprisingly, even a superficial scrutiny of the educational landscape reveals that academic institutions differ from one another not only in size, public or private status, denominational or secular character, and so forth, but also, arguably, in terms of basic character and mission. The role of the two-year community college, as a case in point, is discernibly different from that of a four-year liberal arts institution; and both differ substantially in certain respects from that of a research-focused graduate university.

COMMUNITY COLLEGES

The first level of the multi-tiered institutional hierarchy comprising American higher education is represented by two-year community colleges (formerly called junior colleges). Relatively few in number until after World War II, community colleges thereafter increased in numbers and enrollments (by a factor of about twenty) faster than did any other sector of higher education throughout the third quarter of the century and beyond. Between 1966 and 1976, their numbers rose by 82 percent, from 565 to 1,030, multiplying at the rate of about one a week, with enrollments rising throughout that period from 1.3 million to almost 4 million, a nearly 200 percent increase. Over the next decade, between 1976 and 1986, enrollments increased by another 4 percent, with 38 new colleges added to the roster, for a total of 1,068. Between 1971 and 1983 the number of associate degrees awarded by two-year schools increased by over 81 percent.[3] In 1989 public two-year colleges accounted for over one-quarter of all higher education institutions in the nation, numbering 967. In that year two-year colleges enrolled 4.8 million students, 35.8 percent of all students attending college, and 44.3 percent of all college freshmen.[4] Less than a decade later, the comparable percentage totals had risen even further.

By the mid-1990s there were 1,024 two-year public colleges in existence, with an aggregate enrollment of about 5.5 million. Another 445 two-year private schools enrolled upward of 238,000 students, for a combined total approaching nearly 6 million. Today two-year community colleges serve well over one-third of all students enrolled in American higher education and employ over a third of all faculty.[5] Projections for the end of the century foresee still further growth, attaining a total of slightly over 1,400 two-year institutions by the year 2000. By that time their combined student enrollments are expected to exceed six million. So spectacular a record of growth suggests that community colleges have answered needs in postsecondary education not fulfilled adequately by traditional four-year colleges or universities. Looking at two-year schools as they have evolved today reveals both the nature of those needs and the problematic character of the response they offer.

Two-year colleges have long been touted as agencies for the democratization of opportunity in higher education. Less costly, more numerous, and usually more accessible that most four-year institutions, they continue to attract students who presumably would be less well served by four-year colleges or universities. Community colleges typically have an open-door admission policy, requiring only that entrants be at least seventeen or eighteen years of age. In some cases, candidates for admission need not even hold a high school diploma or its equivalent.[6] They offer both daytime and evening classes; some provide day care for the children of students enrolled; and most are focused on the needs of commuters who neither want nor need a traditional residential campus. Community college students are more heavily of working-class origins, more likely to be members of a minority group (over one-fifth), female (variously estimated at 57 to 65 percent), and older (the average age in 1986 was twenty-nine; in 1991, 37 percent were over the age of thirty) than their peers admitted to four-year institutions.[7] Many—upwards of 40 percent—are enrolled part time.[8]

Because community colleges are less restrictive in their admissions and offer instruction at considerably less cost than most four-year colleges, they afford a point of entry into postsecondary education otherwise limited or lacking entirely for low-income youth, high school graduates with poor academic records, underrepresented ethnic and racial minorities, working adults, recent immigrants, and senior citizens, among others. They attract adults who want or need to upgrade job skills, workers contemplating career changes who require retraining, those seeking basic adult education and literacy skills, and students hoping to acquire specific skills or competencies not tied to any specific degree program. Some do attend in pursuit of a terminal two-year associate degree. Others hope to transfer eventually to a four-year institution and seek a baccalaureate degree.

Community colleges have always sought to offer a broad range of courses. Mindful of predictions that the greatest increase in employment opportunities into the twenty-first century will not be in occupations demanding a bachelor's degree but may require training beyond the high school level, many two-year schools have made occupational preparation their primary focus. Programs emphasize trades and crafts, business and commerce, applied graphic arts, applied engineering skills, data management and computer technology, and so on. Somewhere between 40 to 60 percent of all students attending a typical two-year community college are enrolled in some type of preparatory training program for a specific career or vocation.

Many community colleges provide basic adult literacy training besides other forms of remedial education. Non-English-speaking immigrants find they can turn to their local community college as a place to enroll for English-language instruction. Young and old alike are apt to find an array of specialized noncredit courses adapted to leisure pursuits and hobbies. Meanwhile, most two-year schools continue to offer general education courses that substantially duplicate the offerings of the freshman and sophomore years at a four-year institution. Considering that fully three-quarters of all community college students profess an interest in transferring to a four-year school eventually and continuing on for a baccalaureate-level degree, two-year colleges are heavily invested in the work of college preparation. In theory, what the two-year community college offers is a noncompetitive, lower-cost chance for many students to complete the first half of a bachelor's degree program. The upper-level, more specialized portion is then to be handled by the four-year school to which the candidate transfers at the end of his or her second year of study.

Statistics suggest, however, that while 75 percent of those who attend the community college aspire to go on for a bachelor's degree, fewer than one in every five actually succeed.[9] Over the past two decades the number of community college transfers to four-year schools actually has shown a continuous and marked decline, in both absolute and relative numbers. Whereas in the early 1970s, about one in every three who intended to move on to a four-year school in fact gained admission and went on to graduate from a full-fledged baccalaureate-degree program, by the early 1990s the figure had dropped to less than one-fifth of all those indicating a desire to transfer. By comparison, high school graduates who go straight to a four-year school are two to three times more likely to attain a bachelor's degree than are transfer students of comparable ability who began in a two-year institution.

Factors accounting for the difference are complex and a subject of impassioned debate. Students enrolled in community colleges are allegedly less well socialized to academic life and less well integrated into the routines of an academic institution than are those attending four-year schools. They do not reside on campus and are more likely to be occupied with family responsibilities and the demands of a job. Their dropout rate is much higher. Moreover, given the pervasive vocational orientation of most community colleges, many who began with the intention of transferring to a four-year school are soon deflected from their goal by the availability of aggressively promoted and attractively packaged vocational preparation programs. Others discover or decide they lack the academic ability to succeed in a four-year academic regimen.

Some critics characterize the process as a "cooling out" phenomenon, whereby the aspirations of working-class and minority students are lowered by the allure of employment and short-term financial reward. The alleged result (and perhaps the intent) is to slot lower-class students into the lower echelons of business and industry and thus to reproduce socioeconomic class inequality across generations. Although it promises opportunities for upward socioeconomic mobility and status, or so it has been argued, the community college amounts to a sort of academic cul-de-sac. Its real if latent functions are to protect class privilege, to serve as a sieve of academic aptitude, and, ultimately, to help restrict admissions to four-year colleges and universities.

Regardless of whether any such characterization is plausible, the fact remains that when students are deterred from pursuing academic goals, the likelihood increases that in the long run they will ultimately command less prestigious jobs and have lower incomes than students who complete a four-year course of study and attain a baccalaureate degree. Some argue nevertheless that the community college must reaffirm its historic role as a terminal two-year institution dedicated to career preparation and retraining. So long as it emphasizes academic remediation, transfer courses, and preparation for entry into a four-year college, to precisely that degree the community college weakens and undermines its efforts to supply high-quality job training. The community college intent on serving as a transfer institution cannot escape falling captive to the academic interests and values of four-year schools.

If two-year colleges were not distracted by the task of preparing people for more advanced study, or so it is argued, they might be more likely to concentrate their resources on serving the needs of the vast majority of their students who, realistically, will never attain bachelor degrees and should not be pressured into aspiring to education beyond the associate-degree level. Phrased bluntly, not everyone should be encouraged to attend college for a full four years. By jettisoning its involvement in prebaccalaureate preparation, the community college could allegedly focus on what no other type of school does as well: noncollegiate education and outreach in general, vocational training in particular.

According to this view, if community colleges would play to their strengths, they would embrace job training as a worthy and legitimate undertaking in its own right. Attempting to balance out general academic preparation, adult basic education, literacy training, community extension work, and occupational training was bound to generate just the sort of conflicts and contradictions now prevailing. Not only does the emphasis on prebaccalaureate college work inevitably devalue the status of career preparation, it forces two-year schools to model themselves after, and to compete more directly with, four-year institutions. To maintain its credibility as an institution from which significant numbers of students will be able to transfer elsewhere, the community college is forced to allocate resources to support college preparatory courses. Furthermore, if community colleges continue trying to function as feeders to four-year schools, so the argument continues, they will have to redouble their efforts at lowering student attrition. To accomplish that end, in turn, they will have to work far-reaching changes they can ill afford at present: better advisement, more student support services, the building up of campus residential life, and the offering of more diversified academic curricula.[10]

Community colleges, critics claim, cannot continue to have it both ways. If they stress the college preparatory function, they undermine the status of vocational training. Conversely, by recruiting students into programs of immediate occupational relevance, they divert large numbers of those who aspire to earn a baccalaureate degree into shorter-term courses of study geared to vocations. Hence, the wisest course would be for community colleges to divest themselves of those functions they are least well fitted to carrying out, such as preparing student transfers, and to concentrate on the major task for which there is a genuine societal need: postsecondary career preparation and development below the baccalaureate level.

On the opposite side are critics who turn the argument upside down. Historically, it is alleged, the wholesale vocationalization of the public community college from the 1940s onward did not necessarily spring from any grass-roots movement within the general populace. It did not originate in some broad popular demand for job training. Nor was it a conspiracy entered into by corporate business and industry bent on securing publicly subsidized employee training. Still less was the growth in vocational programs among two-year schools a diversionary tactic led by four-year colleges and universities to protect admission selectivity by channeling students into career preparation.

Simplifying somewhat, large-scale vocationalization was, instead, a development stimulated and led by state and local governments. Providing job skills at the postsecondary level was a political imperative of growing importance in the postwar years, and the two-year community college seemed the most logical and appropriate place to house job preparatory programs. Public officials further believed occupational education offered a means of leveraging the political and monetary support of business and industry needed for achieving that goal. According to this particular analysis, community colleges therefore did not set out intentionally to supply a terminal alternative to four-year schools. Basically, their job training role evolved more in response to external political demands. It was neither the inevitable nor deliberate outcome of a conscious policy decision on their part.

In opposition to those who urge that community colleges renew their commitment to vocational preparation, some critics allege they should now pursue exactly the opposite course: emphasize general academic education. Three out of every four students enrolled in two-year colleges profess an intention to transfer to a four-year college. The challenge, accordingly, is to facilitate the transfer function performed by the community college, not to set up barriers or obstacles for students to overcome. What is needed are closer working relationships between two-year and four-year schools and better articulation agreements. The transition from the first two years of postsecondary learning to enroll-ment in a baccalaureate institution should be made as seamless as possible. Move job preparation down to the secondary level where it belongs, the argument goes, or leave specialized technical training to private proprietary schools. Meanwhile, two-year community colleges should cease thinking of themselves as terminal institutions. They should begin to envision themselves more as halfway houses between high school and college.

Some critics go so far as to suggest that some of the larger public community colleges should themselves be transformed into four-year colleges, and that smaller public two-year institutions, many of them located in rural areas, should be reconstituted as branches of state universities. (A few states already have begun to move in this direction.) Proponents readily concede it is not clear whether popular demand for four-year undergraduate education would warrant any such institutional expansion. Nor is it certain that the public would support the cost of expanding two-year schools into full-fledged four-year institutions, even if the need to do so were compelling.

Arguments on behalf of strengthening and reinforcing the two-year school as a more direct link between high school and the last two years of an undergraduate education vary.[11] In opposition to the notion that two-year schools should be exclusively vocational, for example, some hold that deemphasizing academic preparation would spell the end of general learning in a two-year setting. Democratic theory, it is pointed out, affirms that a literate and informed citizenry is essential in a free and open society. High schools by themselves cannot supply the mini-mal level of knowledge required for citizens to participate effectively in democratic decision making. Citizens need to be critical and reflective thinkers. They need cultural awareness and appreciation for society's traditions. They require full awareness of the social and natural environ-ment in which they live. Vocational education by its very nature is poorly adapted to such broad social purposes; its function is purely instrumental. Hence, general interdisciplinary courses of an academic character have a vital role to play in educating the populace at the postsecondary level. If community colleges abandon their college pre-paratory role, their all-important civic function would be lost. The trade-off, some hold, is unacceptable.

In the late 1990s there appeared to be little consensus on which perspective would hold sway. Assuming that community colleges,

Janus-like, cannot continue indefinitely facing in two directions at once—backward toward secondary education and forward toward collegiate-level academic learning—the question remains what their primary mission will be in the years ahead. On the other hand, some analysts claim that the two opposing views have become so polarized that a false dichotomy has been created. Perhaps community colleges need *not decide* between making academic preparation for baccalaureate-level education their top priority and providing terminal vocational preparation. In reality, the two enterprises may not be as mutually exclusive as certain critics have claimed. Success in preparing people to attend the last two years of a four-year college need not inevitably undermine the equally important task of supplying people with skills needed in the job market. Possibly, it is said, the alleged "blurred identity" of the two-year school does not embody a fundamental contradiction awaiting some definitive resolution. Perhaps, instead, it simply points to the broad and diverse nature of a multipurpose, comprehensive institution.

Regardless of the merits of the respective arguments surrounding two-year schools, for the foreseeable future the community college is most likely to remain an institution attempting to fulfill several missions at the same time, much as it has done in the past. Demands for academic remediation, adult basic literacy, and supplemental career preparation or retraining will all undoubtedly remain strong in future years. Simultaneously, the two-year school will be expected to continue serving as a "feeder" to four-year schools. On this view, its destiny does not lie in striving to become an autonomous, independent two-year alternative to four-year institutions, one emphasizing career education and vocational retraining alone. But neither should the goal of the community college be one of acting as a dependent partner with four-year schools devoted exclusively to academic pursuits. However untidy the logic and ambiguous the arrangement, the community college will continue much as it has previously, commingling many different functions.

Even if this judgment holds true, however, some caveats seem in order. First, if the community college is to preserve its legitimacy as a transitional institution, measures will be needed to ensure that its introductory-level academic course offerings conform to standards prevailing in four-year colleges and universities. Simply facilitating the transfer of academic credits earned will be futile unless all parties involved are assured that the quality of academic work completed in a community college is comparable with that in a four-year college.

So far many two-year schools have not been able to offer any such assurance. Whether the college can maintain high standards without restricting entry based on proven academic ability likewise remains an open question.

Second, community colleges will need to decide how important is their role in providing general education as an integral component of an associate degree program. Possibly the best way of conferring legitimacy upon the two-year associate of arts or sciences certificate as a recognized degree is to ensure that programs are neither unduly narrow nor exclusively technical in content. Required patterns of study will need to accommodate liberal learning as well, possibly in the form of broad interdisciplinary courses in the physical, biological, and social sciences; in literature and the humanities; in English composition and grammar; in political science and economics. But will students whose interests are focused closely on career-related interests in applied fields and specialized technologies—a major reason why many elected to attend a community college in the first place—accept the need for general nonspecialized learning as a mandated part of their courses of study? Once again, the answer seems unclear.

Third, two-year technical colleges will need to improve their record of adapting instructional programs to short-term job market demands. Historically, the congruence between the types of training that schools have offered and what the labor market could absorb at any given time has left much to be desired. Community colleges on occasion have helped glut the market with a surplus of graduates in a given field while failing to respond adequately to the problem of a scarcity of trained workers in other fields. Matching up labor supply and demand in a volatile market, one characterized by rapidly changing technology, poses a formidable challenge. It is an issue community colleges will continue to face for some time to come.

Despite deep divisions of opinion over their priorities, in a very real sense community colleges may be said to have come of age. It used to be that those teaching in two-year schools typically would have preferred to be employed in four-year institutions had the opportunity been available. Today, a faculty position in a two-year institution is a career goal actively sought by academics; and possibly a majority of those so employed have elected a community college setting over the alternatives. For certain purposes, as standards have risen, the associate degree has gained a measure of academic status it once lacked. Finally, although it is true that community colleges lack the stringent admission standards of some of their four-year counterparts, many of those who attend the former do so by choice. They perceive the two-year school as offering training better suited to their needs than the sort of educational experience the traditional four-year college or university typically supplies.

FOUR-YEAR COLLEGES

If it is valid to claim that controversy surrounds the mission of the two-year community school, no less may be said of the four-year college. Included under this generic rubric are many different kinds of academic institutions. Some are private (about 1,569 of them as of the late 1990s). Upward of 600 are classified as public, many of which are former teachers' colleges now designated as regional institutions. Private colleges in recent years have found themselves in direct competition with these publicly subsidized schools, usually to their distinct disadvantage.

Probably no more than 200 four-year institutions are liberal arts colleges in the traditional sense (that is, they award a majority of their baccalaureate degrees in a liberal discipline rather than a prepro-fessional specialty such as business administration or education). Some schools are extremely prestigious and highly selective; most are not. Certain colleges retain a more or less attenuated connection with a religious body, while a few sectarian colleges are rigidly wedded to a particular religious orthodoxy. In any event, while community colleges have grown dramatically in numbers and enrollments in recent decades, exactly the opposite holds true of independent and church-related private schools.

The proportion of students attending liberal arts colleges has declined steadily throughout the twentieth century. In 1900 undergrad-uate colleges enrolled two-thirds of all students attending institutions of higher learning. Even then, however, there were gloomy prognostica-tions about the future of the small college in an era increasingly domi-nated by mass higher education and giant universities. President William Rainey Harper of the fledgling University of Chicago fully expected that three out of every four colleges then in existence would soon be reduced to the status of academies or modified into two-year institutions. Presi-dent Nicholas Murray Butler of Columbia similarly was convinced free-standing colleges would be obliged to reduce their courses of study to two or three years. David Starr Jordan of Stanford, commenting in 1903, declared confidently that "as time goes on the college will disappear, in fact, if not in name. The best will become universities, the others will return to their places as academies."[12]

As it turned out, the apocalyptic predictions of those early university presidents were not fulfilled immediately. Still, it is difficult to argue with the judgment that the twentieth century has not been kind to the four-year college. In 1955 colleges, public and private, still accounted for nearly 40 percent of all institutions of higher learning in operation but enrolled no more than 26 percent of all students.[13] Another half century later, in the last decade of the twentieth century, their "market share" had dropped even further: to just below 20 percent, or slightly less than one in every five undergraduates enrolled in a postsecondary institution. Their combined enrollments as of 1995-96 were estimated at no more than 2.9 million, out of a enrollment total of almost 15 million. Some estimates placed their numbers and enrollments considerably lower.[14] Today, the small independent four-year liberal arts college in particular occupies a much-reduced place within the landscape of American higher education compared with its position a century ago.

More than a few observers today foresee a precarious future for the small private or independent college in the twenty-first century. Beset by escalating costs, capital shortages, and increased competition, scores of such colleges now struggle just to keep their doors open. Yet at the same time many continue to flourish. Despite increasing marginalization as their numbers and influence have dwindled, some private colleges still thrive today much as they did when they dominated American higher learning. To paraphrase Mark Twain, though the death knell of the liberal arts college has often been sounded, reports of its demise have been greatly exaggerated.

Some of the independent, church-related, or state-supported colleges in existence today can trace their origins back as far back as the seventeenth and eighteenth centuries. Harvard University (formerly Harvard College) heads the list of distinguished pioneers founded during the colonial era, dating back to 1636. Other pre-Revolutionary colleges of the same period include William and Mary (founded in 1693), Yale (1701), Pennsylvania (1740), Columbia (1754), Brown (1765), Rutgers (1766), Dartmouth (1769), Salem (1772), Dickinson (1773), and Hampton-Sydney (1776).

For two and a half centuries, until the last quarter of the nineteenth century, the predominant institution of higher learning in North America *was* the liberal arts college—usually a small, church-related institution nestled in a rural setting. "Going to college" meant four years spent on an elm-shaded campus in ivy-covered buildings, under close supervision by college officials, far from the temptations of city life.[15] Virtually all were residential boarding schools serving in loco parentis—which is to say, colleges accepted full responsibility for the social, recreational, and spiritual development of the young men entrusted to their care as well as for their academic instruction.

Harvard, the prototypical liberal arts college, was modeled after one of the established colleges at Cambridge. At both Oxford and Cambridge, individual colleges were semi-autonomous tutorial and residential units. The functions of the university as the overarching structure were limited to not much more than the administration of examinations and the formal conferring of degrees. In colonial New England, of course, there was no existing university with which Harvard could affiliate as a subsidiary unit. It was obliged to stand alone, offering instruction and granting degrees on the authority of its own charter. Harvard's standing as an independent entity supplied the template for virtually all the colleges to follow.

Scores of colleges steeped in the traditions of Christian piety and classical learning were founded throughout the first half of the nineteenth century. Estimates differ as to the total number founded, only to disappear not long afterward into oblivion.[16] Those that survived and persisted shared much in common. First, they tended to be small, with student enrollments numbering a few hundred at most. Second, they were (with a few later exceptions) exclusively male-dominated. The age of coeducation had not yet arrived. Third, liberal arts colleges were relatively inexpensive to attend. Operating costs in all but a select few were deliberately kept to a minimum by relying on retired clergymen and returning foreign missionaries to serve as faculty, supplemented by tutors to hear students' class recitations, the ranks of which were filled with young divinity aspirants awaiting admission to seminary. Fourth, in their early period at least, colleges offered a narrow, rigidly conceived academic regimen consisting of an ordered sequence of classical works in philology, rhetoric, formal logic or dialectic, grammar, ancient history, Greco-Roman literature, geography, ethics, and theology. Electives were unheard of, and all students were obliged to complete the same curriculum in lock-step fashion. Finally, antebellum colleges seem to have been prone to a peculiarly lifeless pedagogy, one consisting of little more than formal lectures, exercises in rote memorization, and formal disputations and recitations.

A report from Charles Francis Adams, Jr., reflecting on his under-graduate days at Harvard in the 1850s, was not atypical. "Our professors," he later recalled, "were a set of rather eminent scholars and highly respectable men. They attended to their duties with commendable assiduity, and drudged along in a dreary humdrum sort of way in a stereotyped method of classroom instruction. But as for giving direction to, in the sense of shaping, the individual minds of young men in their most plastic state, so far as I know nothing of the kind was even dreamed of; it never entered into the professorial mind. . . ." Adams added, "No instructor produced, or endeavored to produce, the slightest impression on me; no spark of enthusiasm was sought to be infused into me."[17]

But if the pedagogy prevalent in the old-time college was inadequate to its purpose, the goal of providing those enrolled with a broad training in the liberal arts was certainly well intended. As the famous Yale Report of 1828 expressed it, the aim was not to teach that which is peculiar to any one of the professions but to "lay the foundation which is common to them all." What the Report termed "classical discipline" was said to constitute "the best preparation for [the] professions of divinity and law. . . ." It was "especially adopted to form the taste, and to discipline the mind, both in thought and diction, to the relish of what is elevated, chaste and simple."

The Columbia Report of 1858 echoed the same theme. The mission of the college, its authors declared, was "to make perfect the intellect in all its parts and functions; by means of a thorough training of all the intellectual faculties, to attain their full development, and by the proper guidance of the moral functions, to direct them to a proper exertion. To form the mind, in short, is the high design of education as sought in [the college]."[18]

Classicist E. K. Rand, writing in the 1940s, summed up the prime objective of the old-time college as one of training the mind to think well and the tongue to speak eloquently. This, he suggested, was "not so bad for the seventeenth century, and it is not an unworthy goal for education today."[19] Some of the lofty pronouncements of academics defining the purpose of collegiate education in an earlier day admittedly sound more than a little overblown to the modern ear. But for all their seeming pomposity, they did reflect a spirit of assurance, a sublime confidence in the formative powers of a liberal education less often advanced with the same degree of certitude today. Two hundred years ago Provost Smith of the College of Philadelphia could accept as a self-evident truth that "thinking, writing, and acting well" was the "grand aim" of liberal learning. Again, the founding charter of the College of Rhode Island in 1764 proclaimed "Institutions for liberal education are highly beneficial to society, by forming the rising generation to virtue, knowledge and useful literature and thus preserving in the community a succession of men duly qualified for discharging the offices of life with usefulness and reputation. . . ."[20]

The colonial and antebellum college from which the modern liberal arts institution is descended was obviously neither vocationally oriented nor directly professionalized. Its function was one of academic, intellectual, and moral preparation for professional life; and most of its students were studying for the major occupations of law, medicine, or divinity. The point to be emphasized, however, is that students' specific career goals notwithstanding, broad liberal learning was *thought to be* the best possible preprofessional training. As an 1829 faculty report at Amherst College expressed it, "Our colleges are designed to give youth a general education, classical, literary, and scientific, as comprehensive as an education can well be, which is professedly preparatory alike for all the professions. They afford the means of instruction in all the branches, with which it is desirable for a youth to have a general acquaintance before directing his attention to a particular course of study. . . ."[21]

Many other statements might be cited to illustrate what historian Carl Becker has caused the "lost cause" of the old-time college in defending this traditional conception of collegiate learning.[22] In the early nineteenth century, the college curriculum was still limited in scope, prescribed, and heavily weighted with classical studies. The typical course was an amalgam of the medieval arts and sciences as well as literature and belles-lettres. Its fundamental discipline was Latin—the language of the law, of the church, and of medicine. Taking its place beside Latin was Greek, the language of classical humanism.[23] Together with Hebrew, logic, rhetoric, mathematics, metaphysics, and moral and natural philosophy, Latin and Greek furnished the staples of a type of learning that, as President Noah Porter of Yale put it, was "preeminently designed to give power to acquire and to think, rather than to impart special knowledge."[24] However it was not the sort of curriculum calculated to win broad popular appeal.

The classic defense for the view that even professional preparation should be nonspecific and general in character was supplied in the Yale Report of 1828 alluded to previously, a faculty manifesto that with almost Olympian assurance laid down the dictum that the true end of higher education was the production of a "disciplined and informed mind." In a document authored chiefly by Yale President Jeremiah Day, the argument was advanced that "the two great points to be gained in intellectual culture, are the *discipline* and the *furniture* of the mind, expanding its powers, and storing it with knowledge." In response to the question as to why each student should not "be allowed to select those branches of study which are most to his taste, which are best adapted to his peculiar talents, and which are most nearly connected with his intended profession," the Report insisted, "Our prescribed course contains those subjects only which ought to be understood . . . by everyone who aims at a thorough education."[25]

Gradually divested of its association with the now-discredited theory of the mind as something akin to a muscle capable of being strengthened through the mental "discipline" afforded by classical learning, the basic goal of the old-time college enunciated in the Yale Report proved enduring. Today as in the early nineteenth century, the notion that the unique role of the college at its best is to offer an undergraduate education of a truly liberal but nonspecialized nature continues to exercise a powerful appeal. Faith in liberal learning remains the same, even though, of course, the traditional curriculum dominated by classical languages and literature has mostly been abandoned or radically broadened to include modern disciplines.[26]

The idea that the best preparation for the world of work is absorption in a broad range of liberal studies rather than concentration in a specific professional specialization certainly has not gone unchallenged. On the contrary, it has been under more or less constant attack for almost two centuries. The seeming intransigence of nineteenth-century colleges in their reluctance to accept curricular change probably only exacerbated the problem. For decades there had been mounting demands for education more directly adapted to the needs of all classes of society. As early as the 1820s, loud and clamorous voices were being heard on all sides calling for a "more practical" type of higher education. Reformers urged a broadening of courses of study to include, in addition to the traditional linguistic, mathematical, and literary subjects, more scientific and technical courses. Yet for their own reasons colleges seemed unwilling to accommodate to the rising pressure for curricular diversification and change. And when reforms were instituted, they were made grudgingly and only halfheartedly.

Francis Wayland of Brown University in 1850 posed the issue in the starkest of terms. The choice, he said, was between adopting a course of study that would appeal to all classes and clinging to a course that served one class only. Summing up half a century of collegiate experience, he observed, "We have produced an article for which the demand is diminishing. We sell it at less than cost, and the deficiency is made up by charity. We give it away, and still the demand diminishes." He then asked rhetorically, "Is it not time to inquire whether we cannot furnish an article for which the demand will be, at least, somewhat more remunerative?"[27]

Responses to Wayland's question varied. South Carolina's president James H. Thornwell, for one, rather defiantly proclaimed, "While others are veering to the popular pressure . . . let it be our aim to make scholars and not sappers or miners—apothecaries—doctors or farmers."[28] Henry Tappan, soon to be president of the University of Michigan, advised, "We ought to aim . . . to make apparent the difference between a mere professional and technical education and that large and generous culture which brings out the whole man. . . ." He added, "That is not really the most practical education which leads men soonest and most directly to practice, but that which fits them best for practice."[29]

Throughout the nineteenth century and into the next, the same refrain was sounded. Wrote Charles Eliot Norton of Harvard, "The highest end of the highest education is not anything which can be directly taught, but is the consummation of all studies. It is the final result of intellectual culture in the development of the breadth and . . . solidity of mind, and in the attainment of that complete self-possession which finds expression in character."[30] Agreeing, W. A. Merrill claimed that liberal education was the most practical kind of education a student could acquire, not only because it conferred a knowledge of humane letters but also because liberal studies were useful "in the elevation of character, in the more lively sympathy with the true, the good, and the beautiful, and in the increase of mental power."[31]

Vassar College's president in 1894 similarly spoke of "real, intellectual culture" and the "opening vistas of intellectual interest" as major aspects of academic purpose. Frank Thilly, a professor of philosophy at the University of Missouri, argued in 1901 that an institution of higher learning as trustee "for the general intellectual capital of society" should have as its chief aim "intellectual emancipation." Alexander Meiklejohn, a philosophy professor and dean at Brown who later assumed the presidency at Amherst College, wrote at length on the importance of liberal learning in an age dominated by materialism and crass utilitarianism. The task of the American college, he affirmed, "is not primarily to teach the forms of living, not primarily to give practice in the art of living, but rather to broaden and deepen the insight into life itself, to open up the riches of human experience, of literature, of nature, of art, of religion, and of philosophy, of human relations, social, economic, political, to arouse an understanding and appreciation of these, so that life may be fuller and richer in content, in a word, the primary function of the American college is the arousing of interests."[32]

Apologists for liberal learning in the college repeatedly returned to the same themes. Vocationalism had supplanted authentic education. Professionalism was rampant. Far too many schools were succumbing to the superstitions of the day and hastening to convert themselves into career training centers. Learning was becoming increasingly fragmented. Higher education had lost its moorings and was now adrift. More and more colleges were surrendering to a trade-school mentality, substituting ignoble ends for those higher values that had once given them intellectual purpose and dignity. A line of demarcation should be drawn between "true" colleges of liberal culture and those institutions bent on becoming preparatory schools for entry into the trades and occupations.

A. Lawrence Lowell, a practicing attorney in Boston in 1887 who would later become president at Harvard, spoke for traditionalists when he argued that the highest aim of the college was to promote general learning, not the acquisition of specific information of immediate or narrow practical utility. A "thorough" education, he believed, "ought to make a man familiar with the fundamental conceptions that underlie the various departments of human knowledge, and with the methods of thought of the persons who pursue them." On one point Lowell was insistent: Not all subjects are equally useful or liberal. "Any man who is to touch the world on many sides, or touch it strongly," he argued, "must have at his command as large a stock as possible of the world's store of knowledge and experience; and . . . bookkeeping does not furnish this in the same measure as literature, history, and science."[33]

The basic argument advanced by Meiklejohn, Lowell, and countless others a century or more ago still remains the bulwark of the contemporary liberal arts college today. Rather than attempting to reconstitute themselves as professional preparatory schools, the best of America's independent colleges have remained true to their heritage, believing that learning of a broad and general character, anchored in an array of basic disciplines, still represents the best possible sort of undergraduate education. They have held firm in the face of critics who allege that liberal arts education is an atavism, a vestige of an aristocratic past when liberal learning was the exclusive province of the sons of a leisured elite. Likewise, they have resisted the modern impulse to abandon liberal education as an intrinsic good or to substitute for it direct preprofessional preparation.

Modern liberal arts colleges thus tend not to offer undergraduate courses of obvious vocational utility. Nor have they added extensive graduate and professional programs to their offerings. Attempts by some to boost enrollments by offering degree programs tied directly to future careers have not been notably successful. Lacking the resources to provide specialized professional training, the efforts of the better colleges are concentrated instead on providing high-quality undergraduate courses of study in the humanities, the social and behavioral sciences, mathematics, and the natural sciences.[34]

What the future holds for independent, four-year liberal arts colleges seems uncertain. The poorest among them find it difficult to induce prospective applicants to overlook their decayed facilities, their inadequate libraries and inferior laboratories. Promotional rhetoric about the importance of an intimate learning environment or a low student-teacher ratio can only ring hollow when the basics are lacking. Eventually, sooner or later, some will be forced to close their doors, their fate akin to the "mom and pop" corner grocery overwhelmed by competition from megamarket chains. On the other side, a few dozen highly respected, nationally known colleges retain their appeal and are likely to endure. Amply endowed with funds from private foundations and generous benefactors, they have little difficulty attracting first-rate faculty and as many outstanding students as they care to admit. It is difficult to imagine they might not endure. Finally, in between the two extremes are perhaps two or three hundred institutions suffering from declining enrollments, poor endowments, and aging facilities whose fate appears more problematic. Optimistic assessments suggest, however, that despite the challenges they face, with proper leadership and prudent management, many of them can and will survive as well.[35]

ORIGINS OF THE AMERICAN UNIVERSITY

The emergence of the American university as a distinctive institutional type, separate and apart from the traditional college, was the product of an entire complex of social, economic, political, and cultural factors at work throughout the latter half of the nineteenth century. Its formative period may be said to have extended from the immediate post–Civil War period up to about the eve of World War I. By the midpoint of the twentieth century's second decade, the university had acquired most of its essential features and was set upon the course that would carry it throughout the remainder of the 1900s.

Some of the university's archetypal elements represented a borrowing and subsequent adaptation of English academic traditions of the seventeenth and eighteenth centuries. Others involved an attempted transplant to American soil of root stock taken from Germanic university ideals of the nineteenth century. To these were added certain indigenous features that were uniquely American. The result, it is often noted, has been a highly eclectic institution whose constituent components do not always seem to fit well together.[36] Mirroring its diverse origins have been its multiple functions. In a very fundamental sense, the history of the American university has been the story of the coexistence within a single institution of several incompatible, even contradictory ends.[37]

Beginning in the 1860s, existing institutions of higher learning were subjected to searching scrutiny as never before. Even within academe, educational leaders were engaged in intensive debate among themselves about basic purposes and goals. Change was in the air; and although opinion differed as to what direction reform should assume, there was little doubt that nothing less than a basic and far-reaching transformation of the collegiate system would suffice. Andrew Carnegie, writing in 1889, spoke for many in voicing his dissatisfaction with the old-time college and its alleged preoccupation with classical lore. "While the college student has been learning a little about the barbarous and petty squabbles of a far-distant past, or trying to master languages which are dead, such knowledge as seems adapted for life upon another planet than this as far as business affairs are concerned," he observed acidly, "the future captain of industry is hotly engaged in the school of experience, obtaining the very knowledge required for his future triumphs." He added, "College education as it exists is fatal to success in that domain."[38]

The entire thrust for reform, noted President David Starr Jordan of Stanford, was "toward reality and practicality." A professor at New York University, writing in 1890, similarly called for an end to the seeming insularity of the antebellum college experience: "The college years are no longer conceived of as a period set apart from life. The college has ceased to be a cloister and has become a workshop." J. M. Barker, in an

1894 work entitled *Colleges in America,* professed bewilderment over
the diverse and often conflicting demands increasingly made upon
institutions of higher learning. "On the one hand," Barker commented,
"there is a demand that the work of our colleges should become higher
and more theoretical and scholarly, and, on the other hand, the utilitarian
opinion and ideal of the function of a college is that the work should be
more progressive and practical. One class emphasizes the importance of
. . . making ardent, methodical, and independent search after truth,
irrespective of its application; the other believes that practice should go
along with theory, and that the college should introduce the student into
the practical methods of actual life."[39]

On one point at least, critics of the old-time college were agreed:
The principles and assumptions about culture, knowledge, and the
purpose of higher learning underlying its curricula lacked credibility
in the modern era. An increasingly pluralistic society, reformers argued, was poorly served by institutions that, for the most, were still
under the control and influence of particular religious denominations
and largely devoted to the training of the clergy. Colleges dedicated
to the task of educating gentlemen for positions of social privilege and
respectability likewise did not seem well adapted to serving the needs
of all classes in a democratic social order. A special complaint often
heard was that colleges had been slow to abandon the now-discredited
theory of formal discipline adduced to justify the elaborate mental
gymnastics framing a classical education. A rigid, limited curriculum
dominated by the languages and literature of Greco-Roman antiquity—the standard stock-in-trade of the old-time college—was bound
to seem lacking in utility or relevance in an age marked by expanding
scientific knowledge and technology.

While there may have been consensus on the limitations of the
traditional college, there was little agreement on what should supplant
it. "What we need is a university," declared Thomas Wentworth Higgin-
son in 1867. "Whether this is to be a new creation, or something reared
on the foundations now laid at Cambridge, or New Haven, or Ann Arbor,
is unimportant. Until we have it somewhere, our means of culture are
still provincial."[40] Yet from the 1850s until at least the late 1870s, it was
still quite unclear what a "university" was supposed to be. For some
analysts, the term meant little more than an institution of greater size
offering instruction in a broad range of disciplines. For other commentators, it simply connoted more extensive library holdings. President
John Hiram Lathrop of Missouri in 1864 captured part of the evolving

pattern in claiming that a "true" university was distinguished by a
department of arts and sciences as its core or nucleus, surrounded by
other academic units offering more specialized instruction in practical
arts and various applied sciences.[41] Elsewhere, the position taken was
that a university, as distinct from a college, was primarily a postcollegi-
ate institution to which the diffusion of knowledge through undergraduate instruction was strictly subsidiary.

Whatever its essential attributes or defining characteristics, there
was widespread agreement that the university was still in process of
development. As Henry P. Tappan had observed in 1851, "In our country
we have no universities. Whatever may be the names by which we
choose to call our institutions of learning, still they are not universities.
They have neither libraries and material of learning, generally, nor the
number of professors and courses of lectures, nor the large and free
organization which go to make up Universities."[42] Tappan's judgment
was to hold true for several decades thereafter.

Early on, it was apparent that the twin ideals of practical learning
and public service would come to define one of the university's most
basic aims. "We must carefully survey the wants of the various classes
of the community," avowed President Wayland of Brown, and build
courses of study which will meet the needs of all classes, including
those of the "useful arts."[43] "We are done with the conservatism of the
past," declared a state senate committee on education in Wisconsin.
"We draw our inspiration from our present principles and build our
hopes upon the future. . . . It is not by poring over the dreamy and
mystical pages of classical lore that the student is to develop . . . energy
of character and strength of purpose. . . ." The citizens of the state, the
committee went on to affirm, expected that their university should
"primarily be adapted to popular needs, that its courses of instruction
shall be arranged to meet as fully as possible the wants of the greatest
number of our citizens. The farmers, mechanics, miners, merchants
and teachers of Wisconsin . . . have a right to ask that [the state] shall
aid them in securing to themselves and their posterity, such educational advantages as shall fit them for their pursuits in life, and which
by an infusion of intelligence and power, shall elevate those pursuits
to a social dignity commensurate with their value."[44]

Not everyone was prepared to go as far as did Ezra Cornell in 1868
when he reportedly proclaimed that he would found an institution
"where any person could find instruction in any study."[45] President
Charles W. Eliot of Harvard came close, however, in his insistence that

practical professional training would define the purpose of the evolving university. "No subject of human inquiry can be out of place in the program of a real university," Eliot asserted. "It is only necessary that every subject should be taught at the university on a higher plane than elsewhere." Other academic leaders sounded variations on the same theme. Whatever else the university was to be, it should aspire to become an agency devoted to practical public service, reaching out to encompass the needs of all classes within society and meeting the practical vocational demands of the modern age. This message was embraced by scores of state colleges and universities from the 1870s onward, in Illinois, Virginia, Minnesota, California, Michigan, and elsewhere.

Nowhere was the trend toward occupational utility more pronounced or more vividly illustrated than in the development of land grant colleges and universities.[46] As early as 1848 Congressman Justin Smith Morrill of Vermont had suggested that colleges should "lop off a portion of the studies established centuries ago as the mark of European scholarship and replace the vacancy . . . by those of a less antique and more practical value." Years later he finally succeeded in winning approval for a bill providing grants of federal land to the states, the income from the sale of which was to be used to help fund state colleges. Every state was to receive 30,000 acres of land for each state senator and representative, and would be obliged to establish a land grant college within a five-year period. Each college so founded, it was stipulated, was to be a place "where the leading object shall be, without excluding other scientific or classical studies, to teach such branches of learning as are related to agriculture and the mechanic arts." The bill was signed into law by President Lincoln in July of 1862. The Land Grant College Act (together with a second Morrill Act enacted in 1890, which extended more funding to the states for the same purpose) was to give powerful impetus to the movement to vocationalize collegiate curricula.

Pennsylvania, Michigan, Maryland, and Iowa lost no time in converting existing agricultural schools into land grant "A & M" universities. Rhode Island, Connecticut, Kentucky, Delaware, Indiana and New York assumed control over private institutions and turned them into state universities. Minnesota, Georgia, Missouri, Wisconsin, and North Carolina all reconstituted existing public colleges as state land grant schools. Arkansas and West Virginia founded new public universities, adding agricultural and mechanical engineering elements. Brand-new institutions likewise were formed in Iowa, Kansas, Oregon, Texas, Washington, and South Dakota. Some of them, in apparent defiance of all logic, were founded in direct competition with existing state colleges or universities.

State land grant universities did not necessarily enjoy the immediate popular favor and acceptance originally anticipated by their supporters. In fact, for several decades their careers as institutions of higher learning were both precarious and uncertain. Substantial enrollments, for example, failed to materialize as quickly as had been expected. Confusion persisted over the question of how prominent a role was to be assumed by agricultural education and the mechanical arts, as compared with more traditional subjects. Nonetheless, from the perspective of 1890, a House Committee on Education was still able to claim with some justification that land grant schools had "turned out a body of men who, as teachers, investigators, and leaders of industry, rank well up with the same class of men everywhere in the world." Their further contribution, the committee's report held, was that they had served to bring older institutions "more closely into harmony with the spirit and purpose of the age."[47]

Reflecting back over the previous quarter century, Michigan's James B. Angell in 1891 rightly observed that state land grant universities "very early . . . began to show a broader and more liberal spirit in the arrangement of their curricula of study than the colleges which were modeled on the New England type. They made ample provision for instruction in science and the application of science to the arts. . . . They founded schools of engineering, pharmacy, medicine, dentistry and law. They opened their doors at an early day to both sexes," and, finally, "attained a development almost unprecedented in the history of colleges and universities."[48]

Clearly, state-assisted universities were in process of distinguishing themselves by their emphasis on practical, applied knowledge as a staple of instruction and, correlatively, a public service orientation. By the end of the century almost all of the basic elements of the public university's service role existed in embryonic form: university-sponsored colloquia and conferences open to the public; short courses; extension work; off-campus practica and student internships; and faculty consultation with business, industry, and agricultural organizations. Academic expertise was no longer something to be found exclusively within some campus enclave. Now it was moving off into society, sometimes—literally—into the field. During the Progressive era especially, scores of universities were caught up in the movement to enhance the social and civic relevance of academe, to bring scholarly expertise to bear on the pressing issues of the day, to recruit faculty and students to lend direct assistance in addressing the challenges of societal reform. The University of Wisconsin was a pioneer; scores of other institutions soon followed its lead.

Even as state-assisted land grant schools were beginning to claim their place in American higher education, a parallel development was taking place with the founding of private universities. As historian Page Smith notes, vast fortunes accumulated by business and industrial tycoons in nineteenth-century America provided just the sort of surplus capital needed to stimulate the formation of private institutions of higher learning. The process had begun with the founding of Johns Hopkins in 1876 in Baltimore, Maryland, under the inspired presidential leadership of Daniel Coit Gilman. Looking to Johns Hopkins as a kind of model or exemplar of what a modern university should strive to become, scores of wealthy philanthropists hastened to endow institutions of their own. As Smith phrases it, "Universities became more popular than yachts or Newport mansions (and much more expensive; colleges were passé or for lesser tycoons)."[49] Commodore Cornelius Vanderbilt offered a million-dollar endowment in 1875 to open the university that was to bear his name. In 1887 Jonas Gilman Clark helped inaugurate Clark University at Worcester, Massachusetts. Meanwhile, Ezra Cornell had initiated his own university at Ithaca, New York, with a grant of about $500,000. Railroad baron Leland Stanford donated $20 million to get his institution started in 1891; and a year later John D. Rockefeller's donation of more than $30 million had made possible the opening of the University of Chicago.

From the very outset, it was not at all clear whether undergraduate education of any sort would have a role to play within the modern university. At Johns Hopkins, as at Chicago, sentiment ran strong for a time that the university ought not to feel obliged to assume any of the functions of the old-time college, undergraduate instruction in particular. Clark University, as one of several examples, refused admission to undergraduates throughout the first fifteen years of its existence, until 1902 when the first freshmen were admitted. The idea that preprofessional preparation could be acquired elsewhere, but certainly not in a university, commanded broad assent in many influential academic circles. The university, it was avowed, should be exclusively a graduate-level institution dedicated to professional training—and to research.

Scholarship and research as a second major function of the university was basically an ideal imported from Germany, albeit in much modified form. What stimulated the adaptation more than anything else were the academic sojourns spent at German universities throughout the 1860s and 1870s by such pioneer scholars as George Bancroft and Charles W. Eliot. Hard on their heels came others, in constantly expanding numbers, drawn by the allure and reputation of German scholarship at Heidelberg, Halle, Leipzig, Breslau, Göttingen, and, above all, the famous University of Berlin. American academics who had visited or studied in Germany returned home filled with effusive praise for the Germanic notion of the university as a place for pure research. Their common resolve was to transform the American institutions to which they returned along the same lines.

American visitors to German universities found several features in particular admirable. First and foremost, they were drawn to the idea that the university could be a seat of learning where pure scholarship and inquiry were encouraged, where professors were free to pursue their research without hindrance or interference of any sort. Whereas academic freedom, or *Lehrfreiheit,* was already well established in Germany and had been for centuries, to American observers it was still a novel idea. Second, at a time when American collegiate courses of study were still mostly rigid and wholly prescribed, the Germanic theme of *Lernfreiheit* or the freedom of students to learn, to select what lectures to attend, to do independent work, and otherwise to prepare themselves for matriculation examinations as they best saw fit, was like a breath of fresh air blowing through the musty corridors of academe. Third, they were impressed by the possibilities of an institution not encumbered by undergraduate responsibilities. More specifically, the thinking was that if the university was absolved of the burden of teaching undergraduates, more resources could be made available to support research and scientific scholarship. Fourth, and finally, for some, the dedication of the German institution of higher learning to direct professional training offered a dramatic and welcome contrast with American collegiate institutions back home.

Some reformers, like Eliot, seemed to be unaware of the implicit tension—if not outright contradiction—between the populist ideal of the university as a body dedicated to practical public service and specialized professional training, on the one hand, and the regulative idea of the university as a haven for "disinterested" or non-utilitarian inquiry, on the other. "Truth and right are above utility in all realms of thought and action," Eliot confidently declared.[50] G. Stanley Hall, a professor of psychology at Johns Hopkins and later president of Clark University, was possibly more cognizant of the dichotomy. Pure research, he insisted, was the "native breath" of the university, its "vital air," and he found that air fouled by those who, as he phrased it, constantly prattled on about "the duty of bringing the university to the people."[51]

It is important, however, to note the unique construction American thinking placed on Germanic practices and ideals so far as the university was concerned. The German ideal of non-utilitarian or disinterested learning was summed up by the term *Wissenschaft,* or "integrated learning." In its nineteenth-century German context, the word was a richly textured concept possessing multiple meanings. At its simplest level it meant "science" in the archaic but all-encompassing sense of any type of "knowledge" in general. At another, *Wissenschaft,* connoted "integrated knowledge," which is to say products of inquiry informed by some coherent scheme of human values. German Idealism further lent it the idea of an underlying spiritual unity or synthesizing "worldview" *(Weltanschauung)* as a regulative guide for inquiry. American interpreters, however, missed the more subtle connotations of *Wissenschaft* and, further, what many German intellectuals considered its highest manifestation, namely *Geisteswissenschaft,* or, approximately, "spiritual knowledge." To them, the former term simply meant "science" in the narrower, modern sense of an enterprise of empirical investigation. Hence, ironically enough, in its English-language rendition, *"Wissenschaft"* came to be conceived of solely as "scientific knowledge," and its pursuit was enshrined as a cardinal university aim. The contemplative and integrative side of the term in its original German context was lost sight of altogether; and for it was substituted empiricism, a connotation it had lacked. The long-term consequences of this shift in thought proved momentous.

The idea that a university should be a place for scientific research and scholarship took hold rather quickly in the United States. Such was the prestige associated with empirical "science" that before long virtually every academic discipline and subspecialty was aspiring to be as "scientific" as possible—and at least the appearance of scientific method was to be adhered to rigidly, not only in the hard sciences, but in the emerging human or behavioral disciplines as well. Indeed, the cachet of academic respectability attained by any given subject or field within the university seemed to depend directly on the success with which it was able to take on the quantitative appurtenances and modes of investigation associated with hard science (as distinct from the broader sense of *Wissenschaft).* Nor was it enough that psychology, sociology, anthropology, and similar fields should seek to become social "sciences." The same imperative was felt in the humanities: in textual criticism and literary interpretation, in historical analysis, in theory-building, in hermeneutics, and so on *ad infinitum*. More than a few modern commentators would argue that the same impulse, already apparent in the waning years of the nineteenth century, still remains a controlling principle in contemporary academe at the end of the twentieth century.

Closely allied with the ideology of scientism was a tendency toward intellectual fragmentation and the "carving up" of knowledge domains into ever smaller and more manageable pieces. As one modern writer has aptly observed, "American paeans to the scientific spirit supplied the rhetorical accompaniment to institutional specialization."[52] Once it became widely accepted that scientific investigation in any subject field was best achieved by concentration and specialization, the principle that ought to govern the university seemed obvious: "That each member as a thinker, investigator, and teacher shall be a law unto himself, in his own department," as Henry Tappan at Michigan phrased it. The university accordingly should aim to be, in his view, a "cyclopedia" of education "where in libraries, cabinets, apparatus, and professors, provision is made for studying every branch of knowledge in full . . . where study may be extended without limit."[53]

Inevitably, not everyone welcomed as an unalloyed good the advent of departmentalization, the division of the university community into smaller and smaller administrative units, or the retreat of scholars into ever more minute specializations.[54] Something important was being lost, it was alleged: a sense of community, of wholeness, a feeling of intellectual connectedness and interdependence. "The prevailing method of university work today is distinctly the German method," Hugo Münsterberg conceded in 1913. But, he added pointedly, many "miss in the technique of that new university method the liberalizing culture which was the leading trait of Oxford and Cambridge. This longing for the gentleman's scholarship after the English pattern has entered many a heart." John Bascom of Wisconsin, writing in the same year, registered a similar point. "The most serious evil, associated with the present tendency in education to special departments," he claimed, was that "the immediate uses of knowledge are allowed to take the place of its widest spiritual ministration. The mind is made microscopic in vision and minute in method, rather than truly comprehensive and penetrating."[55]

Specialization as a dominant tendency or trend within academe at the turn of the century had far-reaching effects. Closely allied with it was yet another social movement that originated in the latter half of the nineteenth century and has continued virtually undiminished ever since: a drive toward the "professionalization" of occupations and vocations. Its impact upon the emerging university was profound. Formerly, it had been possible to speak of the "learned" professions; and they were assumed to be few in number, namely, law, medicine, and theology. But insofar as American middle-class culture was egalitarian and democratic in its basic orientation and committed to upward socioeconomic mobility via careers, the popular tendency as the nineteenth century wore on was to elevate an ever-increasing number of vocations by conferring "professional" status upon them. At once the means and official confirmation of success in this respect was the installation of an extended preparatory program for a particular career within a university curriculum.

The Morrill Acts of 1862 and 1890 supplied the opening wedge. If agricultural pursuits required formal preparatory training in the university, and "mechanics," or engineering, was also to become an academic discipline, the same logic could be applied to practically any other vocation with equal force. Business administration, journalism, nursing, teacher education, library science, home economics, and the domestic arts—all began clamoring for a place within the university. If the university as a seat of learning was to be the place where the specialized knowledge required by emergent professions would be acquired, no occupation aspiring to recognition as a true profession wanted to be left out.

A sort of semantic legerdemain helped the process, conferring prestigious-sounding appellations on once-lowly occupational roles. In the twentieth century the process continued unimpeded. Today one comes to the university to learn how to become a sanitation engineer, an information specialist, a financial analyst, a health-services coordinator, an emergency medical sciences technician, a recreational manager, a production expeditor, a retail sales consultant, and so on *ad nauseam,* to mention only a few of the more egregious examples. Housing preparatory programs for these occupations within the halls of ivy, it might be observed, has both legitimated and facilitated the phenomenon of title inflation that reigns supreme today.

Professionalization and specialization transformed the internal structure of the university quite as much as they did the organization of instruction and research. Just as an increasing division of academic labor according to specialty led to departmentalization, so, too, did administrative management come to resemble more closely the hierarchical, pyramidal bureaucracies of business and industry. The day when a jack-of-all-trades college president could superintend the work of the entire institution with minimal clerical assistance was fast disappearing. By the 1920s and 1930s specialized bureaucratic functionaries were to be found at every administrative level, from the president's office at the top down through the graduated ranks of chancellors, provosts, deans, bursars, registrars, fiscal officers, financial aid analysts, investment counselors, institutional development and public affairs specialists, academic department heads, and program coordinators.

Politically, as critics increasingly took note, the university was coming to resemble nothing so much as a loose assemblage of interest groups, with authority and power distributed in varying measure at different levels throughout the whole. By the 1930s the trend was sufficiently pronounced to prompt University of Chicago Chancellor Robert Maynard Hutchins to quip that a university was a collection of separate colleges and departments sharing little more than a central heating system. Years later Clark Kerr wondered whether the only factor holding the university's various factions together was a common grievance over parking.[56]

Still left unresolved in the midst of change was the long-standing question over whether specialized graduate training for the professions and advanced scientific research should be separated completely from undergraduate teaching. Daniel Coit Gilman of Johns Hopkins had left no doubt about where he stood. An authentic university, he insisted, should be exclusively a graduate research institution; it should have nothing whatsoever to do with undergraduate education. Independent colleges, he felt, should abbreviate their courses of instruction and become three-year preparatory institutions. Others, such as William W. Folwell of the University of Minnesota, advanced the suggestion that the German model be adopted in its entirety. That is, secondary schools would assume responsibility for the equivalent of the freshman and sophomore years of college, whereupon universities would take over at the beginning of the junior year. William Rainey Harper of the University of Chicago, who justly deserves his title as father to the junior college movement, was of the same mind.

Harvard's Charles W. Eliot felt both proposals were impractical. For him and a growing number of others, the economic advantage of combining undergraduate and graduate teaching offered the only feasible alternative. Universities, Eliot declared, should aspire to be nothing less than comprehensive institutions of higher learning, encompassing both undergraduate education of a relatively nonspecific character and specialized graduate training. In 1890 Harvard took the lead by charging its Faculty of Arts and Sciences with responsibility for all nonprofessional education from the first year on up through the doctoral level. In light of this and other initiatives of the period, it was confirmed that teaching, both graduate and undergraduate, general and professional, henceforth would command acceptance as a third general aim of the university, coexisting somewhat uneasily along with public service and research.

Eventually, something close to what Eliot and similar-minded advocates had originally recommended as a structure became the standard university pattern. Within less than a decade, scores of colleges had refashioned themselves as universities, but without abandoning their undergraduate divisions. State universities and land grant schools followed suit, leaving intact their respective undergraduate liberal arts departments or colleges. Meanwhile, hundreds of independent or free-standing colleges continued to function as they had formerly. The sole difference now was that they, too, supplied a mode of entry to graduate-level professional training. Students had two choices. They could first complete a four-year general education in some college and then upon graduation apply for more advanced training at the graduate level in a full-fledged university. Or, alternatively, they could enroll as undergraduates in a comprehensive university and subsequently make separate application for admission to that same institution's graduate program to continue with professional training.

What few anticipated was the extent to which professional training would begin to expand and encroach upon general undergraduate education. Whereas most people apparently expected or assumed that the two would remain separate and apart from one another, it was not long before pressures began building to install still more specialized, pre-professional courses of instruction at the undergraduate level, paralleling standard four-year courses of instruction in the liberal arts disciplines. In effect, general or liberal learning soon stood in danger of being overwhelmed by specialized education, whether it was in engineering, agriculture, business administration and public affairs, or any other applied field. The problem has plagued the modern university ever since. According to some, in recent decades the tendency to sacrifice general learning to undergraduate professional specialization has now gone so far as to assume crisis proportions for the liberal arts.

So long as it could be assumed that general learning of a liberal character would continue to define pre-professional undergraduate education, proponents of the liberal arts seemed to have nothing to fear from the development of professional training in the university. Defenders of the more traditional view had long sounded warnings about the "creeping vocationalization" of academe and issued dire predictions about what was to come. Nevertheless, at the outset, the place of a liberal arts college as the dominant core of any university's undergraduate program appeared secure. But even in the early years of the twentieth century, as universities added on more and more professional programs at the undergraduate level, each new school or college began expanding its own academic degree requirements, doing so at the direct expense of general learning. Overall, the history of general learning within the American university since the early 1900s has been the story of a seemingly inexorable diminution of liberal arts education, a constriction of general requirements in favor of more course work demanded within an applied preprofessional or professional field of study, and, in consequence, a steady decrease in liberal arts enrollments as a percentage of total student enrollment.

STRUCTURAL ELEMENTS AND GOALS

Today, the structural constitution of the modern university is more or less taken for granted. It requires both historical perspective and some sense of detachment to step back and look at the institution afresh, to recognize how disparate are its constitutive elements and its aims. First, there is the college of arts and sciences, officially still the nucleus of the typical undergraduate portion of the university, a modified replication of the free-standing or independent liberal arts college that was the forbearer of many universities, but now, as in England, incorporated as only one academic unit or element within a larger, all-embracing university structure.

The typical arts and sciences college of today inevitably encompasses far more subjects and academic specializations than its predecessors, but its basic function remains much the same. Its purpose is to lay out a liberal arts foundation for undergraduate instruction. The aim, variously expressed, is to supply some significant measure of disciplinary breadth or scope (the well-known "distribution" requirement whereby students are obliged to satisfy course requirements in the humanities, social sciences, mathematics, physical and biological sciences, and fine arts). Simultaneously, it allows—and requires—a "concentration" or specialization (that is, an academic "major") in some given discipline. Overall, instruction is not tied directly or closely to any particular occupation or vocation. The presumption is that study is engaged in first and foremost (though not necessarily exclusively) for whatever intrinsic value inheres in the learning acquired; second, for how it presumably conduces to the development of a well-rounded individual; and, third, for its contribution to the formation of a literate and informed citizen.

Some, though not all, of the fundamental ideals and values associated with the liberal arts tradition have been deemphasized in the modern university. Few institutions now attempt to function *in loco parentis* and the paternalism characteristic of the old-time college is notably absent. In public universities especially, officials tend not to try to exercise the same degree of surveillance or supervision over students' lives as they did a generation or so ago. Yet the notion that learning should touch the spirit and heart as well as the intellect is still alive and well. At the level of public rhetoric at least, liberal arts educators still profess a strong commitment to developing civic virtue and literacy, personal character and morality, refinement of judgment, breadth of perspective, catholicity of taste and style, good breeding—all the essentials of the traditional collegiate ideal. Above all, honored in the breach if not always in the observance, is a professed commitment to excellence in instruction. Good teaching, or so it is alleged, remains a *sine qua non* of undergraduate liberal arts education.

Situated astride the undergraduate college, as it were, is the university's graduate school. The latter, of course, represents the institutionalized expression of the Germanic university ideal. Or, more precisely, the graduate division of the typical American university represents a modified adaptation of certain elements of the nineteenth-century German university. At the graduate level, the focus is upon specialized professional training and scholarly research. Most faculty thus live in two worlds, quite unlike their German counterparts of a century or more ago. They teach lower-level courses to undergraduates and at the same time assume responsibility for more specialized instruction at the graduate level. They may serve simultaneously as undergraduate advisors and as mentors to candidates for advanced degrees. At the same time they are expected to be productive scholars engaged in research.

A third structural element of the university edifice is represented by professional schools. A few professional schools or colleges are exclusively or primarily undergraduate-level enterprises; some concentrate on graduate education (for example, law and medicine); an increasing number encompass both undergraduate and graduate levels. Schools of law or medicine, of course, derive most directly from the German model. Schools or colleges of agriculture and engineering, in contrast, trace their origins back to the indigenous American land grant tradition. Professional schools in the American mold generally reflect at one and the same time both the historical emphasis on practical professional training and popular interest in the university as an agency devoted to public service.

REGULATIVE UNIVERSITY IDEALS

It is often lamented that none of the major aims of the university has ever successfully supplied a unifying focus or center for the university as a whole—not research and scholarship, not teaching, not public service. Neither the concept of disinterested inquiry and pure science nor the ideal of applied professional preparation, and still less the idea of the university as a custodian of liberal culture and learning has gained exclusive preeminence and thereby conferred upon the university an anchor point for its identity. The centrifugal forces of specialization, scientism, and professionalism, on the contrary, have worked precisely in the opposite direction, tending to keep it the most pluralist of social institutions in American society. Although attempts have been made repeatedly to elevate one or the other of its many functions at the expense of all others, to declare that teaching or research or service lies at the heart and center of the university, so far all such efforts have failed to win broad acceptance.

Philosopher Karl Jaspers in *The Idea of the University* (1960) once spoke to the same point as follows: "Three things are required at a university: professional training, education of the whole man, research," he observed. "For the university is simultaneously a professional school, a cultural centre and a research institute. People have tried to force the university to choose between these three possibilities. They have asked what it is that we really expect the university to do. Since, so they say, it cannot do everything, it ought to decide upon one of these three alternatives. It was even suggested that the university as such be dissolved, to be replaced by three special types of school: institutes for professional training, institutes for general education and research institutes." Jaspers's verdict was that any such proposal was bound to fail. "In the idea of the university. . . these three are indissolubly united," he insisted. "One cannot be cut off from the others without destroying the intellectual substance of the university, and without at the same time crippling itself. All three are factors of a living whole. By isolating them, the spirit of the university perishes."[57]

Speaking at Princeton in the fall of 1965, President James A. Perkins of Cornell offered a less sanguine interpretation. "The modern university is one of those strange paradoxes of human affairs, dangerously close to becoming the victim of its own success," he avowed. "At a time when there is the greatest clamor among students for admission to the university, there is the greatest dissatisfaction with the conditions of student life and studies. . . . At a time when research is richly supported—and respected—it is being described as the academic Trojan horse whose personnel have all but captured the city of the intellect. And at a time when faculty members are in greatest demand for service. . . there are intimations that their efforts to save the world will cost us our university soul."[58] More than thirty years later Perkins's words still ring true. With only minor modifications to reflect intervening changes, his assessment of the predicament of the modern university seems as apt now at the end of the century as when it was first offered.

The "classic" case for the university as a place of instruction and as a repository of liberal learning and culture, of course, was that first advanced a century and a half ago by Cardinal John Henry Newman (1801-1890). In May of 1852, having been previously called to assume the rectorship of the Catholic University of Ireland, Newman delivered a series of inaugural discourses published as *The Idea of a University*. Newman's views are more often invoked for rhetorical purposes today than actually read, and their complexity renders any brief characterization somewhat hazardous. However, it may be no exaggeration to concur with a modern commentator who flatly asserts that Newman's discourses constitute "the most important treatise on the idea of the university ever written in any language."[59]

Among the many clichés about the university, perhaps none is more worth keeping than the definition of it as a "community of scholars." Well aware even in his own day of the splintering forces already at work, Newman insisted that if the university was to live up to its own ideal, it would strive to nurture and preserve itself as an integrated whole. He strongly criticized those who, as he put it, looked upon the university as "a sort of bazaar, or pantechnicon, in which wares of all kinds are heaped together for sale in stalls independent of each other" and in which "all professions and classes are at liberty to congregate, varying, however, according to the season, each of them strange to each." On the contrary, Newman insisted, "if we would rightly deem of it, a University is the home, it is the mansion-house, of the goodly family of the Sciences, sisters all, and sisterly in their mutual dispositions." Partially cloaked by the archaisms of nineteenth-century prose is a central theme: that the university, properly thought of, ought not to be conceived—and still less should its members think of it—as a random assortment of autonomous units independent of one another. Disciplines housed within the university must be seen as fundamentally interdependent and allied in furtherance of a common unifying purpose.

That common purpose, Newman asserted repeatedly, was to impart to students through careful instruction all of the essential elements of a liberal education. He was well aware that critics would attack his view that education at its finest consists of a set of speculative activities that are not to be justified by their being directly useful to society, nor by their tendency to further the betterment of humankind in some immediate fashion. The notion, he realized, that education is not concerned directly with the social good, and only incidentally serves purposes that go beyond the activities in which education consists, might seem nonsensical to many. But Newman was persuaded that there are experiences and states of mind that characteristically repel any question of their utility. "Knowledge is capable of being its own end," he declared. "Such is the constitution of the human mind, that any kind of knowledge, if it really be such, is its own reward."[60]

Elsewhere in his discourses, Newman registered basically the same point. "Knowledge is, not merely a means to something beyond it, or the preliminary of certain arts into which it naturally resolves, but an end sufficient to rest in and to pursue for its own sake," he declared. "That alone is liberal knowledge, which stands alone on its own pretensions, which is independent of sequel [that is, of practical consequences], expects no complement, refuses to be informed . . . by any end, or absorbed into any art, in order duly to present itself to our contemplation."[61] Contrary to what later critics alleged, Newman was not opposed to applied knowledge, either as a subject of instruction or on its own account. But he did distinguish more carefully than others between knowledge pursued primarily as its own end and learning acquired in pursuit of some extrinsic end.

In the introduction to his seventh discourse, Newman defined liberal education and the mission of the ideal university with exceptional succinctness. The process of shaping and developing the intellect, he claimed,

> instead of being formed or sacrificed to some particular or accidental purpose, some specific trade or profession, or study or science, is disciplined for its own sake, for the perception of its own proper object, and for its own highest culture, is called Liberal Education; and though there is no one in whom it is carried as far as is conceivable, or whose intellect would be a pattern of what intellects should be made . . . there is scarcely any one but may gain an idea of what real training is, and at least look towards it, and make its true scope and result, not something else, his standard of excellence; and numbers there are who may submit themselves to it, and secure it to themselves in good measure. And to set forth the right standard, and to train according to it, and to help forward all students towards it according to their various capacities, this I conceive to be the business of a University.[62]

The product of liberal learning Newman called "intellectual culture." Although he was wholly convinced that the value of that culture was intrinsic or self-contained, he did not preclude the possibility that it might also have utility of an indirect sort. Liberal learning, he wrote, represents "the best aid to professional and scientific study," for

> the man who has learned to think and to reason and to compare and to discriminate and to analyze, who has refined his taste, and formed his judgment, and sharpened his mental vision, will not indeed at once be a lawyer . . . or an orator, or a statesman, or a physician, or a good landlord, or a man of business, or a soldier, or an engineer, or a chemist, or a geologist, or an antiquarian, but he will be placed in that state of intellect in which he can take up any one of the sciences or callings I have referred to . . . with an ease, a grace, a versatility, and a success to which another is a stranger.[63]

Pioneer sociologist Thorstein Veblen, writing some seventy years later in a 1918 work entitled *The Higher Learning in America,* might have accepted parts of Newman's analysis, though his own regulative ideal for the university was actually quite different. His focus was not upon the university as a place of instruction but as an agency of disinterested research and scholarship. Veblen conceded that instruction could be considered a subsidiary function of the university, but he was willing to fit students into his ideal scheme of things only to the extent that teaching aided the work of research. "The conservation and advancement of the higher learning," as Veblen put it, involves "scientific and scholarly inquiry," which is "primary and indispensable." The work of teaching properly belongs in the university "only because and in so far as it incites and facilitates the university's . . . work," he continued. "The instruction necessarily involved in university work, therefore, is only such as can readily be combined with the work of inquiry, at the same time that it goes directly to further the higher learning in that it trains the incoming generation of scholars and scientists for the further pursuit of knowledge."[64]

The university Veblen defined as "a corporation of learning, disinterested and dispassionate" giving itself over to "the single-minded pursuit of science and scholarship, without afterthought and without a view to interests subsidiary or extraneous to the higher learning." Universities therefore ought not to serve as "seminaries for training of a vocational kind." The authentic institution, in Veblen's view, was to be thought of rather as "a body of mature scholars and scientists, the 'faculty,'—with whatever plant and other equipment may incidentally serve as appliances for their work in any given case." It should be, he reiterated, "the one great institution of modern times that works to no ulterior end and is controlled by no consideration of expediency beyond its own [65]

Veblen's exclusionary view of what a university should be left room for little besides its research-related functions. An undergraduate college within a university, he felt, was "an appendage, a side issue, to be taken care of by afterthought." The very presence of an "undergraduate training school" within a university was suspect in his eyes, suggesting perhaps that the faculty was only "a body of secondary-school teachers masquerading under the assumed name of a university." So too, professional and technical schools, like the college, "in their aims, methods and achievements are in the nature of the case, foreign to the higher learning," he avowed. Incorporating professional schools within the university, he claimed, "does not set aside the substantial discrepancy between their purpose, work and animus and those of the university proper. It can only serve to trouble the singlemindedness of both. It leaves both the pursuit of learning and the work of preparation for the professions somewhat at loose ends, confused with the bootless illusion that they are, in some recondite way, parallel variants of a single line of work." Professional schools are about practicality, while the pursuit of scholarship, he insisted, "is not 'practical' in the slightest degree."[66]

Veblen reserved his strongest criticism for what he called "the submergence of the university" in the "edification of the unlearned by 'university extension' and similar excursions into the field of public amusement, training of secondary school teachers, encouragement of amateurs by 'correspondence,' etc." He admitted that the question about "how much these extraneous activities the university should allow itself" was "a matter on which there is no general agreement even among those whose inclinations go far in that direction." Nevertheless, Veblen avowed, "What is taken for granted . . . is the secure premise that the university is in the first place a seminary of the higher learning, and that no school can make good its pretensions to university standing except by proving its fitness in this respect."

As for the state universities of his own day, Veblen professed nothing but contempt. The "greater number of these state schools," he observed, "are not . . . universities except in name. These establishments have been founded, commonly, with a professed utilitarian purpose, and have started out with professional training as their chief avowed aim." Their function, as he characterized it, was "to train young men for proficiency in some gainful occupation; along with this have gone many half-articulate professions of solicitude for cultural interests to be taken care of by the same means. They have been installed by politicians looking for popular acclaim, rather than by men of scholarly or scientific insight, and their management has not infrequently been entrusted to political masters of intrigue, with scant academic qualifications their foundation has been the work of practical politicians with a view to conciliate the good will of a lay constituency clamoring for things tangibly 'useful'—that is to say, pecuniarily gainful." Thus, Veblen concluded, "these experts in short-term political prestige have made provision for schools" and designated them as universities "because the name carries an air of scholarly repute, of a higher, more substantial kind than any naked avowal of material practicality would give."[67] So far as he was concerned, the misrepresentation of mundane training centers as universities was nothing short of scandalous.

To the objection that his vision was "fantastic and unpractical, useless and undesirable; that such has not been the mission of the university in the past, nor its accepted place and use in the educational system of today and yesterday; that the universities of Christendom have from their first foundation been occupied with professional training and useful knowledge and their work has been guided mainly or altogether by utilitarian considerations," Veblen's response was that he conceded as much without argument. But he thought it would be "a gratuitous imbecility" to "prune back the modern university to that inchoate phase of its life-history" and make it again a corporation for professional training. "The historical argument," Veblen observed, "does not enjoin a return to the beginning of things, but rather an intelligent appreciation of what things are coming to."[68] Veblen believed—wrongly, as it turned out—that history was on his side, and that "the barbarian animus of utilitarianism" would be overcome, thereby clearing the way for the emergence of the university as an institution given over exclusively to basic research.

A third major regulative ideal of the university, one standing somewhere between Newman's and Veblen's and combining elements of both, was that enunciated by Robert Maynard Hutchins, a former chancellor at the University of Chicago in the 1930s who subsequently directed the Center for the Study of Democratic Institutions in Santa Barbara, California. In a series of essays, articles, and books spanning four decades, Hutchins advanced one of the most controversial and hotly contested positions respecting the work of the university to appear in the twentieth century. Most widely read among his many works was a collection of manifesto-like addresses delivered at Yale and published originally in 1936 as *The Higher Learning in America.*

At the root of the confusion over academic missions and aims, Hutchins asserted there and elsewhere, was the lack of any regulative *idea* of the university itself: "An idea enables you to tell what is appropriate and what not, what is to be included and what left out. The idea shapes the constitution, the external and internal relationships, and the activities of the university. It holds the place together and defines and protects it." In the United States, he observed, "All we have to do to decide whether we have an idea of a university is to ask ourselves whether there is anything imaginable that would seem inappropriate in an American institution of higher learning."[69]

Hutchins's judgment was that in the absence of a defining idea, the university as an institution has tried to be all things to all people, with nothing at its core to give it identity or to furnish it with limits and priorities. Comparing American institutions of higher learning with those elsewhere in the world, Hutchins commented, "Nowhere else is it automatically assumed that everything anybody wants by way of educational experience beyond the high school or anything anybody would like to see done by way of solving practical problems, collecting data, investigating the universe, or cleaning up the landscape may as a matter of course be a function of the university."[70]

Hutchins was fond of recounting anecdotes to adduce examples of the alleged superficiality and lack of coherence he felt was characteristic throughout American higher education. As he observed in 1941, "I attacked triviality, and forty-two students enrolled in the Oklahoma University short course for drum majors. I attacked vocationalism, and the University of California announced a course in cosmetology, saying, 'The profession of beautician is the fastest growing in this state.'"[71] A University of Michigan president in 1952 at a meeting of university executive officers reportedly asked, "Say, I want to ask you fellows, what we are going to do about embalming?" He went on to explain that the embalmers in his state wanted to become a profession for the dual purpose of limiting competition and raising their social standing. This they proposed to accomplish by establishing a school of embalming at the University of Michigan and requiring all practitioners to have a degree from the school before being allowed to embalm any state resident. Hutchins noted pointedly that no one could think of any reason why the request should not be granted.[72]

As he surveyed the state of academe, Hutchins professed to find only rampant confusion, capitulation to materialism and consumerism, and craven institutions distinguished chiefly for their unabashed vocationalism and unprincipled opportunism. "Love of money," he alleged, had the practical effect of creating a "service-station" university. Scrambling to satisfy anyone and everyone, he claimed, the typical university had bent its energies to flattering the spirit of the age by accommodating to popular demands of the basest sort. And he excoriated that tendency of the university to try to frame responses to each and every exigency in the name of social utility. In its headlong rush to meet miscellaneous, immediate, low-level needs of every kind, Hutchins judged, curricula had proliferated mindlessly. "One of the easiest things in the world," he remarked, "is to assemble a list of hilarious courses offered in the colleges and universities of the United States. Such courses reflect the total lack of coherent, rational purpose in these institutions."[73]

As Hutchins viewed it, once begun, the process of social accommodation would continue with no end in sight. More and more, the service-station university was framing its policies to suit those who pay the bills. "Whatever the society wants the university will do, provided it gets the money to pay for it. And it is not even what the society wants. It is what the most vocal pressure groups demand."[74] Hence the university is neither free nor independent; it is always obliged to pursue money to support its multitudinous tasks.[75] Repeatedly Hutchins returned to his central theme. Contemporary society, he insisted, was confused in its assumption that education should serve a vocational purpose. "Every group in the community that is well enough organized to have an audible voice wants the university to spare it the necessity of training its own recruits," he complained. "They want to get from the university a product as nearly finished as possible."

The problem as he saw it was that in acceding to that pressure, the university had lost sight of itself. "An institution is defined by its task. Its task is defined by asking what it alone can do, or what it can do better than any other institution. The functions of the service station can be carried out by training schools, junior colleges, research institutes, hospitals, commercial laboratories, experiment stations, or what you will."[76] But the question of what the university can do best, he judged, remained unanswered.

Although conceding the need for job training, Hutchins felt the university was a very poor place to attempt direct instruction for employment. "Turning professional schools into vocational schools degrades the universities and does not elevate the professions," he emphasized. The inherent ambiguity in any training program is how to secure immediate technical proficiency and at the same time promote a larger understanding of general principles underlying a craft or profession. As he put it, "My contention is that the tricks of the trade cannot be learned in a university, and that if they can be they should not be. They cannot be learned in a university because they get out of date and new tricks take their place, because the teachers get out of date and cannot keep up with current tricks, and because tricks can be learned only in the actual situation in which they can be employed."[77] What the university should concentrate on, as Hutchins saw it, was promoting the broad understanding that would constitute the basis or foundation for specific skills and place their application in some intelligible context.

Hutchins's decidedly unfashionable prescription was for a forthright return to "a common intellectual training." Without it, he asserted, a university was condemned to remain a series of disparate academic units lacking any common understanding, language, or shared sense of purpose. More specifically, what was needed, in his view, was a "common stock of fundamental ideas" to overcome the "disunity, discord, and disorder" he believed had overcome academe. Higher learning rightly understood should address "the cultivation of the intellect" and devote itself to the single-minded pursuit of intellectual virtues: "The heart of any course of study designed for the whole people will be . . . the same at any time, in any place, under any political, social, or economic conditions."[78] What the university can and must do for society, ultimately, is to furnish intellectual leadership, to fashion the mind of the age.

An ideal university, as Hutchins conceived it, would be "a center of independent thought and criticism, an autonomous thinking community." If the university were to disgorge the vast range of miscellaneous, irrelevant activities it had swallowed; if it would abandon the freshman and sophomore years of instruction; and if it would limit its professors and students to those capable of independent thought, it would get rid of "many aspects of immaturity that now confuse it and its supporters." The object of the university, Hutchins claimed, "is to see knowledge, life, the world, or truth whole. The aim of the university is to tame the pretensions and excesses of experts and specialists by drawing them into the academic circle and subjecting them to the criticism of other disciplines. Everything in the university is to be seen in the light of everything else." Professional study need not be excluded, he felt, but he added, "If the sole object in view is to train reasonably successful lawyers, doctors, administrators, engineers, or technicians of any kind, there is no reason for burdening the university with the task. History has repeatedly shown that this can be done on the job or in separate training schools."[79]

For Hutchins, the ideal university would be a relatively small institution, a community of advanced-level students and scholars bound together for purposes of shared inquiry and instruction of a very broad and generic character. It would not be a professional trade school, though it might seek to provide the underlying intellectual foundation for professional development. The university would accommodate teaching, but only in connection with a general or liberal course of study. University scholars might elect to engage in research, but their labors would be disinterested and not necessarily tied to immediate utilitarian considerations. As for the university's service function, Hutchins's settled conclusion was that society would be better advised to look elsewhere or to devise new institutions for the purpose.

To a roster of seminal works on university aims and goals, besides Newman's, Veblen's, and Hutchins' offerings, one might add many other twentieth-century contributions, including analyses proffered by Abraham Flexner, Jacques Barzun, Daniel Bell, Derek Bok, Ernest Boyer, Theodore Greene, Talcott Parsons, Lewis Mayhew, Henry Rosovsky, Christopher Jencks and David Riesman, and Allan Bloom, among others. The list of distinguished titles meriting consideration could be a lengthy one. But among them one additional perspective stands out, not so much for its advocacy of a particular regulative university ideal but, rather, because of the power of its descriptive analysis. In Clark Kerr's *The Uses of the University* (1963), contradictions and tensions within the modern "multiversity" were laid out with exceptional clarity and insight.

Kerr, formerly president of the University of California, opened his discussion with the observation, "Although it is one of our oldest social institutions, the university today finds itself in a quite novel position in society. It faces its new role with few precedents to fall back on, with little but platitudes to mask the nakedness of the change."[80] Today, he went on to observe, the large American university consists of "a whole series of communities and activities held together by a common name, a common governing board"—and perhaps little else.[81] Because the university has been called upon to be so many things to so many different people, "it must, of necessity, be partially at war with itself." The "multiversity," as Kerr characterized it, "is an imperative rather than a reasoned choice among elegant alternatives."[82]

Following a lengthy historical review of the British tradition of undergraduate education, the German tradition of research and specialized graduate training, and the American emphasis upon public service which jointly have formed the modern university, Kerr noted that its tendency had been to try to transcend the contradictions among its several missions by doing everything at once. "Universities," he commented wryly, "have a unique capacity for riding off in all directions and still staying in the same place."[83] Research, graduate training, and service, Kerr argued, have proved fairly compatible with one another. All are carried forward through specialization, and they increasingly relate also to the outside community, to government, to industry, to the professions. All are best carried out in an institution large enough to accommodate an increasing number of specialties and to provide large laboratories and libraries. But undergraduate education finds it harder to coexist with other university missions. Undergraduate instruction is more internally oriented—toward the student—and typically needs to focus on generalization more than on specialization. Further, in large institutions, mass instruction tends to become impersonal and alienating to the very students it is intended to serve.[84]

Kerr stopped well short of offering any comprehensive prescription for reform other than his often-quoted, semifacetious dictum, "A university anywhere can aim no higher than to be as British as possible for the sake of the undergraduates, as German as possible for the sake of the graduates and the research personnel, as American as possible for the sake of the public at large—and as confused as possible for the sake of the preservation of the whole uneasy balance." Summing up the paradoxes, Kerr noted how "a vast transformation" had taken place without a revolution, for a time almost without notice being taken. "The multiversity has demonstrated," he observed, "how adaptive it can be to new opportunities for creativity; how responsive to money; how eagerly it can play a new and useful role; how fast it can change while pretending that nothing has happened at all; how fast it can neglect some of its ancient virtues."[85] Kerr concluded sounding sympathetic to others' efforts to advance an integrative theory of the university's functions. But he did not attempt to offer one of his own, other than to note that popular opinion seemed to be that the university should continue to perform any tasks society assigns to it.

Cameron Fincher of the University of Georgia offers a useful set of summaries illustrating the contrasts among the views of Newman, Hutchins, Veblen, and Kerr. For Newman and Hutchins, to the extent they share a tendency to emphasize the university's teaching role, the ideal is an institution "in which inspired teachers and aspiring students convene in search of truth. Knowledge, wisdom and truth are . . . transmitted with good fidelity to willing students who read, study, and discuss the best that has been thought and written in the annals of western civilization." Veblen's ideal (as well as that of Jaspers, Flexner, and others) is of a university whose mission is "the creation, discovery, and advancement of knowledge. . . . Knowledge and truth are the quest of an intellectual elite." Kerr's "multiversity," on the other hand, is not the expression of a normative ideal so much as it is a matter-of-fact effort to describe the contemporary university in all its dimensions, but without critically assessing relationships among its many functions.[86]

RECONCILING OBJECTIVES
AND FUNCTIONS

Toward the close of the twentieth century, there still seems to be scant consensus on university priorities and aims. Partisans of the research function continue to press their case, as do advocates for placing greater stress on teaching, many of whom allege that neglect of undergraduate education now constitutes the contemporary university's single greatest failing. Likewise, those wishing to emphasize the university's civic purposes have renewed their calls for enlisting the help of universities in addressing society's most pressing social, economic and political problems through research and applied scholarship.[87]

Charles J. Sykes, author of a muckraking exposé entitled *Profscam: Professors and the Demise of Higher Education* (1988) and a follow-up work, *The Hollow Men: Politics and Corruption in Higher Education* (1990), has been only one of many journalistic critics over the past decade or so who with unaccustomed ferocity have lashed out at current conditions prevailing in academe. As a professional class, he alleges, university teachers are typically neglectful of their teaching duties, "unapproachable, uncommunicative and unavailable" to their students, obsessed with research, and prone to turning over their classroom duties to an underpaid and overworked lumpenproletariat—graduate assistants. Worse yet, as Sykes portrays them, professors have been guilty of inflicting thousands of useless articles and books upon the world, written in "stupefying and inscrutable jargon" that serves only to mask the vacuous and trivial character of their content. In their eagerness to pursue their own professional career goals, he claims, professors are busily engaged filling up entire libraries with "masses of unread, unreadable and worthless pablum."[88] The sadness of it all, critics claim, is that so many academics have allowed themselves to become part of a system that forces them to write when, as is painfully obvious, they have nothing of any great importance to say.[89]

Even as arguments rage back and forth over the publish-or-perish syndrome, there are others who assail the university for its neglect of its historic service role. As Ira Harkavy and John Puckett of the University of Pennsylvania noted some few years ago, "During the past decade a small but growing number of educators, scholars, and influential citizens have begun to criticize. . . universities for having lost their civic purpose. Some are calling for a radical reorientation of American higher education to become, once again, a collection of mission-oriented institutions using reason and research to improve the human condition." In 1990 retiring Harvard president Derek Bok claimed in *Universities and the Future of America* that universities are failing to do what they are supposed to do: help society alleviate its most painful and threatening problems. Many of them, he observed, expend the least effort in those areas where society's needs are most urgent. Harkavy and Puckett concluded, "Colleges and universities can no longer afford the luxury of being inward-looking, relatively self-contained, and unconcerned about producing useful knowledge. . . ."[90]

By the mid-1990s such prestigious bodies as the Education Commission of the States and the American Association for Higher Education had begun lending their active support to initiatives aimed at enhancing the university's service mission.[91] Former U.S. Commissioner of Education Ernest Boyer, president of the Carnegie Commission for the Advancement of Teaching, observed that "the conviction is growing that the vision of service that once so energized the nation's campuses must be given a new legitimacy." He framed the challenge as a question: "Can America's colleges and universities, with all the richness of their resources, be of greater service to the nation and the world . . . [and] respond more adequately to the urgent new realities both within the academy and beyond?"[92] Boyer, among others, was persuaded that American higher education at the end of the twentieth century could become a vital force for social renewal. What was needed, he believed, was a commitment and a resolve on the part of the professoriate to focus its efforts more closely on the production and dissemination of socially useful knowledge and its application to the pressing social issues of the day.

Sir Eric Ashby, master of Clare College at Cambridge and an astute observer of academe on both sides of the Atlantic, offers an interesting perspective on these and other debates that have so wracked the American university in recent years. "Let us try to cast a balance for the modern university," he has urged. "It is the very success of universities which endangers their cohesion internally and their integrity from outside. It does not matter much if the external structure of universities changes . . . provided always that the thin stream of excellence on which the intellectual health of the nation ultimately depends is not contaminated."[93] Ashby's considered judgment on the future of the university as an institution is basically an optimistic one, akin to Cardinal Newman's judgment about the Church when he declared that he kept "an unruffled faith in it, coupled with a conviction of the miserable deficiencies that exist." For Ashby, the issue is not one of deciding *which* roles the university will choose to play but *how competently* it performs with respect to whatever involvements society demands, all the while maintaining some viable balance among them.

First and foremost, however, universities must rededicate themselves to the task of providing quality instruction to students at both the undergraduate and graduate levels. It does not follow that each and every member of the faculty of a given university must be an outstanding classroom teacher. Nor is it realistic to suppose that some good purpose would be served by dragging productive researchers from their clinics and laboratories and hauling them under protest into classrooms. What the imperative demands is that the institution as a whole acknowledge the priority of instruction over all other activities, and then foster an institutional environment or climate directly supportive of that priority, including allowing those faculty members who wish to teach (and who are good at it) to build their careers as teachers.

Second, not in spite of but precisely because they tend to be gigantic in size, universities must become places where students as individuals are mentored and nurtured. Academic advisement must become an integral part of the professorial role, not merely in the narrow or formal sense of assisting students plan specific programs of study, but in counseling with them about their interests and academic concerns. In short, universities must become true communities of scholarship within which students are encouraged to take their place as active participants, both within and outside the classroom. Under present circumstances, given the constraints and pressures under which faculty members work, time spent with students is apt to be regarded at best as a distraction or diversion from more rewarding pursuits. But the sad truth is, literally thousands of students graduate after four or more years spent on campus and depart without being able to claim anything more than a nodding acquaintance, if that, with a single professor. There is something pathetic about a graduating senior in search of someone to write a letter of recommendation on his or her behalf—who then discovers no one is in a position to supply one.

Third, tomorrow's universities, if they are to flourish, must sharpen and refocus much of what goes on in the name of academic research. Here a distinction is useful: that between "scholarship" in the sense of investigation, inquiry, and analysis associated with arts and letters, as well as with certain aspects of the social sciences, and empirical experimentation of the sort long associated with the hard sciences. Respecting the former, if the university does not provide a place in which such inquiry can be sustained, it is difficult to imagine where else it might find an appropriate home. On the other hand, even a generous assessment of what goes on in the name of humane research must conclude that very little of it is the product of disinterested scholarship.

By and large, here the critics of the publish-or-perish syndrome seem to have the better argument. What percentage of the hundreds of thousands of articles and monographs produced yearly are generated by faculty in pursuit of tenure, promotion, or salary increments is anyone's guess. That university faculty have an obligation to demonstrate their scholarship and share it in some public way is unquestioned. That faculty scholarship must find its sole or primary expression through an endless outpouring of books, book chapters, monographs, paper presentations, and journal articles, much of it seemingly of scant significance or import, is another proposition altogether.

Sponsored research of the type typically conducted in the sciences and applied technologies offers a different set of considerations. Considering the funding sources—corporate business, industry, and above all government agencies—most of it can hardly be called disinterested either. Basic or "pure" research needs a university base. "Applied" research within a university context may also be appropriate, though possibly to a lesser degree. What arouses the ire of critics is not that universities sponsor so much research activity, but that they do so to such an extent that some academic institutions to all intents and purposes are converted into R & D arms of sponsoring agencies. Exacerbating matters further is the relatively new phenomenon of proprietary research conducted under the auspices of semi-autonomous institutes and centers that function unto themselves, separate and apart from any larger university governance structure. Some of these new entities appear to exist more for the purpose of enriching the academic entrepreneurs who work within them than to further any legitimate academic purpose of the university at large.

Employing academic expertise for leverage against pressing social problems has a long if not always honorable lineage. Where universities can perform valuable social services, they probably ought to be encouraged to do so. Once again, the issue is one of proportion. Where the university's external involvements assist other agencies and institutions within society to address problems of discrimination, poverty, the environment, human welfare concerns, or urban renewal and so forth, only a hidebound reactionary might object. But when consulting, partnership arrangements, consortia, and other vehicles for public service unduly monopolize faculty time and energy, or otherwise serve to deflect the institution away from its primary academic purposes, then there is cause for legitimate concern.

At the most fundamental level, the question of deciding what the university's aims and priorities ought to be seems insoluble, if only because empirically there is so little agreement at present about them within society and even less prospect for achieving some general consensus among all the protagonists involved. At another level of discourse, the problem of reconciling priorities and objectives is a challenge each academic institution must face on its own, and within each, a question of what stance individuals are prepared to assume. The terms under which seemingly incompatible or contradictory pressures are reconciled amounts to an ongoing challenge, one worked out anew by each successive generation. For the immediate future, it seems unlikely the university will abandon any of its multiple tasks. The real and most meaningful choices, possibly, have to do not with including certain activities at the expense of other involvements, but instead working out and negotiating the terms under which competing but legitimate interests may all be honored in appropriate measure.

III.

ENTRANCE STANDARDS: WHO SHALL BE ADMITTED?

INCLUSION AND EXCLUSION: THE PERENNIAL TENSION

"The seriousness Americans attach to the performance of their academic institutions," observes Stephen Balch, former president of the National Association of Scholars and professor of government at the City University of New York, "reflects the key role those institutions play in realizing the ideals of a liberal and democratic society." As tools for helping people achieve upward social mobility, universities in concert with lower schools are expected to sustain equality of opportunity. "As sharpeners of the mind, they prepare rising generations for the responsibilities of citizenship. As purveyors of cultural understanding and technical skill, they further assimilation, national community, and the increase of the country's productive resources." Finally, Balch notes, "As instruments for the discovery of new knowledge, they bolster expectations of material progress and ratify popular confidence in the powers of reason and science."[1]

To the enumeration of university functions Balch supplies, others might add still other aims and functions—without necessarily agreeing on their relative importance. In spite of disagreement over specifics, what unites most Americans is a sense that education represents both a personal and a social good. More broadly, there is popular appreciation for the important role institutions of higher learning play in advancing that good. As a result, much importance is attached to policy issues involving higher education. Nowhere is that interest and concern so vividly illustrated than in public debate over the question of who should attend college. Practically everyone at some abstract level feels he or she is a stakeholder in how the question is decided. At a more personal or intimate level, especially perhaps for an adolescent aspiring to enter college, acceptance or rejection from the institution of choice (and the reasons thereof) sometimes seems to assume life-defining significance.

Looked at one way, the question "Who should go to college?" appears moot, since practically everyone who wants to attend a postsecondary institution seems already to be there.[2] A good case can be made that everyone and anyone of the requisite minimum age who holds a high school diploma or its equivalent, if sufficiently motivated and possessed of the means to pay tuition (or a willingness to incur debt for the same purpose), can attend college, more or less irrespective of his or her qualifications and abilities. A candidate may not always succeed in gaining entry to his or her specific institution of choice, or even to a second or third preference. Yet somehow, somewhere, there is always a school willing to accept a determined applicant.

Again, any meaningful response to the question about who ought to be allowed or denied admission to higher education needs to take into consideration the sort of institution one has in mind. It can be argued, for example, that admission to two-year community colleges should be completely open to anyone who applies. Then, without contradiction, it could be held that more selective admissions should apply in the case of four-year institutions. Whether the institution is public or private also might be deemed a relevant consideration. Naturally, an answer might hinge on the qualifications and potential for success (or perceived lack thereof) of the individual applicant relative to the degree program sought. Accordingly, the specific course of studies to which the person seeks admission would be taken into account in determining eligibility. Some would say an answer to the question also turns on the individual's motivation in seeking entry, or on the cost to society involved, or what the prospects might be of that person's collegiate preparation helping to fulfill some larger social need or requirement.

However it is framed, the question is still pertinent—if only because there are those who believe that too many people have been admitted into academe, students who have no business being there and who should never have been accepted in the first place. With equal passion others argue that no one should be denied an opportunity to pursue a higher education if they so choose. Two ideals, both of them essential parts of the American way of thinking, thus seem to be in conflict with each other.[3] Reduced to their essentials, one point of view holds that higher learning should be reserved for the few; the other insists that it should be for the many. The former is inspired by the ideal of individual distinction and achievement. The latter invokes the ideal of democracy, of equal rights for all.

The difficulty, as the argument usually is presented, is that the more democratic education becomes, the less it favors excellence; and the more it raises and refines its standards, the less democratic it becomes. Throwing wide the portals of colleges and universities to all who seek entry allegedly increases chances that higher education will devolve into some type of "lower" learning, that academic standards and expectations somehow will be fatally compromised. Conversely, elevating learning to a level where it is stringent and exacting could serve to exclude the great majority of those who otherwise might profit from a college education. Alternatively, setting achievement standards too high might result in an unconscionable rate of failure among those granted admission, assuming some large portion thereof were never fully qualified for acceptance. Hence, in matters involving higher education, so the argument proceeds, there seems to be an inverse relationship between democracy and distinction. Quantity and quality, forever mutually exclusive and irreconcilable, seem to be at war with one another.

As it is typically formulated, making the case for the populist or egalitarian point of view is by far the easier task. Americans traditionally have been suspicious of anything smacking of "elitism." They tend to be profoundly distrustful of any viewpoint serving to legitimate the elevation of any one class of persons over another, or one allowing invidious comparisons to be made between them. Whereas Americans accept radical disparities in income and social class as the inevitable price of a free market economy (and at the very extremes, on a scale approaching that of oil-soaked Middle Eastern sheikdoms and other Third World countries), the common presumption is that in some other, usually ill-defined sense, all people should be considered "equal." Everyone should enjoy equal rights. No one is "better" than anyone else; and therefore no group of people should be allowed to claim privilege or superiority over others. Hence the proposition that some people are more deserving of access to higher education than others is apt to be greeted with skepticism.

At the same time, and without any apparent sense of paradox or contradiction, the American ethos also emphasizes the theme of the "self-made" person, the individual who, by dint of hard work, ability, and perhaps extraordinary effort, succeeds in claiming a position of distinction and preeminence in his or her chosen field of endeavor. Any such person is unmistakably "better" (more skilled, more talented, more proficient, more successful) than are others. Americans profess to admire and honor achievement in its myriad forms and applications. "Excellence" is held out as a goal to be striven after; and it is assumed that those who attain it deserve whatever rewards accrue. The successful corporate entrepreneur, the star athlete, the performing artist who wins fame and fortune—each is admired, held up as a model, and perhaps deemed worthy of emulation. Implicit in this view is the notion that in the rough-and-tumble competition framing the game of life, there must be "winners" as well as "losers." (Less often acknowledged is a possible corollary: Just as the winners are entitled to their victories, somehow, too, the less successful "deserve" their fate, assuming the competition was fair and not rigged.)

Either position can be oversimplified easily and the conflict between them exaggerated. Nevertheless, there can be little doubt that, taken together as formal arguments, they do embody an enduring tension, a paradox even, one not easily resolved. Pursued to their logical conclusion, the two points of view lead in diametrically opposed directions so far as college and university admission policies are concerned. Needless to say, the democratic ideal pursued to its radical extreme favors a completely inclusive approach to collegiate admissions. The meritocratic ideal of individual distinction and achievement, on the other hand, lends support to a more exclusionary position.

OPEN ADMISSIONS:
THE EGALITARIAN VIEW

Academic mythology holds there was once a time when rigorous intellectual standards were maintained, and mediocre or unqualified students were appropriately excluded from the citadels of higher learning. Even a superficial look to the past, however, offers only qualified support for this view. It may have been the case that students in colonial colleges were a fairly serious lot and tended to remain so up until the end of the eighteenth century. (On the other hand, it is worth recalling that they represented an infinitesimally small fraction of the total population.) Thereafter the evidence is more mixed. Most of the antebellum colleges founded in the early years of the nineteenth century were shoestring operations, forced to accept any student who came along. The practical necessity they faced was to carry each entrant forward at whatever point his (less frequently, her) ignorance and limited preparation required.[4] The situation did not change materially in the post–Civil War era, marked as it was by burgeoning enrollments and the opening of scores of new colleges and universities.

There are enough recorded complaints about nineteenth-century students as indifferent scholars to suggest that enforcing standards was forever an uphill struggle. Nor do the enrollment statistics point to much selectivity in admissions. As always, there were good students and bad, just as there were a few favored institutions blessed with an overabundance of qualified applicants and alongside them marginal colleges struggling to attract enough applicants to keep their doors open.[5] The advent of land grant colleges and state universities made possible by passage of the Morrill Acts did little to change matters. Ingrained in the land grant idea was the concept of collegiate education for practically everyone at public expense. This was hardly a prescription for much selectivity or competitiveness. As historian Frederick Rudolph comments with some understatement, "Against this popular democratic ideal, standards of excellence quite obviously would be at a disadvantage."[6]

The appearance in large numbers of publicly supported state institutions of higher learning boded ill for the hundreds of small denominational colleges that still dotted the educational landscape in the 1880s and 1890s. Forced into direct competition with state colossuses for students, private colleges had little choice but to accept most of those who sought admission, even if it meant both a lowering of entry criteria and a certain erosion of academic achievement standards.[7] Meanwhile, during their formative period even privately endowed universities such as Stanford, Cornell, and Chicago were compelled to welcome nearly all comers, no matter how poorly prepared they might be.[8]

The picture becomes clearer still around the turn of the century. Anecdotal lore and the recorded lamentations of innumerable university presidents offer ample testimony to the persistence of a student culture not much attuned to academic rigor and high achievement. At more than a few academic institutions, the general feeling was that it was "bad

form" to earn more than a gentleman's "C" in class lest one be held up
to ridicule by peers as a "grade grind." Students reportedly took it as a
point of pride to rely on cram sessions alone in preparing for examinations. Stories abound of students who boasted of never having visited
the library and of undergraduates who seldom if ever opened a book.
"Don't let studies interfere with your education," advised one light-
hearted student motto.[9] Generally speaking, the impression left is one
of academic laxity and lackluster performance even within the better
universities. How much worse the situation might have been at less
prestigious institutions is more difficult to judge. The fact that by the
1890s nearly all denominational colleges, dependent as they were on
tuition income, were actively recruiting students wherever they could
find them does not suggest much admission selectivity.

What was apparent in the early 1900s was the growing concern
among educational leaders that inclusiveness and quality were proving
incompatible with one another. William T. Foster, who taught at Columbia University, to cite but one instance, believed entrance requirements were far too lax, and he assailed what he characterized as a
"democratic leniency toward the unfit."[10] A German student who visited
the United States in 1906 similarly criticized the "easy, superficial"
character of American universities as compared with their German
counterparts.[11] Countless others echoed the same refrain.

The point of examining historical precedent in this connection,
of course, is simply to illustrate the fact that, for good or for ill,
so-called open admissions are nothing new. As Henry Rosovsky,
former dean of the Faculty of Arts and Sciences at Harvard, points out,
selectivity in admissions was essentially a postwar phenomenon and
it has been limited in its scope ever since. Prior to World War II,
Harvard routinely accepted almost half of all who applied. Comparable
institutions did about the same. Only gradually in the 1940s and 1950s
did certain institutions begin to inaugurate more selective and competitive admission policies. Throughout the decade of the 1960s others
had begun to do the same. By the mid-1980s, chiefly because of
expanded demand, Harvard, Princeton, and Yale were able to accept
no more than about 17 to 19 percent of those who applied; Stanford
was selecting about 15 percent of its applicant pool; and MIT and
Cal-Tech took in between 30 and 34 percent of a much smaller number
seeking admission. At major state universities such as Wisconsin,
Berkeley, and Michigan, the acceptance rate ran considerably higher,
around 50 to 80 percent.

As Rosovsky attests, overall there has been a comparative lack of selectivity in almost 95 percent of all institutions of higher education over the past half century or so.[12] Hence, the case for selective admission on historical grounds is not a strong one. The facts more nearly support the interpretation that, rightly or wrongly, maximal access to American higher education always has been the common pattern. Phrasing the same point differently, invoking some idyllic past as a time when selectivity and rigor prevailed as a way of offering a contrast with present usage lacks much in the way of historical foundation. Something approximating nonselective admissions to colleges and universities more nearly represents a well-established tradition in American higher education. Perhaps only between the late 1940s and the mid-1960s have their been periods when admission to college was an achievement reserved for a relatively select few, and then only certain institutions were involved. On the other hand, for a variety of other reasons, it was not until the late 1960s that the percentage of graduating high school seniors seeking admission to college began to increase dramatically.

Historical considerations aside, advocates of egalitarianism in higher education tend to base their arguments on a combination of social need and the concept of individual rights or entitlements within a democracy. A democratic social order, it is argued, demands nothing less than equality of opportunity for all its citizenry, not just for a privileged few. The same principle of equal opportunity applies with respect to access to higher education. All—or nearly all—must be admitted equally to higher education and treated equally once they get there. Not many commentators would argue that eligibility to attend college is an inalienable and wholly unqualified "right." But according to populist theory, it is certainly more than a "privilege" to be extended or witheld at will.

In today's complex society, for all practical purposes it is essential that as many people as possible be encouraged to extend their education beyond high school. In a simpler, less demanding era, a secondary education sufficed for the needs of most people. This is no longer the case. Effective, meaningful participation in contemporary social, political, and economic life demands the greater awareness and broader understanding that only postsecondary education can supply. From the individual's perspective, higher education offers the prospect of more career options, better choices, an enhanced quality of life. From society's perspective, higher learning amounts to an investment promising better-informed citizens and more highly skilled workers. It is an expenditure no developed economy can afford to do without.

As for the argument that mass higher education amounts to a contradiction in terms, or that standards inevitably will be compromised as more and more people are admitted to campus, proponents of the inclusive view offer several possible rejoinders. First, it is said, traditional academic learning samples only a small fraction of the total range of human abilities, interests, and skills represented within the total population. It has been in the main overly intellectualist, abstract, and conceptual. Only good can come from the pressure to enlarge and expand curricula, to open up new courses of study, to broaden the diversity of approaches to teaching and learning necessitated by the presence of large numbers of those formerly discouraged from attending college. New knowledge paradigms and ways of knowing need to be honored; novel forms of applying knowledge in concrete situations need to be developed; and innovative ways of linking up personal and social needs remain to be explored.

Second, it is asserted, insofar as traditional ways of determining college eligibility have fallen short of predicting success or failure in individual cases, they must be employed with even greater caution. Better yet, democratic ideals should furnish the impetus for abandoning exclusionary measures almost entirely. Always the burden of proof should fall on the institution to show why someone is incapable of learning, not on the individual to demonstrate his or her potential to profit from the collegiate experience. The safest and fairest approach is to allow virtually everyone admission. Provided always that the institution affords a genuine welcome to all, with a view toward nurturing students and affording them genuine opportunities to succeed, the individuals involved and society at large alike benefit.

That academic standards of accomplishment must *change* is undoubted. Whether change of itself implies degradation or deterioration is another matter. America will have moved closer to applying its democratic values to the fullest only when colleges and universities are compelled to adapt themselves to the real needs of those who seek entry, rather than compelling people to conform to internal standards established on the basis of academic considerations alone. The vitality and dynamism of many two-year community colleges, to adduce one possible example, offer dramatic testimony to the transformative possibilities latent in opening up academe to the masses.

Finally, according to egalitarian theorists, the demand for more open admissions need not oblige each and every institution to adhere to precisely the same policies and practices. There is no irreconcilable contradiction inherent in the movement toward encouraging more and more nontraditional applicants to pursue higher education, on the one hand, and the legitimate expectation that some academic institutions may find it appropriate to retain selective admissions, on the other. The ideal would be akin to an open marketplace in which colleges and universities offer many different kinds of experiences and opportunities. So long as everyone's aspirations and needs are addressed to the fullest practical extent feasible, the democratic imperative of equal opportunity can and will be satisfied.

"The only sensible admissions policy is an 'open,' nonrestrictive admissions policy," declare Robert and Jon Solomon, authors of *Up the University: Re-Creating Higher Education in America* (1993).

> Let them all in. There are no good predictors for university performance, nor are there any noncontroversial standards for 'success.' The criteria used today—SAT scores, high school grade point averages—are only self-fulfilling, they prove that people who do well on tests before they begin university tend to do well on tests in the university as well. There are no good tests for readiness and willingness, no computer-graded exams to measure enthusiasm or creativity or intellectual curiosity. There is no way to tell which students are late bloomers. . . . The only sure test for college preparedness is college.[13]

The egalitarian critique denies that quality and quantity are inherently in conflict, sometimes going so far as to dismiss their supposed incompatibility as a false antithesis. The argument essentially is that schools *can* have it both ways: The academic achievements of the outstanding few are not necessarily affected adversely by the more modest successes of the many. Both are possible. "It has been proved on the campuses of great American universities that excellence and mediocrity can coexist, sharing the same dormitories and cafeterias and central heating plants," Eric Ashby has observed. Even those sanctuaries of British elitism, Oxford and Cambridge, as he takes pains to point out, until quite recently nurtured "agreeable and moneyed boneheads" alongside "the most brilliant intellects of the nation." "The mathematical genius and the hearty oarsman lived on the same college staircase."

Basically, the degree signifying no more than modest achievement does not drive out the elite degree: "It is only because public demand for the modest degree is satisfied that the elite degree can hold its standard."[14]

What of the argument then that it is a cruel hoax to admit students unprepared or otherwise lacking the necessary ability to succeed? Assuming academic standards remained rigorous and demanding, would not the inevitable result be a mass exodus of those who could not meet those standards? What would be the consequences, political and social, of a skyrocketing attrition rate? Here, too, populist critics have an answer. "Opening up admissions will let in the riffraff along with the neglected," concede Solomon and Solomon. "But the riffraff will be quickly discouraged or marginalized. We do not need to run the sadistic 'weed-out' courses that some departments notoriously inflict on their students to eliminate the unpromising enthusiast. It is enough that the culture of the university stays focused on education, so those who are not interested will soon find themselves with no point in being there." Again, the conclusion: "The sole requirement for study at the university should be interest and dedication, and those get tested only in the actual process of education."[15]

But *can* the university "stay focused on education" if it is inundated with hundreds of students of modest abilities and limited potential, a distressingly high percentage of whom will arrive on campus poorly motivated and often inadequately prepared as well? Can academic institutions hold the line, all the while adhering to stringent standards of academic achievement? Can or will they do so in spite of their having admitted many of these types of students who, even with the aid of remedial programs and special help, are unlikely to perform at a level sufficient to meet those standards? Or do historical experience and empirical evidence indicate that it is nearly impossible to hold the many accountable to scholastic criteria normed against the accomplishments of the few? The considered judgment of those who argue for selective admission policies is that colleges and universities always face choices: opening admissions and lowering achievement standards, or maintaining standards and allowing higher rates of attrition.

Second, the implication that unsuccessful students would simply pack up en masse and make an unobtrusive departure seems unrealistic. Already, the student failure rate at publicly assisted institutions has occasioned strong criticism and outcries of alarm, forcing universities to redouble their efforts to keep attrition rates down to a level the body politic is prepared to tolerate. One approach has been to deploy elaborate support systems and special coaching for students identified "at risk."[16] Opinion remains divided over the possible limits of their efficacy. Well-designed retention programs appear to offer help for competent students who, for a variety of reasons, are not living up to their potential. But they afford no panacea in meeting the needs of students who probably never should have been allowed in originally.

Meanwhile the suspicion persists—with little hard evidence to buttress either side of the argument—that many students are able to make their way through to graduation only because they have completed a less demanding regimen than their forbears of a generation or more ago. Advocates of nonrestrictive enrollment strenuously deny the allegation. But as one critic has expressed it, "Ultimately it is the yearning to believe that anyone can be brought up to college level that has brought colleges down to everyone's level."[17]

RESTRICTIVE ADMISSIONS: THE MERITOCRATIC VIEW

Terms such as "elite" and "elitism" invoke decidedly pejorative connotations in popular thought. Their associations imply suggestions of unearned privilege, of hereditary aristocracy, of snobbery even. To brand someone an "elitist" is thus often tantamount to condemning the person for excessive self-importance or, possibly, for harboring undemocratic pretensions. The label is rarely used in its more neutral dictionary sense to refer to "the choice or best of anything considered collectively, as of a group or class of persons." More commonly, "elitist" is employed as an invective epithet or as an expression of disapprobation, intended to cast the person or group of persons against whom it is directed on the defensive. The argument that higher education ought to be reserved for the relative few rather than for the many, however, is ultimately and inevitably an elitist view. (Less well appreciated is the point that elitism in this connection is one founded on academic merit or exceptional scholastic ability, not arbitrary privilege.)

The notion that higher learning should be held exclusive to an elite has an ancient lineage, extending back into classical antiquity.[18] Aristotle, for example, gave voice to the established opinion of his day when he estimated that only a small minority was capable of high-order learning. Because it involves mental abstraction and generalization, he judged, all but a talented few would find true higher learning literally incomprehensible. Plato's *Republic* similarly outlines an ideal just state presided over by a small group of philosophers whose intellectual powers have fitted them to their responsibilities as rulers over all other classes. Overall, so far as received opinion among the ancient Greeks and Romans was concerned, liberal learning in the context of a slave economy was necessarily reserved for those with the freedom and leisure to pursue it, namely, the brightest among those who were "free" citizens.

Down through the centuries, the same presumption dominated the pedagogical wisdom of virtually all writers on education: that advanced learning of any sort is the unique province of the few—courtiers, governors, members of the privileged classes of society. Virtually no consideration was given to the possibility that commoners or members of the emergent bourgeoisie would seek, or even possess the capability of profiting from, much beyond the rudiments of basic literacy. Even in colonial America, when Thomas Jefferson proposed a comprehensive system of education for his native Virginia, he assumed that only the unusually talented would be culled or "raked from the rubbish" of the masses and ushered into a university. Abraham Flexner's well-known dictum issued early in the twentieth century summed up the common perspective of the two preceding millennia—that higher education not only is and has been the privilege of the few, but of right ought to be.[19]

The American Declaration of Independence enunciated the principle that "all men are created equal." Then and ever since it has not always been entirely clear *in what specific sense* all are or should be equal, because it is manifestly the case that people are *not* equal in terms of their life circumstances. Early in the nineteenth century the theory gained credence that inequalities among people were due primarily to inequalities in their education. It seemed to follow, therefore, that the corrective for inequality was more education. "Education, then, beyond all other devices of human origin," declared Horace Mann, "is the great equalizer of the conditions of men—the balance wheel of the social machinery."[20] Most reformers of the period had mass elementary schooling in mind; later, secondary-level instruction. By the same token, however, especially in the Jacksonian era, it was not difficult to extend the argument to encompass higher learning for the "common man" as well. The founding of land grant colleges dedicated to imparting applied knowledge to the masses was partly a self-conscious repudiation of the older tradition of classical learning for a leisured, gentlemanly elite.

Democracy, it was held, demanded nothing less than the extension to all the academic privileges formerly monopolized by the few.

Some of the practical consequences following from the mass popularization of higher education in the nineteenth and early twentieth centuries are not hard to identify. Enrollments swelled to record proportions. Included within the multitudes clamoring for admission were students whose abilities were limited at best. Second, curricula and courses of study changed, usually for the better. Had colleges not been forced to accede to the preferences and needs of their "nontraditional" students, it seems unlikely they would have been willing to abandon the classical curriculum that had served as their mainstay throughout the hundred years or so preceding. Even as it was, colleges were exceedingly slow in admitting new subjects—modern history, modern languages, and literature; geography; the fledgling experimental sciences; the infant social science disciplines—and they did so chiefly in response to popular pressures for reform.

Otherwise, the historical record can be read several ways. Indicative of how admission standards were declining was the case of South Dakota College, where in 1888 applicants were required to have only one year of preparatory work beyond the eighth grade. Nor was this an isolated or extreme instance. State colleges and universities as a whole were rarely able to impose entry standards of much stringency and still fill their facilities. For a brief time a few holdouts operated in procrustean fashion, demanding that students adapt themselves to existing strictures. But so few students were able to comply that the numbers thrown on the academic scrap heap soon grew alarming. Attempting to reverse the process, institutions of higher education began fitting their offerings to the students, even the most mediocre among them. Yet the more popular this policy became, the more a kind of Gresham's law seemed to operate, driving away the talented.[21] With equality rapidly gaining ascendancy over quality, many foresaw a time when higher learning in its traditional sense would disappear at all but a very few isolated academic enclaves.

By 1905 Henry Seidel Canby of Yale was expressing wonderment over the extent to which the American university had been transformed by its popularization, terming it "this unheard of combination of sporting resort, beer garden, political convention, laboratory, and factory for research" that left everyone's minds, in his words, "as confused as a Spanish omelet."[22] Norman Foerster, writing in 1931, likewise commented on what had happened to collegiate curricula in the face of popular pressures toward intellectual democratization. At the University of Nebraska, he reported, a student could enroll for courses in, among other subjects, early Irish, creative thinking, American English, first aid, advanced clothing, ice cream and ices, third-year Czechoslovakian, football, sewerage, and problems in the modern home.[23]

The mystique, the aura of esoteric lore, long associated with higher learning had been dealt a decisive blow. "As long as college was something for a small minority," Peter Schrag observes with poetic irony, "as long as it was associated with an aristocracy, it was possible to maintain the belief that the special privileges which higher education conferred or certified were legitimate . . . that somewhere in those ivy halls, those libraries, and laboratories, there burned a special light . . . that there existed a special commitment which enabled men to control spirits and to master powers and incantations which were not shared by ordinary mortals."[24]

But the "demystification" of academe and the consequent opening of higher learning to all "ordinary mortals" came at a price. As the twentieth century wore on, few people wanted to repudiate entirely the whole process of democratizing higher education begun with the enactment of the Morrill Acts, if not long before. On the other hand, psychological research had clearly and irrefutably established the fact of individual differences. Increasingly, empirical evidence was mounting to show that people differ in terms of motivation, learning styles and preferences, the ways in which they process and integrate information— and basic intelligence. "Intelligence" as a psychometric concept did not seem to admit of any unitary or precise definition. But the point that people are different, and that, however it is defined, intelligence is distributed throughout the population along a statistical normal curve, could no longer be doubted. That realization more than anything else dealt a coup de grace to the notion that college students all possess roughly equal abilities. And if nothing else, it necessitated reconsideration of the Jacksonian egalitarianism which had spurred unchecked growth in American higher education for a century and more.

Today's proponents of more restrictive admission standards in academe point out that fifty years ago a high school diploma was still a meaningful credential, and college was a privilege for the relatively few. Now high school graduation is virtually assured for adolescents outside the ghettos and barrios. As for the college degree, it clearly is no longer held to be the mark of distinction or proof of achievement it once was. Completing college nowadays is regarded more as a routine or a rite of passage young persons must go through en route to careers and adulthood. According to recent calculations, fully 63 percent of all American high school graduates—nearly two-thirds of each graduating class—now continue on to some form of further education, and the bulk of them attain at least an associate's degree.[25] Nearly one-third of all secondary graduates ultimately obtain a four-year baccalaureate degree, a percentage figure far exceeding comparable statistics for virtually all of the world's other developed nations. This is, as critic William Henry points out, "inclusiveness at its most extreme and most peculiarly American."[26]

The egalitarian movement to open the doors of academe began with a grand premise, that equality of opportunity requires that the many and the few, the mediocre and the exceptional, should all have their due. Each should be afforded the chance to enter college and demonstrate his or her ability to succeed. Yet no matter how noble the sentiments, critics argue, the actual outcome of that great experiment has been to impose tremendous economic costs on the American people while delivering questionable benefits to many of the individuals supposedly being helped. The total bill for higher education currently runs at about $150 to $175 billion annually, with almost two-thirds of that total expended by taxpayer-supported institutions. Private colleges and universities also access public funds by serving as conduits for subsidized student loans, grants, and other forms of financial assistance. According to Henry and many others, "At its present size, the American style of mass higher education probably ought to be judged a mistake—and one based on a giant lie."[27]

The alleged lie, or deception, has to do with economic benefits promised those who complete a college degree. It remains valid to claim that college graduates on average are more likely to become better off economically than those who do not attend college at all. But the relationship between attending college and economic affluence is neither simple nor straightforward. At the extremes, those with five or more years of college earn about three times the income as those whose formal education ends with high school. Those who attain bachelor's degrees may expect to earn half as much again as those whose education terminates at the secondary level. However, these outcomes reflect other factors besides the impact of the degree itself. It is not unreasonable to assume that college graduates achieve more and earn more partly because colleges and universities tend to attract people who have sufficient intelligence and drive to excel with or without a formal credential.

A more difficult but important question is whether students of limited abilities who have flooded onto the nation's college campuses do better than they otherwise would have had they not elected to attend college. Here reliable answers are elusive. If it could be documented that graduates' economic opportunities were enhanced by having pursued a postsecondary degree, the question would still remain whether they were better job-holders for having attended college or whether the credential they earned *simply facilitated their getting interviewed and hired by employers.* In individual cases, completing college may well be a credential without being a qualification, required without being requisite.[28] In any event, it is by no means clear that the college degree does enhance economic opportunities to anywhere near the extent commonly alleged. Furthermore, even to the extent that it does, that degree of enhancement may be fast disappearing.

The fact of the matter is that formal education *by itself* seems to play a relatively modest role in an individual's advancement as measured in terms of lifetime income; and the income differences resulting from education appear to be small when compared with the total picture. For example, it has been estimated that the median incomes separating the 80 percent of families in the United States that fall along the income spectrum from the bottom fifth to the upper four-fifths represent a ratio of about five to one. Not much of that difference appears to be explained or accounted for by educational attainment.[29] The total ratio, to say nothing of the component explained by education, is minuscule when compared to the extremes of income in America between the richest and poorest households. Yet the five-to-one ratio is sufficient to inspire enormous efforts on the part of parents and their offspring in pursuing college degrees. Formal education operates, as it were, on the margins of the ratio, but its marginal advantage is one few people feel they can afford to be without in the competitive struggle for socioeconomic status.

Meanwhile, it has been suggested, whereas income and education are only modestly correlated, education and occupational status are more highly correlated—but the latter correlation may actually be decreasing. The United States Labor Department's Bureau of Labor Statistics reports that of one-fifth or more of all college graduates work in fields not requiring a college degree. This total is expected to grow, exceeding 30 percent by the year 2005. What was long predicted, that a college degree would afford no guarantee of higher-status employment, is now coming true for an ever-expanding percentage of college graduates.[30]

As the movement toward something beginning to approach universal higher education has progressed, it has become increasingly apparent that the college degree open to many no longer affords automatic entry to desirable, white-collar employment. Relative to the actual educational requirements of the job market, there is already a plethora or surfeit of highly credentialed people in the labor pool; and if current enrollment projections hold up, their numbers are destined to increase considerably in the years ahead. Many jobs formerly open to nongraduates are now being filled by college graduates. Prospects are that in future even more such positions will not make full use of the training people bring to them.

The much-debated phenomenon of "credential inflation" affords another perspective on the same trend. As the scarcity value of the college degree has decreased because an ever-expanding percentage of the population possesses it, the tendency has been to raise the educational requirements of positions well above the actual levels of knowledge and skill needed for satisfactory performance. Hence, many jobs once open to anyone with a high school diploma now require a two-year associate's degree. Positions that formerly did not require a baccalaureate degree now are closed to anyone lacking the four-year credential. Employment opportunities once open to holders of the undergraduate degree are now reserved increasingly for those with graduate degrees, and so on.

The logic of the dynamic is as inexorable as it is transparent. As more people achieve a particular level of educational attainment, the relative advantage or benefit of having done so decreases. Thus, as more students acquire high school diplomas, the economic value of the diploma goes down. Relative advantage erodes due to oversaturation. An individual's predicament is roughly akin to what happens using a stair-stepping exercise machine, where one "ascends" the stairs yet always maintains a stationary spacial position. Loss of differential benefit at any given educational level is an extremely powerful factor in efforts to gain access (and to limit access) to higher levels of the educational system. Erosion of relative advantage at one level of the educational system simply drives up demand for access to the next. When everyone has a high school degree, enormous pressure is generated to continue on to college. But, again, as more and more people obtain college degrees, the benefits of that degree diminish also.[31]

Accompanying this expansion of credentialing is the corollary previously noted, that college graduates are now being compelled more and more frequently to accept positions once considered inappropriate for those possessing college degrees. More significantly, the trend is toward a reduction in the wage and salary differentials of college graduates and nongraduates. Meanwhile, proponents of exclusionary admission standards for higher education are prone to underscore the point that, employment and salary trends notwithstanding, institutions of higher education still continue blithely turning out many more prospective white-collar managers and narrowly trained professionals than the future labor market can possibly accommodate, even by the most optimistic projections.

At present, to cite a case in point, there reportedly are more undergraduate students majoring in the field of journalism than the total number of full-time professional journalists currently employed. Until quite recently, there were more students enrolled in law schools than the total number of partners in all of the nation's law firms. Oversupplies in other fields as well have become commonplace. William Henry remarks, "Inevitably many students of limited talent spend huge amounts of time and money pursuing some brass-ring occupation, only to see their dreams denied. As a society we consider it cruel not to give them every chance at success. It may be more cruel to let them go on fooling themselves."[32]

SELECTIVE ADMISSIONS RECONSIDERED

Extreme egalitarians seek to enlarge the circle of those admitted to higher education as widely as possible, to the point even where everyone desiring collegiate admission is granted entry. (Some observers would claim that, to all intents and purposes, this goal already has been achieved, and with disastrous results.) Extreme elitists want to contract the circle and make postsecondary admissions far more stringent, even if it means turning away literally thousands of prospective applicants in favor of the exceptional few. Neither view in its most extreme form has succeeded in commanding broad consensus. Between the two points of view, colleges and universities must pick their way. Powerful pressures work against exclusive practices, rendering the prospect of truly elitist higher education somewhat improbable. By the same token, there is growing popular awareness that open admission has not been an unmitigated blessing either.

Elementary schooling for everyone at public expense has long since won near-universal acceptance. Free public education for all up through high school is equally well supported (even though there are abundant indications to suggest that a certain percentage of the population is neither able nor willing to conform to the standards of academic achievement formerly associated with obtaining a high school diploma). As for higher learning, opinion is divided, for reasons already mentioned. The suspicion persists that in today's academic environment, if truly high standards were maintained, a brutal "slaughter of the innocents" in the first year of college would ensue.[33] No such slaughter occurs. Hence, persistent and recurrent claims of a general degradation of standards throughout many of the nation's colleges and universities do seem credible.

"In an egalitarian environment," William Henry insists, "the influx of mediocrities relentlessly lowers the general standards at colleges to levels the weak ones can meet."[34] Evidence to support his contention is necessarily sketchy and impressionistic, but it cannot be ignored altogether. The prevalence of remediation programs for freshmen, even at the most prestigious institutions, where students are taught skills formerly mastered in junior high school, represents one straw in the wind. Periodic reports of declining scores on national academic achievement examinations represent another. The erosion or abandonment of once-common collegiate requirements in mathematics, experimental sciences, and foreign languages fits the same pattern, as does the tendency at some institutions to allow so-called applied vocational courses to substitute for courses in basic academic disciplines. Journalistic accounts of rampant grade inflation and of what happened at schools where open admission policies have been adopted offer still other illustrations.

John Leo, writing for a popular news magazine not many years ago, for example, publicly lamented what he termed "the race to the bottom" at the City University of New York after it had acceded to political demands that it give up selective admissions and allow enrollment by everyone applying from any of the city's municipal boroughs.[35] Caught up in charges that all academic norms were elitist, the institution reportedly lowered its standards and accepted large numbers of poorly prepared students. Within a matter of months, as Leo describes it, the distinction between remedial and regular courses had largely evaporated. Enrollments in English literature courses allegedly dropped precipitously, to be replaced by swelling numbers enrolled in high school level remedial English. "Consumer mathematics" began to replace standard offerings in the field. Before long, remediation had "swallowed up" most of the rest of the curriculum, but even abysmally low standards in other disciplines were not being met. Gradually the entire institutional infrastructure began to organize itself around trying to meet the needs of the low-ability students the school had attracted.

As Leo represented it, the university's failure to maintain even minimal standards required some official rationalization. One argument heard was that "deficiency" and "remediation" were mere social constructs intended to marginalize unwanted groups. "Competence in one's own culture" rather than academic proficiency was promoted to the status of a goal. Cooperation, connectedness, and subjectivity were elevated over objectivity and achievement as dominant academic values. The new pedagogy, born of necessity and through a process of political alchemy transmuted into a virtue, now began touting the advantages of the nonhierarchical, collaborative, and nonjudgmental classroom. Various and sundry forms of self-esteem therapy reputedly came to substitute for solid accomplishment in the mastery of disciplinary subject matter.

Protests from those alarmed by the erosion of standards went unheeded. Word of what was going on soon began to spread beyond the university's precincts. Inevitably, as doubts over the integrity of the academic process grew stronger, degrees granted by the institution became suspect. In the final analysis, according to Leo, CUNY's predicament came down to a failure to challenge the claim from radical egalitarians that a college degree as a social good was something that elites were withholding from the disadvantaged and that could be extracted by the naked exercise of political pressure. Leo's case study of an institution gone wrong (even allowing for possible journalistic license and a degree of rhetorical excess) offers a cautionary tale worth heeding.

What of the argument that the opportunity to pursue a college degree is a basic "right"? From a legal perspective, it has been argued before the courts that access to higher education is a right of every citizen, protected under the Constitution's Fourteenth Amendment, and that any denial or abrogation of that right is a violation under the equal-protection clause. To date, no such argument has won legal sanction. At most, courts have held that admission policies and criteria must be neither arbitrary nor capricious; that under contract theory an institution of higher learning is bound to adhere to its published standards and to honor its own admission decisions; and, finally, that entrance requirements may not be formulated so as to discriminate on the base of race, ethnicity, age, or physical exceptionality.[36] But the principle that denial of access to higher education amounts to an abridge-ment of a constitutional right has not been upheld.

Even in a broader extralegal sense, the argument that higher education is an inherent "right" lacks plausibility, and for much the same reasons that not everyone has a "right" to run a four-minute mile or throw a javelin a record-breaking distance. The argument from "equality of opportunity" to support open admissions similarly requires scant con-sideration. If memory, intelligence, and whatever other personal attri-butes needed for academic success are unequally distributed throughout the prospective college-attending population, it follows that two indi-viduals admitted to college, one brilliant and one of mediocre ability, cannot be said to enjoy equal opportunity. Their respective prospects for achieving success are neither even nor equal—any more than are the prospects that an amateur in poor physical condition could compete successfully with an Olympic long-distance runner, even though both have been admitted to a race. (The counterargument that higher educa-tion is not a "race" does not necessarily invalidate the point served by the metaphor.)

A person of high intelligence may be expected to profit from instruction in a wide range of demanding subjects, including calculus, physics, philosophy, or law. The person of lower intelligence, defined in any plausible way, will make little or nothing of these subjects, for they all require intellectual powers of abstraction and analysis he or she lacks. To demand of the latter student that he or she master difficult subjects when the native capacity for doing so is missing is therefore to encourage a waste of time, energy, and resources.

To this line of argument it might be objected that academic performance is not dichotomous at all—that is, the prospect so far as an individual student is concerned is not simply one of failing or succeed-ing. Instead, it is said, one should think of a broad spectrum of academic accomplishment, along which students arrange themselves continuously according to their respective efforts and abilities (the results calculated in terms of a cumulative grade point average, ranging from a minimal 2.0 to 4.0 on the four-point scale). Still less is it a question of "winning" or "losing," considered as mutually exclusive outcomes. College stu-dents achieve in varying measure, ranging from marginally acceptable to truly distinguished, and everyone who continues to perform at or above the minimal level can be said to enjoy some degree of success.

The observation may be well taken, but it is still somewhat beside the point. For all practical purposes, the real questions have to do with what constitutes minimally acceptable performance within a college or university and what qualifications, academic or otherwise, are required to achieve that basic performance level. The bottom line consideration is just that—a question about a floor or bottom level of ability and achievement.

Once again, it seems necessary to emphasize the starting point that American higher education today *is* extremely nonselective in terms of who gains entry to a college or university. When the American College Test (ACT) or Scholastic Aptitude Test (SAT) scores of all graduating seniors who take the test at any given time are compared with the scores of those who actually become college freshmen, for example, the reported difference between the two groups is insignificant enough to demonstrate marked nonselectivity overall on the part of admitting institutions of higher learning. The vast majority of high school seniors who apply to college are admitted, regardless of test scores; and a very large percentage of those who do enter come with below-average test scores. Eight out of every ten with an SAT score one full standard deviation below the mean, for example, do gain admittance.

In short, colleges demonstrate ample willingness to ignore test scores, or to consider them only in conjunction with a host of other factors, including letters of recommendation and high school grades. In no way are they alone decisive in the admissions process—and properly so. But the entire debate in recent years about what the Scholastic Aptitude Test actually measures, how reliable it is as a predictor of college success, and whether it is culturally biased is therefore irrelevant from a practical point of view if few admissions officers place much weight on test scores in making selections. Furthermore, it has been noted, by themselves scores predict no statistical advantage in the quest for employment, job success, or lifetime income.[37]

Just as admissions criteria do not appear particularly stringent, neither are the standards against which performance is judged subsequent to admission. Leaving aside the much-discussed phenomenon of grade inflation that is alleged to have infected academe over the past two or three decades, analysis of attrition statistics lends credence to the proposition that, all things being equal, a student of markedly inferior ability is unlikely to flunk out or leave college for reasons having to do directly or primarily with academic nonperformance. Very bright students (as measured by test scores and collegiate grade point averages) have a very high probability of graduating from college. But even students with low test scores and indifferent collegiate records of achievement, once admitted, still have better than one chance in three of graduating. Tens of thousands of such people are being admitted to higher education; and their chances of graduating do not fall much below the overall average. If academic standards were demanding, a greater differential in noncompletion rates would be expected. The evidence supports no such difference. Among other consequences, the upshot is that employers are reportedly being forced to do what they once relied on colleges for, namely, to sort out large numbers of college graduates whose verbal and quantitative skills are unequal to the challenges of the workplace. Estimates vary, though it has been alleged that upward of about sixteen out of every hundred graduates may be considered academically deficient.[38]

What would happen if four-year colleges and universities across the country became more selective? An analysis of the social composition of entering freshman in relation to College Board or ACT scores for five different years by Timothy Weaver of Boston University some few years ago offers one intriguing possibility. Under prevailing conditions, he judged, deemphasizing test scores in the admission process works to the advantage of applicants from above-average income households and African American families. It tends to work against those of white working-class backgrounds or those from poor households. Weaver postulated a hypothetical policy in place that would restrict admission only to graduating seniors who scored in the upper half of the distribution of scores of all who took the ACT test. He found that under such conditions, the social condition of all college-bound seniors would change—not dramatically, but significantly.

In all cases he ascertained that the offspring of middle- and upper-income families, who currently provide approximately three times as many college freshmen as students of poor or blue-collar working-class background, would bear the brunt of a tougher admission standard in the form of a test-score cutoff.[39] This would be the case because students with low tests scores but coming from advantaged backgrounds are still much more likely to attend college than students with high scores from lower-income families. Hence, as Weaver noted, the assumption that poor and working-class students are currently in college only because of lenient standards, while the same is not true of middle-class students, is ill-founded. The reverse is more nearly the case, since it would not be the few high-achieving students of low socioeconomic background but the larger numbers of lower-achieving students from above-average income households who would fail to make the fiftieth-percentile cutoff.

Advocates for more demanding admission standards have advanced several alternative suggestions. One commonly mentioned is to adjust entry criteria so as to reduce the percentage of high school graduates who go on to a four-year institution of higher learning from the current figure of over 60 percent down to a still-generous 33, or 40, or even 50 percent. If necessary—though the very idea is anathema to many people—high school students lacking the desire and ability to attend college, it has been argued, should be encouraged to enter vocational training programs as a worthwhile and more cost-effective alternative. "This is where most of them are headed in life anyway," asserts William Henry. "Why should they wait until they are older and must enroll in high-priced proprietary vocational programs of often dubious efficacy—frequently throwing away not only their own funds but federal loans in the process—because they emerged from high school heading nowhere and knowing nothing useful in the marketplace?"[40] Sounding the same theme, Brand Blanshard comments, "Perhaps the chief problem for educational administrators in decades ahead is to think out the ways in which the majority of our youth whose gifts and tastes are not academic can be prepared for their own thousandfold walks in life."[41]

A major contention of those who oppose any such move to limit opportunities to attend college is that society at large would be the major loser, not just the thousands of individuals denied admission if more stringent standards were in place. The argument typically assumes two forms, one economic, and one cultural or social. The economic version holds that America's competitive position in world markets and its high-tech infrastructure might be threatened if a decreasing percentage of its population was excluded from the chance to benefit from a four-year college education. The rejoinder proffered by meritocratic partisans is that no direct link has yet been established between rate of participation in higher education and the general condition of any nation's economy. The United States, Canada, Israel, and Russia have very different economies but similarly high proportions of populations formally schooled. Japan and Germany allow a much lower proportion of each student cohort to attend college, but without apparent injury to their national economies. India and Taiwan, among other countries, each have an oversupply of college graduates, without apparent benefit (and possibly incurring some harm) to their economies. Despite decades of efforts aimed at demonstrating that causal relationships exist, national economic indicators have not yet been shown to be tied in any precise way to participation rates in higher education.

The second version of the argument fastens on the presumed non-economic benefits of having an extensively schooled citizenry. There are many ways of estimating the value of a college education, it is held, and not all of them have to do with economic advantage. Whereas it may be true that economic incentives drive large numbers of people to pursue a higher education, there are other equally valid reasons for attending college. Higher learning serves many purposes, among them the fostering of a literate and informed citizenry. Democracy depends on the wide diffusion of civic literacy; and traditionally it has been assumed that the years a student spends on campus contribute meaningfully to the inculcation and development of such democratic values. Empirical evidence to support that claim is not altogether lacking.[42] Hence, the public but noneconomic advantage of having a high percentage of graduating seniors go on to college ought not to be discounted.

Proponents stress the point that decades of research on how the collegiate experience affects students indicates that profound and far-reaching changes typically occur—changes that might not happen in most of the hundreds of thousands of instances where strengthened admission and achievement standards would work to preclude students from attending college. Over a four-year period, college students register large gains in their general intellectual competencies and skills, including those involving abstract reasoning, reflective judgment, and critical thinking. Students' interests and activities—aesthetic, cultural, and intellectual—begin to expand. Lifelong habits of appreciation and understanding are laid down during the college years. There is an unmistakable shift toward more openness and tolerance for diversity. A stronger "other-person orientation" develops, as does concern for individual rights and human welfare. There is a marked decline in doctrinaire opinions and dogma, coupled with a certain liberalization of attitudes and values. The shift reportedly is away from a narrow personal outlook characterized by constraint, exclusiveness, simplicity, and intolerance, and toward a perspective emphasizing greater individual freedom, breadth, inclusiveness, complexity, and tolerance.[43]

Between the freshman and senior years, research suggests, students form a stronger sense of self-identity. Their intellectual interests expand, as does their general psychological maturity. Individual autonomy increases. The individual's skill in maintaining positive interpersonal relationships is reportedly enhanced. Not only do college students become more tolerant and accepting of others, but they grow and develop in their ability to form and defend their own reasoned opinions and convictions.[44] Although the applicable research fails to demonstrate irrefutably that some of this development might not take place anyway, outside the campus environment, it would be hazardous to assume that no connection holds between personal maturation and years spent in academic pursuits.

More important, what the evidence falls short of showing is that such changes occur to an approximately equal extent among all college students, independent of academic ability or achievement. It might be the case, for example, that brighter students are affected more profoundly by the total collegiate experience than are students of lesser academic talent, and marginal students might remain unaffected at all. In other words, the beneficial effects may not be uniformly distributed. Then again, the converse might hold true, and that mediocre students may have the most to gain in the course of pursuing a four-year degree. The point is, no one knows with any certainty. The appeal to the common good as a rationale for encouraging a very large percentage of the population to attend college, in any event, ought not to be dismissed entirely. On the other hand, there is counter-evidence to suggest that many of the collegians crowding the nation's campuses today are not necessarily seeking to expand their intellectual or spiritual horizons. Student pressures to relax degree requirements affords one possible indication. Another is the demand by students for courses that purport to assist them in affirming their own identities in the most literal way possible, in terms of gender or ethnicity or sexual orientation. A marked decline in the amount and quality of work expected in class, as reported by administrators and faculty alike, also does not seem especially encouraging. The inclination of most college students to frame their studies in the narrowest of vocational terms serves also to suggest that "intellectual enlightenment" does not figure conspicuously as a major college goal.

Possibly the single greatest challenge to proposals for more exclusionary standards in academe is the adverse effect they might have on minority access to higher education. Since members of certain ethnic and racial minority groups typically score lower on average on SAT and ACT scores, any proposal to limit admission to colleges and universities based on test scores might serve only to exacerbate the problem of underrepresentation of African Americans and Hispanics already plaguing colleges and universities. A report by the American Council on Education released in 1995, for example, reported that the actual number of minorities going to college had risen only slightly two years previously, up 1.3 percent for African Americans, 3.6 percent for Hispanics, and 3.9 percent for Asian Americans over the preceding year. But because Blacks and Hispanics also make up a growing percentage of all young Americans, the proportion in college remained flat. Just 33 percent of all eighteen to twenty-four-year-old Black high school graduates and 36 percent of Hispanic graduates had enrolled in college in 1993, compared with a much higher percentage of Whites, according to the Council's study.

No initiative to limit college enrollments could win popular support under circumstances where equality of educational opportunity was limited by extraneous factors such as race, gender, or ethnicity. Ideally, academic ability, and ability alone, should be the sole deciding factor in determining admission to college. This consideration has long been acknowledged, even by advocates for more stringent standards. Writing in 1927, philosopher T. V. Smith argued that educational opportunity must be made as "equal" and equitable as possible. His contention was that a person's ability should never be reckoned by what it is at any one time but instead by what it might be if given a favorable opportunity to develop. The only way society can be sure that circumstances are favorable to such an outcome is when adequate compensation or allowance is made for such social accidents of birth as race or economic circumstances, when these factors can be shown to prevent youths from revealing the true extent of their talents. Otherwise, Smith observed, "any judgment before actual trial that persons cannot profit equally from the same opportunity lends itself too obviously to prejudice and unfairness."[45] Precisely this logic inspired what came to be known in the United States from the 1960s onward as affirmative action. No analysis of collegiate admissions would be adequate without consideration of affirmative action programs in academe, the rationale adduced on their behalf, and the recent backlash they appear to have provoked.

AFFIRMATIVE ACTION AND ITS CRITICS: AN ALTERNATIVE

The concept of affirmative action was first unveiled by President Lyndon Johnson in a June 1965 address at Howard University, although the principle behind it was enunciated as early as 1941. In a speech drafted by Daniel Moynihan, Johnson spoke of the need to aid those "hobbled" in life by past discrimination, disadvantaged young African

Americans in particular. Executive Order 11246, issued not long thereafter, called for "affirmative action" among federal contractors and
required hiring without respect to race. Subsequent initiatives broadened
the applications of affirmative action, though efforts were made to avoid
any explicit suggestion that racial quotas as such should be employed.

A 1974 case argued before the Supreme Court, *DeFunis v
Odegaard,* posed the question of whether a system of racial preferences
in law school admissions was permissible under law. Justice William O.
Douglas, for one, argued that racial preferences were unconstitutional
and suggested instead that preferences be based on disadvantage. Four
years later, in the celebrated *Bakke* case, affirmative action as a means
to achieve "diversity" gained credibility as defensible public policy. By
the mid-1970s American institutions of higher education commonly
adjusted admissions rules so as to fill a sizable portion of their freshman
classes each year with students from certified minority groups—mainly
African Americans and Hispanics—who sometimes had lower grade
point averages and standardized test scores than White and Asian
American applicants who were refused admission.

The task confronting a university's admissions officer ever since
typically has been to achieve the goal of admitting appropriate ratios
of Whites, Blacks, Hispanics, Asians, and Native Americans. The
principle advanced is one of "proportional representation." Applying
academic criteria uniformly will not suffice to produce the desired
distribution or mix of students, since the number of minority applicants
who would normally qualify under regular standards is likely to be
small. Hence, admissions requirements must be manipulated to alter
the outcome and academic standards subordinated to the mandate to
achieve ethnic and racial diversity. The admissions director may feel
uneasy about denying places to otherwise-deserving Asian and major-
ity-culture applicants. Nevertheless, the logic of affirmative action
requires preferential treatment for some on the grounds that social
justice must take precedence over individual rights.[46]

Whereas critics assail affirmative action as a form of reverse
discrimination, supporters claim that nothing less offers sufficient
compensation to the disadvantaged for the historic discrimination they
have suffered. Further, it is alleged, if preferential treatment for
minorities leads to their fuller representation within the academic
community, the university ultimately benefits more through the im-
portation of minority perspectives. The higher good, namely, cultural
"diversity," is thereby achieved for the benefit of all.

There are several problems with this argument, of course, not the least of which are the tacit assumptions that racial or ethnic diversity amounts to the same thing as cultural or intellectual pluralism; that intellectual diversity in its most fundamental dimensions is reducible to the categories of race, ethnicity, or gender; and that one must personally embody an ascribed trait, quality, or condition in order to appreciate or understand it in some authentic way. As critic Dinesh D'Souza comments, "The problem with the idea of ethnically determined 'perspectives' is that it condemns us to an intellectual and moral universe in which people of different backgrounds can never really hope to understand each other." According to this atomized view of life, "we are forever resigned to seeing fellow human beings from the outside—empathy becomes difficult, if not impossible."[47]

Critics of affirmative action readily concede there may be circumstances when preferential treatment in admitting certain students may be justified: when it is obvious, for example, that measurable indices of merit do not adequately reflect a student's true academic ability and potential. "Every admissions officer knows that a 1,200 SAT score by a student from Harlem or Anacostia, who comes from a broken family and has struggled against peer pressure and a terrible school system, means something entirely different from a 1,200 score from a student from Scarsdale or Georgetown, whose privileges include private tutors and SAT prep courses," D'Souza observes.[48] Universities thus may well be justified in offering concessions to students who may not have registered high test scores but for whom there is evidence to suggest that low scores are not due to lack of ability or diligence but rather to demonstrated disadvantage.

Increasingly, growing numbers of political conservatives and liberals alike have proposed an alternative to racially based ratios of representation. Universities should retain their policies of preferential treatment, it is urged, but switch their criteria for admission from race to socioeconomic disadvantage. Hence, in decisions about who should be admitted, colleges and universities would take into account such factors as the applicant's family background and financial condition, giving preference to disadvantaged students, provided it was apparent that the beneficiaries could reasonably be expected to meet the academic challenge once admitted. Race or ethnicity, however, would cease to count for or against any given applicant.[49]

Basing admission preferences on class, not race, while adhering strictly to the principle of race neutrality would allegedly carry several advantages. In the first place, class-based affirmative action could help defuse White racism. Because proportional representation according to racial and ethnic categories violates the democratic principle of equal opportunity for individuals, an end to the concept of "group justice" might lessen the indignation and sense of unfairness experienced by those victimized by proportional quotas. Second, basing preferences on socioeconomic factors would more nearly restore the principle of treating applicants as individuals and not simply as members of an ethnic group. Ethnicity or skin color would no longer be utilized as an index of merit or provide an automatic justification for compensation. Third, to the extent that minorities are overrepresented among the disadvantaged, they would still benefit disproportionately from class-based affirmative action programs. The victimization imposed by past discrimination would still weigh heavily as a plus factor in an applicant's favor if it could be shown to translate into socioeconomic disadvantage currently suffered by the student applicant. Finally, as D'Souza remarks, "This kind of affirmative action loses the special stigma that is attached to racial preference. No longer would universities be forced to explain the anomaly of enforcing racial discrimination as a means to combat racial discrimination. The euphemism and mendacity currently employed to justify preferential treatment can stop. . . . [and] the rationale for racial grievance among groups dissolves."[50]

Opponents argue that giving priority to class over race would solve very little since it would afford no guidance in deciding, all other things being equal, between a black sharecropper's son or daughter and the offspring of a white unemployed miner from Appalachia. Yet in the case of some universities, such "apples-and-oranges" questions are already commonplace. Graduate admissions committees regularly must decide between an applicant with a 3.2 cumulative grade point average from Yale and one with a 3.3 from Georgetown or Stanford.[51] In fact, some institutions, among them Berkeley and Temple University Law School, already give preferences for disadvantaged students in addition to racial minorities. Proponents of class-based affirmative action simply call for the more consistent application of socioeconomic criteria instead of those involving race or ethnicity. True, class preferences would mean continuing to treat prospective students as members of a group rather than as individuals. But social-class membership, it is argued, is a far more relevant categorical affiliation than race or ethnicity so far as hidden academic potential is concerned. Moreover, although there always has been a social consensus to support the notion that students from poor backgrounds deserve special consideration, the same cannot be said for class-blind racial preferences.

The calculus of determining class status or disadvantage might be difficult, but not impossible. Income could be made to serve as a good proxy for a whole host of economic disadvantages (such as poor schools and hence inadequate preparation for college). The occupation of an applicant's parents or guardian also might be found to be relevant. The point is not that any given list of variables would fix class status or degree of disadvantage precisely, but that it *is* possible to devise a series of tests that would be indicative of the extent to which an individual's academic potential has been obscured by socioeconomic factors. "It's just not true," argues writer Richard Kahlenberg, "that a system of class preferences is inherently harder to administer than a system based on race."[52] Ultimately, or so it is now increasingly alleged, widespread adoption of class-sensitive admission criteria might go further to promote genuine equality of educational opportunity than has been achieved so far by all the cumbersome and divisive machinery of proportional representation, quotas, and other forms of preference based on race or ethnicity heretofore placed in service.

FUTURE PROSPECTS

Formidable obstacles stand in the way of any movement toward a significant decrease in collegiate enrollments resulting from stricter standards for admission and retention. So long as formal schooling at the postsecondary level is popularly regarded as a symbol of accomplishment as well as the means of attaining or securing socioeconomic status, few will give up whatever differential advantage it is thought to afford, even if it turns out to be a marginal one at best. At the same time, colleges and universities have strong instincts for self preservation. All will make the attempt to attract as many bright students as they can, but failing that, they will accept duller minds in numbers sufficient to fill their classrooms and residence halls. Given a choice between mediocre students and no students at all, institutions of higher learning have consistently demonstrated their willingness to make do with whomever applies.

For many, the prospect that some institutions of higher learning might be forced to close their doors is a chilling one. Nevertheless, it has happened in the past many times before, and closures today still occur periodically, albeit mostly out at the margins of academe. Just as the hulks of former factories, abandoned or converted to new uses, dot the landscape, so, too, it is not entirely impossible to imagine a time when the same fate might befall many colleges or universities. The prospect of empty high-rise residence halls or deserted campuses is not an especially pleasant one to contemplate. Yet keeping the enterprise going for the sole purpose of protecting investments in physical facilities or catering to the loyalties of dedicated alumni, some might argue, offers little justification for retaining a system that has been overbuilt and expanded far beyond the requirements of any authentic social need.

Members of minority groups will not easily or willingly forsake recruitment systems that seem to afford them special advantages where there is strong competition for admission to selective colleges and universities. The notion that everyone deserves a chance to succeed at college, even if it means running the risk of debasing the intellectual currency of academe, will not soon disappear. And so long as the perception obtains that society's needs are well served in proportion to the number of people who seek college degrees, the argument for exclusion (even to a modest extent) is not likely to be received sympathetically.

On the other side, there are some indications that the present system cannot be long sustained without major structural change or modification. The frequency with which institutions of higher learning have resorted to declarations of financial exigency has increased in recent years, sending shock waves reverberating throughout the normally placid groves of academe. Hard-pressed state legislatures have balked at the high cost of maintaining far-flung systems of mass public higher education; and economic circumstances in the years ahead may force them to become more penurious still. Demands for greater "accountability" from institutions of higher education, which had seemed to abate temporarily in the late 1980s and early 1990s, have now been renewed with greater urgency and insistency than ever before.

The appearance in recent years of literally scores of books bearing apocalyptic titles highly critical of academe is likewise worthy of note, especially considering the fact that some few, quite improbably, have attained the status of national best-sellers and, rightly or wrongly, serve to mold public opinion. In any event, the popular suspicion grows that all is not right in the country's colleges and universities, as does the conviction in certain quarters that drastic measures will be called for to set things aright. Hence the possibility should not be lost sight of that the American public will conclude that the nation and its citizenry have, in effect, "overinvested" in higher learning of the traditional sort. Should any such idea attract a wide-spread following, support might build for a quite different academic system in the century ahead, one characterized by considerably greater selectivity than has been common in decades past.

A number of scenarios offer themselves for consideration. It may turn out that any further enrollment increases in two-year community colleges will be purchased at the expense of enrollments at four-year institutions, particularly if the college-attending percentage of the total population flattens out or even begins to decline. If costs continue to escalate, outpacing increases in the cost of living, and if these coincide with any marked decrease in the level of support extended publicly assisted institutions, private colleges and universities may enjoy a renaissance of sorts, competing on a more nearly equal basis with their public-sector counterparts. By the same token, if private institutions find it impossible to keep expenses down, it is highly probable that their position in the academic marketplace will continue to erode.

It is impossible to predict which schools, if any, might be willing to experiment with more selective and competitive admission policies and stricter academic standards. (The proven fact over time is that when certain institutions of high repute have inaugurated more stringent standards, typically enrollments have gone up, not down.) In the public sphere, it has been suggested more than once that public funding should give special consideration to schools serving a high percentage of disadvantaged students and that taxpayers' dollars ought not to subsidize and artificially depress the real cost of public higher education for those who otherwise might turn to private alternatives. As William Henry sardonically comments, "Even ardent egalitarians should recognize the injustice of taxing people who wash dishes or mop floors for a living to pay for the below-cost public higher education of the children of lawyers so that they can go on to become lawyers too."[53]

Already in some states the first tentative steps have been taken to compare schools based on the general academic level attained by their respective student bodies, as measured by some type of uniform assessment examination. Others have suggested that graduating college seniors should all be required to take the Graduate Record Examination or some equivalent evaluation instrument; and if the results prove to be inadequate at any given school, public funding should be withheld forthwith from that institution. Similarly, if the achievement record of students attending a private college or university were shown to be deficient, the school's eligibility to process subsidized student loans and grants-in-aid should be terminated summarily.

In the final analysis, massive—some would say, draconian—initiatives are not likely to be pursued so far as restricting college and university enrollments are concerned, at least not in any immediately foreseeable future. More likely by far is cautious, piecemeal experimentation on the part of scattered institutions here and there. It is possible that financial and political considerations may end up driving public policy to a far greater extent than matters of considered principle. But however achieved, if institutions of higher learning grew resolved to become more selective and competitive in their admissions policies and procedures, and if some of those same institutions were determined to insist on high standards of academic achievement, the ultimate results could turn out to be both dramatic and far-reaching. At the very least, public debate over what college students should be taught, over the shape of undergraduate curricula, would assume entirely new dimensions.

IV.

THE CURRICULUM:
WHAT SHALL BE
TAUGHT?

LIBERAL LEARNING AND GENERAL
EDUCATION: ROOTS OF CRISIS

"Crisis" is an immensely overworked term, often invoked rhetorically to lend urgency to, or to heighten popular interest in, a particular subject. It attracts attention. It also helps sell books. Yet some would argue the word "crisis" needs the protective embrace of quotation marks when used to characterize the present condition of the undergraduate curriculum in American higher education.[1] To proclaim yet another crisis in higher education seems alarmist, histrionic even, if only because crisis seemingly has been the norm for decades. When the Soviets first sent *Sputnik* aloft toward the end of the Eisenhower era and the nation's preeminence in world affairs appeared threatened, pundits hastened to proclaim the advent of a major crisis in education. A decade later, when college campuses were thronged with student protesters and the legitimacy of all forms of authority seemed thrown into doubt, critics once again announced a state of crisis.[2] In the 1970s and 1980s yet another alleged crisis loomed large, this one stemming from revelations of downward academic achievement scores and the apparent disintegration of the traditional canon long thought to dominate collegiate curricula. In short, reports of crisis in matters academic have become chronic.

If there is an authentic crisis at present, or if one seems to threaten on the horizon, it is that the wrangling and contention, the endless disputations and hand-wringing, over the state of undergraduate education in America have become so routine as to obscure rather than to reveal what has actually taken place over the span of the last quarter century or so in American academe. Moreover, indications are that much of the present debate over the curriculum has been politicized to the point where the locus has shifted away from educational considerations almost entirely.[3] Questions about the collegiate course of studies, in other words, increasingly furnish the occasion for fighting out social divisions with society at large. But if this trend continues—if, that is, the politics of the debate assume precedence over all else—the result may very well turn out to be a full-blown crisis in the true sense of the word.

The fact of the matter is, there has hardly been a time when consensus was achieved over the content and organization of the undergraduate curriculum.[4] Historians will look in vain to some former golden age when broad agreement prevailed about texts, organizational patterns, or undergirding assumptions and practices—which is to say, simply, that curricular issues have always and forever been contentious, with very little about them commanding universal assent. Nowadays the sweep of debate has been greatly magnified by the sheer scale upon which mass higher education is conducted. The urgency with which certain issues are prosecuted likewise also may be said to have increased dramatically in comparison with the past. Yet when all is said and done, few if any of the elements of controversy are genuinely novel. They reduce, in some final analysis, to questions about purposes and goals; about conceptions of what the educated person is supposed to know and to be and to do (though some disputants will deny even this claim); about the worth of, and priorities among, different types of knowledge; about the meaning and function of the baccalaureate degree, and, for that matter, by extension, about the purpose of undergraduate collegiate experience as a whole.

Harvard president Charles William Eliot's inaugural address of 1869 furnishes a convenient vantage point from which to gain a certain perspective on today's curricular debates. Throughout the first half of the nineteenth century, academic leaders had been locked in debate over the respective merits of a fixed curriculum built on classical learning as compared with a more flexible, open-ended course of studies incorporating modern subjects. At the time Eliot assumed his new post, Harvard freshmen were still required to enroll for a rigidly prescribed curriculum, one including Latin, Greek, mathematics, French, elocution, and ethics.

Victor Duray's *Historie Grecque* was required reading. Entering students were further compelled to familiarize themselves with at least twenty chapters of Gibbon's *Decline and Fall of the Roman Empire* and some 350 pages of a philosophic work entitled *The Philosophy of the Active and Moral Powers of Man* (1828) by the now-obscure Scottish philosopher Duglad Stewart (1753-1828).

Second-year students took physics, chemistry, German, elocution, and "themes." Juniors and seniors were allowed a limited number of elective choices, though the bulk of their studies was still prescribed. Surveying the scene as he found it upon his arrival, and taking note of the debates still swirling throughout the halls of academe, Eliot professed to discern no inherent conflict between defenders of the older classical conception of liberal learning and protagonists of curricular reform. "The endless controversies whether language, philosophy, mathematics, or science supplies the best mental training, whether general education should be chiefly literary or chiefly scientific, have no practical lesson for us today," he asserted. "This university recognizes no real antagonism between literature and science, and consents to no such narrow alternatives as mathematics or classics, science or metaphysics," he declared. "We would have them all, and at their best."

The vexing question, of course, was precisely how to "have them all." Eliot's answer, in frank acknowledgment of the expansion of human knowledge and the growing impossibility of anyone's encompassing all that could be known, was an elective system permitting students for the first time to select from among alternative courses and programs of study. Defending what at the time was a radical proposal, Eliot observed, "In education the individual traits of different minds have not been sufficiently attended to . . . [and] the young man of nineteen or twenty ought to know what he likes best and is most fit for. . . ."[5] Gone would be the uniform curriculum of Harvard's yesterday. For it would be substituted a multiplicity of individual specializations.

"The elective system," Eliot alleged, "fosters scholarship, because it gives free play to natural preferences and inborn aptitudes, takes possible enthusiasm for a chosen work, [and] relieves the professor. . . of the presence of a body of students who are compelled to an unwelcome task." As if to dispel any remaining doubts about his intentions, President Eliot concluded, "The college therefore proposes to persevere in its efforts to establish, improve, and extend the elective system."[6] Here, all unknowingly, Eliot was giving expression to a rationale that has been appealed to ever since by certain modernists:

that choice enhances learner motivation and that heterogeneity or "diversity" within the student body demands multiple curricular options and greater freedom of choice.

Eliot's dethronement of the prescribed classical curriculum provoked strong reactions. Conservatives were appalled, branding the new elective system inaugurated at a national trend-setter among the nation's colleges and fledgling universities a "fraud" and a "monstrosity."[7] The verdict of Princeton's James McCosh as he declared it in 1885: "I cannot allow that it is an advance in scholarship. It is a bid for popularity." If broadly implemented, he feared, any plan permitting students wide latitude in selecting classes would lead them to prefer "duck-hunting" to academic endeavors, to idling about instead of concentrating on the studies proper to a well-educated person.[8] Bryn Mawr's president Carey Thomas sarcastically wondered aloud about the extremes to which student choice might lead. "In many colleges everything that is desirable for a human being to learn," she complained, "counts toward the bachelor's degree . . . [including] ladder work in the gymnasium (why not go upstairs?) . . . [or] swimming in the tank (why not one's morning bath?)."[9]

In New Haven, President Noah Porter of Yale flatly denied students were capable of making intelligent and informed choices under an elective system. "Their tastes are either unformed or capricious and prejudiced; if they are decided and strong, they often require correction," he insisted. "The study which is the farthest removed from that which strikes his fancy may be the study which is most needed for the student."[10] Andrew F. West of Princeton denied Eliot's claim that individual differences among students necessarily legitimated multiple instructional patterns and courses. "Minds resemble and differ from each other just as faces and complexions do," he avowed. "They are all different, but all human. It is nothing but fallacious then, to argue that . . . colleges may not prescribe that students shall be trained in the great studies which demonstrably cultivate their essential characteristics before the colleges consent to call such minds liberally educated."[11] Here West was echoing the counterpoint to Eliot's assertion that individual differences necessitate different curricula. Commonalities outweigh differences, West asserted, and the fact of students' shared humanity requires that all be trained in the same "great studies." This argument also has remained virtually unchanged ever since in all but minor detail, and is still invoked in modern debate over the college curriculum.

Part of Eliot's goal in giving students "freedom in choice of studies" was what he termed "the enlargement of the circle of liberal arts." On several occasions he returned to the same theme, avowing "That all branches of sound knowledge are of equal dignity and equal educational value for mature students is the only hopeful and tenable view in our day."[12] Critics remained skeptical. Some believed freedom of choice inevitably would allow too much specialization. Others felt all coherence and integration would be lost and that students left to customize their own studies would be let off far too easily. Most shared the fear that any form of election was inadequate to furnish the values of an authentic liberal education. For his part, McCosh, foremost among the critics of what was happening at Harvard, remained unalterably opposed to the claim that "in a university the student must choose his studies and govern himself," and he repeatedly argued for requiring students to be exposed to a predetermined pattern of study in language, literature, science, and philosophy, "branches which no candidate for the degree should be allowed to avoid." McCosh added, "Every educated man should know so much of one of these."[13]

Scarcely two years following Eliot's address, Noah Porter opened up with his own broadside. "Especially in matters of education should [higher learning] neither pander to popular prejudices nor take advantage of popular humors," he advised in 1871. "If there is any sanctuary where well-grounded convictions should find refuge, and where these should be honored, it is in a place devoted to the higher education." Among his "well-grounded convictions," Porter counted the fixed, prescribed four-year course of collegiate study.[14] The verdict of Charles Francis Adams in a 1906 Phi Beta Kappa address at Columbia was equally plain. The elective system, he declared, was nothing more than a mischievous fad.

Thus the battle between proponents and opponents of a system of curricular choice in higher education was joined. It was a controversy that would rage on throughout the remainder of the century, continuing to arouse strong passions on both sides.[15] Yet one after another leading institutions were beginning to favor the adoption of an elective principle. The larger state universities of the Midwest and West were the most enthusiastic in embracing the innovation, followed by some of the larger universities with private endowments. Least receptive were the old-time colleges of New England. By the 1890s Wisconsin and Michigan counted among the few major institutions still maintaining required freshman and sophomore courses. By 1896

Cornell was allowing a virtually unrestricted system of electives. The next year even Yale, then Wisconsin, permitted unlimited electives after the student's initial year of enrollment.

Gradually, as required courses were abandoned and elective courses of study became even more directly tied to occupational interests, the idea of acquaintance with *any* fixed body of knowledge, classical or otherwise, as the mark of an educated person began to disappear. Still left unanswered was the question as to whether all subjects of study should be weighted equal in value—bookkeeping no less than physics, civil engineering together with Greek poetry, theology and accountancy, metaphysics and domestic science. Increasingly, the tacit presumption was that no one discipline or field of study could be considered more or less important than any other. Each deserved its place within academe. David Starr Jordan, writing in *The Voice of the Scholar* (1899), made the argument explicit. "It is not for the university to decide on the relative merits of knowledge," he declared. "Each man makes his own market, controlled by his own standards. It is for the university to see [only] that all standards are honest, that all work is genuine."[16]

The corollary to curricular egalitarianism was the admission into collegiate courses of study of modern subjects heretofore excluded. This process of accretion had begun well before the midpoint of the nineteenth century, and it was to continue unabated thereafter. Modern languages first appeared as distinct fields for specialized study in the 1870s. In the decade following, modern philosophy, literature, and the fine arts won acceptance as academic studies. By the 1890s a variety of social sciences had appeared and were being enshrined in college curricula. Old barriers continued to tumble. By the late 1880s land grant colleges had expanded their offerings in animal husbandry, agronomy, veterinary medicine, horticulture, plant pathology, farm management, mechanical engineering, and "domestic sciences" beyond anything formerly anticipated. Vocational and technical education were fast becoming legitimate, accepted aspects of American higher education.

Partly as a result, the distinction between professional and vocational education blurred. Universities, it was now apparent, would offer instruction for practically *all* careers for which some formal body of knowledge existed—not just divinity, law, or medicine, but also education, journalism, engineering, and other applied fields. With attendant specialization and departmentalization came fragmentation and the carving up of human knowledge into entirely separate disciplines or domains superintended by distinct, often contending administrative units. This fragmentation of academic life simply underscored the growing conviction symbolized by the elective principle that not all educated people needed to command the same knowledge.[17]

The problem, however, was to decide whether received notions of liberal learning and humanistic thought still had any relevance or applicability whatsoever in the modern age. By 1900, if not well before, the traditional notion that an educated person was distinguished by familiarity with a common body of thought and value was beginning to seem moribund. A felt loss of unity and coherence was widely remarked upon. John Dewey, one among many, writing in 1902, commented at some length on the "multiplication of studies" and "consequent congestion of the curriculum, and the conflict of various studies for a recognized place in the curriculum." The fact that "one cannot get in without crowding something else out; the effort to arrange a compromise in various courses of study by throwing the entire burden of election upon the student so that he shall make his own course of study"—this problem, he concluded, was symptomatic of a deep lack of unity within society itself. It bespoke the need, he felt, to seek "more harmony, more system in our scheme of life."[18]

Unfortunately "unity" within social and intellectual life was not something that could be generated at will or summoned on command, any more than it could be achieved readily within college and university courses of study. Breadth fostering the balanced development of a wide range of human potentialities had been the avowed aim of most American educators throughout the nineteenth century. Whether unrestricted choice could achieve that end in any intelligible way seemed more and more doubtful. A growing feeling among many writers at the turn of the century was that Eliot's elective system, begun three decades before, had borne bitter fruit. Not only had the college curriculum been fragmented beyond repair, but it had become possible now—an unthinkable proposition in earlier days—for two students to attend the same institution over a four-year period and never take a single course in common. Specialization of interest and professionalism, many warned, had advanced to the point where general education of a liberal character was suffering neglect and would soon disappear altogether.

RESTORING CURRICULAR INTEGRATION

By the opening years of the twentieth century, even the most ardent supporters of the idea of a fixed curriculum, uniform and prescribed for all, had to concede that the traditional scheme was no longer supportable. By the same token, there was widespread agreement that uncontrolled application of the elective principle—that all could freely chose whatever attracted their interests—offered no satisfactory alternative. Critics were increasingly agreed that whatever gains were achieved by allowing students almost unlimited personal choice were overshadowed by a loss of coherence and intellectual integration. Eliot's bold scheme, it was said, had led to disintegration, to the taking of courses in isolation from one another, the whole lacking any overall unity or design. The typical course of study, it was now alleged, lacked organic unity, a system of connections and common tasks among disparate disciplines. If the old idea of a shared intellectual and moral "culture," or *paideia* had been too narrowly circumscribed by classical learning, the alternative of a "cafeteria" approach to learning was too open-ended. As reaction to the "smorgasbord" curriculum set in, the consensus of opinion shifted toward seeking a better balance between elective anarchy and rigid curricular prescription.

To make a long story shorter, the practical expedient that eventually won acceptance among most institutions of higher learning was a "concentration and distribution" requirement. That is, as a sort of compromise between two extremes, students were required to "concentrate" their studies in a given field or discipline (the "major") while "distributing" or spreading their other choices across a range of subjects in the arts, humanities, and sciences. The academic major was intended to supply "depth" of content; the distribution, it was expected, would safeguard "scope" or breadth of subject matter. The former would serve to prevent intellectual shallowness or superficiality; the latter would ensure against excessive specialization.

The major advantage of balancing curricular breadth and depth in this fashion, supporters pointed out, was that it mandated exposure to those important fields of knowledge a shortsighted or misguided student might otherwise try to avoid. At the same time it allowed and demanded more than passing acquaintance with one single discipline. Ultimately, some such system of concentration and distribution was adopted by colleges and universities across the country. It remains the single most pervasive way of organizing curricular requirements today.

An alternative approach stressing an even greater degree of synoptic integration was that associated about the time of World War I with what came to be known as "general culture" or "general studies" or "general education." Alexander Meiklejohn at Amherst was among the first to try out the idea of so-called survey courses. In 1914 he first introduced a course entitled "Social and Economic Institutions." It offered a broad perspective on society and was intended to introduce students to virtually all of the "humanistic sciences." Five years later Columbia University introduced a peacetime adaptation of a "war issues" course, now retitled "Contemporary Civilization," which was similar in structure to the survey begun at Amherst. Required of all entering freshmen, it was the first of several offered that emphasized historical, social, and cultural development. "There is a certain minimum of . . . [the Western] intellectual and spiritual tradition that a man must experience and understand if he is to be called educated," a faculty prospectus explained.[19]

By 1936 Columbia was offering in addition an integrative humanities sequence, then also a compendious survey of the sciences. Dartmouth and Reed College followed suit with their own survey courses; and their prototypes, along with those pioneered at Columbia, were widely imitated on scores of campuses across the country. Extensive experimentation followed as colleges and universities attempted to provide their students with the broad outlines of human knowledge through various synoptic surveys and introductory overviews of the disciplines.[20] In the search for organizing principles, some survey courses stressed subject matter *content*. Others emphasized the basic *methods of inquiry* distinctive in various fields. Still others organized material around such *thematic* rubrics as "The Social World," or "Contemporary Issues," "Man and His Environment," or "Problems of Democracy." Especially noteworthy was a social ethics course treating "the ethical foundations of private and public action in human relations" begun at the University of Utah around 1930. Similarly, between 1924 and 1930 a widely emulated "Nature of the World and Man" survey was inaugurated at the University of Chicago.

Even as general survey courses came into vogue, however, they started meeting with strong criticism. Charges of shallowness, of superficiality and lack of depth became almost commonplace. One major complaint was that introductory courses were being misused to recruit prospective student majors into the discipline or disciplines represented, thereby frustrating their original intent of supplying undergraduates with a broad and integrated intellectual overview of diverse fields of study. Others faulted so-called interdisciplinary surveys for their characteristic lack of structure and rigor. Alexander Meiklejohn himself, in criticizing the typical survey course as it had evolved, described it as "a little music, a taste of philosophy, a glimpse into history, some practice in the technique of the laboratory, a thrill or two in the appreciation of poetry."[21] Even those committed to the idea of surveys had to admit that the search for satisfactory ways of bringing knowledge into some kind of unity was proving extraordinarily difficult.

Much of the history of higher education between 1920 and the early 1940s could be written around the theme of how colleges devised new curricula or courses designed to avoid the intellectual anarchy many felt then prevailed throughout academe. Several different approaches were tried. Breadth of experience was a common theme. Some schools retained their "survey" or "orientation" courses. Others fell back on the "distribution and concentration" approach. The amount of freedom permitted students in selecting courses varied, depending on what system was utilized. Oftentimes choices were narrowly circumscribed. At some institutions greater latitude was allowed, but always within the broad constraints of a distribution system.

Either way, after two years of general education, students were obliged to concentrate in greater depth in a single field of study. Choosing a "major," however, unlike current usage, did not necessarily carry the presumption that further specialized study would convert into preparation for a particular occupation or profession. On the contrary, someone might elect to major in history without intending to become a professional historian, or major in psychology without anticipating future employment in the field. The larger purpose almost always was to encourage the student to achieve a greater depth of understanding in some particular discipline without regard for its possible economic applications.

GREAT BOOKS: THE IDEA
OF A CURRICULAR CANON

One of the most remarkable and hotly debated curricular experiments undertaken by a major university was that begun in 1930 at the University of Chicago under the leadership of Chancellor Robert Maynard Hutchins. His was a bold initiative, running counter to all prevailing trends, and it was aimed at nothing less than a revival of the "classical" tradition of the liberal arts. Accompanying the founding of a new undergraduate college within the university structure was a new general education curriculum organized around original sources, the so-called Great Books of Western civilization. Henceforth, it was announced, general learning at Chicago would mean the study "of the greatest books of the Western world and the arts of reading, writing, thinking, and speaking, together with mathematics, the best exemplar of the processes of human reason." The hope expressed was that a curriculum had been framed that would speak to all of the elements of humanity's shared common nature.

The course of study prescribed was both uniform and demanding. It consisted of a series of one-year interdisciplinary survey courses taught through lectures and supplemented by frequent small-group discussions. Course credits and tests were dispensed with entirely. In their place, students were required to submit themselves whenever they felt sufficiently well prepared to pass comprehensive examinations in English composition, humanities, social science, the physical sciences, and biology. Minimal proficiency in a foreign language also was required. Only when all examinations had been passed satisfactorily was a student permitted to extend his or her studies at an upper-divisional level or in another college of the university.[22]

For Hutchins, as for Mortimer Adler, Mark Van Doren, Jacques Maritain, Irving Babbitt, Gilbert Highet, and many others, only Great Books—those works representing "classics" in all field of knowledge—were sufficient to realize the purpose of general or liberal learning to their fullest. A great book, it was said, is one that has survived the test of time. As the prospectus for the Great Books Program published by Encyclopaedia Britannica and the University of Chicago Press phrased it, a truly great book, first, is one that does not have to be written again because, like any great work of art, it succeeds perfectly in accomplishing what it sets out to do. (The world, one wit observed, does not require a sequel to Plato's *Republic, Republic Reconsidered* possibly, any more than does one of Shakespeare's tragedies invite a *Son of Hamlet* or a *Macbeth II.*)

Second, a great book is always contemporary. It is a perennial best-seller, in the long run outlasting (and perhaps outselling) any popular but ephemeral best-seller. It is a work for all times, enjoying the same fundamental appeal and currency in every century, in any place or time, under any political, social, or economic conditions. It endures, long after a lesser work has been consigned to oblivion. A great book is not read for antiquarian purposes. The intent is not archaeological or philological, but contemporary.

Third, a great book, Hutchins and his colleagues insisted, is readable by almost everyone. Its appeal is universal because it deals with the universal themes that always occupy thinking persons. Finally, and most important of all, according to Hutchins, a great book is one capable of helping to develop standards of taste and criticism, one enabling a learner to think and act intelligently, to participate fully in the social and intellectual movements or "conversations" of his or her own time.

Hutchins did not foresee any great inclination on the part of the American public to embrace his program—though he did feel that if the curriculum started at Chicago proved successful, other institutions eventually would fall into line. And for a time in fact some did. Such was the prestige of the University of Chicago and the personal charisma of its chancellor that elements of the Chicago program were indeed replicated in scores of experimental colleges, honors departments, and schools throughout the country. Best known among those that adopted the so-called Chicago Plan almost intact was St. John's College in Annapolis, Maryland, and later a sister campus in Santa Fe, New Mexico.[23]

Two years after its beginning in 1937, Donald P. Cottrell of Teachers College, Columbia University, reported for the National Society for the Study of Education on what was transpiring at St. John's. "In the belief that the power of the great liberal tradition of Europe and America is generally being neglected," he observed, "St. John's proposes to center its program upon the recovery of that tradition . . . through the great classic books—the books of our Western heritage that have been read by the greatest number of readers, the books that have the largest number of possible interpretations, the books that 'raise the persistent unanswerable questions about the great themes in European thought,' the books that are works of fine art, the books that are masterpieces of the liberal arts."[24]

Many commentators spoke approvingly of what Stringfellow Barr, Scott Buchanan, and other innovators were attempting at St. John's. Philosopher John Dewey, on the other hand, most decidedly did not. "The idea that an adequate education of any kind can be obtained by means of a miscellaneous assortment of . . . books is laughable when viewed practically," he commented acidly. "The five-foot bookshelf for adults to be read, reread, and digested at leisure throughout a lifetime, is one thing. Crowded into four years and dealt out in fixed doses, it is quite another thing."[25] Largely undeterred by critics, St. John's introduced few changes over the next four decades. Rejecting claims that the ideal of a specific canon of books was too narrow, too unconnected with the demands of modern life, supporters of the Great Books continued to press for a type of education that would draw out and develop human rationality and the power of reflective thought through firsthand exposure to the timeless classics of Western thought.

Today there are few who remain wedded to a fixed list of books to be mastered by every educated person. Yet the idea of a curricular canon, of an identifiable and substantive content for liberal learning, still claims many ardent proponents. In its modern incarnation, the idea retains its enduring appeal—not to mention its capacity to provoke controversy and dissent. Over the past decade or so, of course, much of the debate has turned on a somewhat different issue, that of cultural inclusion. The issue now is not simply whether there can be a static list of books with which everyone must be able to claim acquaintance in order to deserve being called educated. Rather, the question—one of several—is whether the Western cultural tradition of itself offers a sufficiently generous or commodious framework for general learning. A global society, some argue, requires of its citizenry that all members be conversant with multiple cultural traditions, not just Western civilization to the exclusion of all others. Equally familiar is the demand that the cultural contributions of groups heretofore marginalized or consigned to the periphery (women and minorities especially) be brought into the mainstream and accorded their due.

GENERAL AND COMMON LEARNING: THE "DISASTER"

Some of the attempts to revivify general learning undertaken in the two decades after World War I were inspired by the spirit of the Chicago Plan. Others pursued rather different directions in the quest to restore general and common learning in the undergraduate curriculum. Then as now, general learning, common or otherwise, was touted as a panacea for almost every imaginable academic problem, from overspecialization to excessive vocationalization in higher education. Commenting, Ernest Boyer and Arthur Levine have noted, "General education was seen as an answer to the intolerance and conformity of the 1920s. It would help young people understand and find a useful place in a complex industrial society on an interconnected globe. . . . But above all, for older Americans who were still rooted in the certitudes of the pre-1914 world, general education would revive the heady idealism and sense of national unity that had so suddenly and so mysteriously faded with the signing of the Armistice in November 1918."[26]

Looking back from the perspective of 1939, Stanford's Alvin C. Eurich felt collegiate experimentation had revealed a palpable failure to reach consensus on the meaning or content of general learning. "Each person who uses the term has some definite connotation in mind," he wrote. "Commonly it is thought of in contrast with specialization and as implying an emphasis upon living in a democratic society."[27] Still, considerable confusion continued to prevail over the manner or methods of implementing the concept and making it real.

The release of a 1945 Harvard faculty committee's report, entitled *General Education in a Free Society,* marked the first of several successive postwar attempts to revisit the entire issue anew. Bound with a red cover, the so-called Harvard Redbook stopped short of supplying what its authors claimed was most needed: some "over-all logic, some strong, not easily broken frame" within which institutions of higher learning could simultaneously fulfill their duty to prepare students for their individual careers, while still fitting them "for those common spheres which, as citizens and heirs of a joint culture, they will share with others."[28]

The Report did caution against assuming any single pattern was workable for all colleges and universities. The basic need was to strive for a balance between "general" and "special" (that is, specialized) education. The former should not be thought of as "some airy education in knowledge in general." It should not be formless, consisting merely of the taking of one course after another. Nor should it be defined negatively, in the sense of whatever is left over apart from a field of concentration and specialization, the committee affirmed.[29] Unfortunately, the Redbook offered no positive characterization of what general learning should be either.

What the Report concluded with instead was a series of specific recommendations for required courses in the humanities, social sciences, and natural sciences. One was to be called "Great Texts of Literature." The second was to be "Western Thought and Institutions." A third would be built around physics or biology. Ironically enough, the Harvard faculty ultimately rejected its own committee's report and the proposed courses were never offered. Elsewhere, however, support for the Harvard plan ran strong, and variations were adopted by dozens of colleges and universities. Two years later, a White House Commission on Higher Education for Democracy released a report strongly endorsing general education along the lines sketched out in the Harvard Redbook. A flurry of reform activity ensued.

From the vantage point of 1980, Gresham Riley, dean at the University of Richmond, judged that the mixture of required courses and limited choices within groupings of closely related disciplines inspired by the Harvard Report had for the most part been "seriously flawed." Besides being restricted to Western society and its dominant ethnic and socioeconomic groups, the typical curriculum, he claimed, focused predominantly on the subject matter of various disciplines, with little or no thought given to relationships *among* bodies of knowledge. As for the general introductory course, his feeling was that it tended to stifle rather than to stimulate student interest. "I find it appropriate," he commented, "that we frequently characterized those introductory courses as providing 'an exposure' to the various disciplines. As a matter of fact, they 'exposed' students to disciplines like a smallpox vaccination exposes a child to the disease: One is 'cured for life'—in the latter case of the disease and in the former case of any possible interest in the subject matter."[30]

Horace M. Kallen, author of *The Education of Free Man* (1949), decried the identification of general education with a fixed historical content. "Any thought or thing, any vocation or technique momentous to a mind may become the base of its liberation," he claimed. "Any art or craft, any theme, datum or system of ideas, is an instrument of liberal education when it serves as a road and not as a wall for him who studies it. Whatever be the avowed field and purpose of the study—farming, engineering, business, law, medicine, the ministry, teaching, garbage collecting, archaeology—when it liberates, it is liberal."[31] Kallen criticized what he termed "the mortuary cult" of traditionalists that would impose intact a predefined "body of knowledge" inherited from the past. Liberal education, he concluded, was "one that frees each and all safely and happily to live and to move and have his personal being in fact or in idea among the others of his choice. This is what liberal education must mean in the modern world."[32] The practical implication of Kallen's view, of course, was that liberal or general education would be undefinable in terms of any specific subject matter. The only relevant consideration would be the "spirit" in which learning occurs and the larger purpose it might serve.

Interestingly, in the 1940s and 1950s some writers attempted to introduce a sharp distinction between "general" and "liberal" education, the suggestion being that the former should be thought of in terms of a fixed body of liberal arts disciplines and the latter as any course of study exhibiting breadth and scope of content. This usage was decidedly at odds with earlier interpretations in the 1920s and 1930s, when the two terms were used interchangeably and almost synonymously.[33] As always, various arguments were put forward on behalf of curricula freed from direct ties to vocational considerations. But no one pattern or set of recommendations appeared to command widespread assent in academic circles.

Yet another significant attempt to reexamine the meaning of general education came with Daniel Bell's 1966 study, *The Reforming of General Education*.[34] Basically, what its author recommended were courses for undergraduates designed to illustrate how knowledge is differently generated within mathematics, the sciences, the social sciences, and the humanities. The key to curricular coherence, Bell felt, was a scheme that envisaged the first year of study given over to acquiring a very broad, basic background in a range of disciplines; followed by the second and third years devoted to training in a specific discipline; and the fourth year occupied with a combination of seminar work in a discipline and synoptic courses—a "third-tier" level—which could give the learner a sense for how his or her major subject might be applied to specific problems and how it related to other knowledge domains. Bell denied that he had in mind a set of survey courses or "interdisciplinary" courses, or courses of the type called "great issues." In his proposed sequence, the concluding phase would set the fund of knowledge previously acquired into some large context, showing its possible applications and connections. Though widely discussed at the time, Bell's work did not inspire many specific experiments or practical curricular initiatives.

Some few others beside Bell wrestled with the question of what general or liberal education could mean in contemporary society. Wayne C. Booth, for example, felt the key to deciding what knowledge is most worth having had to begin with the question of what knowledge beyond basic survival lore might be regarded as essential for all persons as human beings.[35] Liberal education, he argued, must encompass, besides basic reasoning skills, knowledge about the individual's own nature and humanity's place in the world. In natural science, philosophy, literature, and the various social sciences, the learner finds accounts of the universe and humankind's place within it. Second, in order to be fully human, a person must be educated to the experience of beauty. A person who has not learned to comprehend, understand, and appreciate creative esthetic endeavor, Booth claimed, is enslaved to caprice, bound to the testimony of others, or ultimately condemned to a life of esthetic impoverishment and ugliness.

Third, a person needs to learn about human intentions and how to make them effective in the world. The individual must come to understand something about what is possible and what is impossible, what is desirable and what undesirable, what is desirable and what is merely desired. In short, people must acquire "practical wisdom" in the realm of human values.

Booth admitted his threefold scheme would not lead to a list of great books that everyone must read, nor to any specific pattern of requirements across the many domains of knowledge. But, he insisted, a college or university must try to help each learner use his or her mind independently in the pursuit of knowledge of truth, beauty, and goodness (or "right choice"), regardless of any particular course of study followed.

Philosopher Richard McKeon's contribution to discussions about general learning in the 1960s was an analysis of four different ways in which education can be "general."[36] In his view, general education could be construed, first, as the search for a *common* learning to be shared by all people—what a fixed and prescribed curriculum seeks to supply. General education also can involve the search for *principles* or *structures* underlying knowledge—what theology or metaphysics allegedly once provided and what proponents of epistemic "unity" and curricular "integration" now look for in modern surrogates. Again, general education could mean the search for learning appropriate to all *experience*—whether sought in great books, "life-adjustment" courses, or interdisciplinary surveys of issues, concepts, and problems. Finally, according to McKeon, general education could be understood as the search for a learning derived from or applicable *to all human cultures.*[37] Unfortunately, McKeon's analysis did not extend to the specifics of curricular organization and planning. Nor did he attempt to prescribe any particular pattern colleges and universities might try out.

The 1970s and 1980s brought renewed attempts to fix the place of general or liberal learning in undergraduate curricula. In the aftermath of the Vietnam conflict and the isolationism that swept the country, pundits began calling for corrective education designed to foster internationalism and a more global perspective among college students. In the wake of political scandal at the national level, others urged more attention to moral training. Amid reports that students were becoming narcissistic and self-absorbed, general education aimed at promoting civic consciousness and democratic citizenship seemed essential to many. Liberal learning was similarly viewed as a palliative for excessive vocationalism on campus and the apparent loss of interest among undergraduates in a liberal arts education.

As Boyer and Levine were to remark in 1981, proponents of general education "consistently have been worried about a society that appeared to be losing cohesion, splintering into countless individual atoms, each flying off in its own direction, each pursuing its own selfish ends." Those who would urge more attention to general learning, they alleged, "have been convinced that our common life must be reaffirmed, our common goals redefined, our common problems confronted. The specific agenda—the preservation of democracy, the promoting of a common heritage, the development of citizen responsibility, a renewed commitment to ethical behavior, the enhancement of global perspectives, the integration of diverse groups into the larger society—has varied. But the underlying concern has remained remarkably constant."[38]

Specific social concerns aside, more than a few observers of American higher education throughout the 1970s were agreed that the state of general learning in academe offered ample cause for alarm. "Contemporary liberal education," declared Willis D. Weatherford, chair of the 1971 Commission on Liberal Learning of the American Association of American Colleges, "seems irrelevant to much of the undergraduate population and, more especially, to middle America. The concept of intellect has not been democratized; the humanities are moribund, unrelated to student interest, and the liberal arts appear headed for stagnation. Narrow vocational education has captured the larger portion of political interest."

Weatherford felt there was blame enough to go around. "The liberal arts colleges," he alleged, "are captives of illiberally educated faculty members who barter with credit hours and pacts of nonaggression among their fiefs and baronies. Illiberally educated politicians, who want a bigger gross national product with scant regard for whether the mind and lives of the persons who produce it are or are not gross, make their own negative contribution, as do illiberally educated students. . . ."[39]

As if to confirm Weatherford's indictment, six years later the Carnegie Council on Policy Studies in Higher Education reported that between 1967 and 1974, general education requirements, as a percentage of undergraduate curricula, had dropped significantly. "Today there is little consensus on what constitutes a liberal education," the Council opined, "and, as if by default, the choices have been left to the student." General education, the report claimed, is now a disaster area. It has been on the defensive and losing ground for more than 100 years."[40]

Efforts to analyze the causes of the alleged "disaster" dominated an ever-growing body of literature. There was broad agreement that the professionalization of scholarship in higher education was a major factor contributing to specialization and fragmentation. Likewise inimical to the cause of the liberal arts, it was said, was the modern tendency to treat knowledge as a commodity, something to be "used" or "consumed." Finally, the bureaucratization of the university itself was identified as a culprit. Robert Paul Wolff in *The Ideal of the University* (1969), Brand Blanshard in *The Uses of a Liberal Education* (1973), and Christopher Jencks and David Riesman in *The Academic Revolution* (1977) all tended to offer the same diagnoses.[41]

Universities, they alleged, had grown complacent, less reflective about their own practices. Bereft of any guiding intellectual vision, most institutions of higher learning had settled for a hodgepodge curriculum, which thinking students rightly disdained as "required irrelevance." Corrupted by populism, professionalism, and assembly-line scholarship, universities had surrendered to pressures to turn students over to specialized preparation for careers as quickly as possible. Having abandoned their integrity to marketplace ebb and flow, colleges and universities had lost the will to insist upon any intellectual coherence or unity in their vast offerings. Universities had become knowledge factories. They were the principal manufacturers and retailers of knowledge as a commodity. Buyers included students shopping mainly for credentials to guarantee themselves a prosperous future, businesses and industries in search of the skills and products of research, and governmental agencies needing an array of specialized services. In their quest for competitive advantage and prestige, critics lamented, academic institutions had simply sold out to the highest bidders.[42]

In the absence of a scheme of values commanding broad assent in society, it was further said, academic disciplines had sought to be value-free, each imitating the neutral discourse of the hard sciences.[43] The American university had committed itself to all that is objective, quantifiable, precise, and publicly verifiable, in process consigning larger questions of human meaning, purpose, or significance to the realm of the unanswerable and the insignificant.[44] Hence institutions of higher education had tacitly acceded to the popular belief that so-called ultimate questions are nonintellectual, subjective, and therefore not amenable to reasoned analysis or discourse.[45]

Herbert U. London of New York University saw a kind of "cult of neutrality" operating in academe, one combining elements of reductive behaviorism and positivism, whose effect was to create a kind of Gresham's law of curriculum design: "That which is measurable will drive . . . what is not measurable out of the curriculum."[46] As he saw it, the tendency of modern life, in other words, was a shift away from liberal educational aims to goals that are measurable and attainable but finite. The "minimalists," he feared, if unopposed, would eventually overwhelm what was left of the liberal arts tradition in higher education with talk of discrete "outcomes," "competencies," and learning "performances."

London, like many others, was not optimistic about prospects for liberal or general learning in the university as currently constituted. Establishing a "core curriculum," for example, he felt was a near impossibility in a climate where specialists continue to press for a wider array of narrowly focused courses, and where "a ballot to determine the complexion of the curriculum is very often simply a pork barrel bid" by competing units more intent on bolstering sagging enrollments and saving faculty positions than on matters of academic principle. Dean Robert H. Chambers at Bucknell University summed up the problem: "The triumph of the academic department as an autonomous unit capable of demanding greater loyalty than the institution of which it is a part is certainly the primary cause of the splintering of the liberal arts curriculum that we see all around us today."[47] American University professor Samuel Lubell served the same point in claiming that the "feudal" structure of the university, with all of its divisive characteristics, was mostly to blame.[48]

REFRAMING THE CORE CURRICULUM

In the fall of 1976 Dean Henry Rosovsky of Harvard devoted his annual report to the topic of undergraduate education. Defining six requirements as basic attributes of a "reasonable standard" for undergraduate instruction, Rosovsky returned to the theme of liberal education and its meaning for American institutions of higher learning. He asked, first, that college graduates "be able to think and write clearly and effectively . . . [and] to communicate with precision, cogency, and force"; second, that they possess "an informed acquaintance with the mathematical and experimental methods of the physical and biological sciences; with the main forms of analysis and the historical and quantitative techniques needed for investigating the workings and development of modern society; with some of the important scholarly, literary, and artistic achievements of the past; and with the major religious and philosophical conceptions" of humankind; and third, that they not be "ignorant of other cultures and other times."

Fourth, Rosovsky stipulated that graduates should possess "some understanding of, and experience in thinking about, moral and ethical problems" and be able to "make discriminating moral choices." Fifth, students ought to possess "the capacity to reject shoddiness in all its many forms, and to explain and defend . . . [their] views effectively and rationally." Finally, he felt, they should have "achieved depth in some field of knowledge."[49]

By the following year, a Harvard Task Force on the Core Curriculum had begun its first comprehensive reappraisal of undergraduate education since the appearance of the landmark Harvard Redbook of 1945. At the conclusion of its deliberations, the task force called for the restoration of a year's study in at least four or five major subject areas: arts and literature, history, social analysis and moral reasoning, the natural and social sciences, and foreign cultures. Instead of such staples as "Central Themes in American History" or "Natural Science I," students would opt from among such courses as "The Function and Criticism of Literature," "The Christianization of the Roman World," "The Theory of a Just War," and "Art, Myth, and Ritual in Africa."[50]

Fulfilling the core curriculum courses was to occupy the equivalent of one academic year. Other requirements involving expository writing, mathematics, a foreign language, and quantitative reasoning would consume a second year; and concentration requirements were planned to take up another two years' of academic work. Associate Dean Charles Whitlock explained, "We think the new core curriculum is a strong, positive restatement of our belief in the value of liberal arts training."[51]

Reactions to the Harvard initiative were mixed, often critical. "Neither original nor particularly distinguished" was one judgment. "At best, a watered-down version of the experiments in general education conducted at Columbia in the 1920s, at Hutchins' Chicago in the 1930s, and at Harvard itself in the late 1940s" was another.

"Disappointingly short of expectations" came still another response. A "rather simple and unimaginative resurrection of distribution requirements" yet another critic asserted.[52] Elizabeth Coleman, writing in the June 1, 1981 *Chronicle of Higher Education,* observed that the history of American higher education was "strewn with the debris of attempts to create a more integrated curriculum . . . to revitalize the liberal arts." She, like many others, questioned whether a lost common heritage or shared culture could be recaptured through simple curricular reform such as had been attempted at Harvard, Yale, and elsewhere, or whether the splintered curriculum could be put back together in any meaningful and coherent way.[53]

Jerry Gaff, director of the Center for General Education, sponsored by the American Association of Colleges, felt that the simple imposition of conventional distribution requirements was a "quick and dirty" approach to curricular reform. While it reasserted the importance of the liberal arts, he felt it did not go nearly far enough. "Distribution requirements," he claimed, "are usually fashioned for political rather than education reasons; more often than not they constitute a trade-off among departments on how to carve up the curricular pie rather than a genuine commitment that certain kinds of knowledge are more important than others."[54] Theodore Lockwood shared Gaff's skepticism. "The current trend at colleges of reviving distribution requirements does not convince me we are improving the quality of education. Giving the curriculum more structure doesn't necessarily give it coherence," he observed.[55]

Similar judgments became almost the norm throughout the 1980s and 1990s; and various studies lamenting the state of general learning in collegiate curricula have been issued with almost monotonous regularity.[56] In practically all cases, recurrent themes included pleas for more stringent academic standards, demands that ethical values be given more attention in learning, reiteration of the need to restore citizenship education to a place of primacy, and arguments in defense of a common learning capable of supplying a more coherent unifying purpose and structure to undergraduate curricula.[57]

Mindful of the criticism, colleges and universities did continue to experiment with alternative models, the pessimism of observers over prospects for their success notwithstanding. Some initiatives went well beyond distribution requirements: new core programs, college-wide courses, tightened skill requirements, integrative and interdisciplinary seminars, the inclusion of global or non-Western studies to help students broaden their predominantly Western worldview, administrative reorganization schemes providing greater centralized authority over general education programs, and other nontraditional arrangements.

Foremost in the minds of many faculty planning committees throughout the last two decades of the twentieth century was the need to upgrade students' ability to read, write, and compute. Beyond this, the problem as many saw it was how to secure a greater measure of agreement over priorities. Jill Kerr Conway, president of Smith College, felt daunted by the search for a common learning. "We can no longer say today what courses ought to be taught and what ones ought not to be taught. We can no longer say, for instance, that students should study the Bible instead of the Koran. Those days are gone forever."[58] Paul L. Dressel of Michigan State agreed that efforts to define a liberal education in terms of some specified content would always run afoul of disagreements over specifics. A better tactic, he argued, was to ask again about the characteristics of a liberally educated person and how to determine whether an individual is broadly educated, much as Rosovsky had proposed.

Dressel's list, for example, specified that an educated college graduate ought to know how to acquire and use knowledge; exhibit mastery of communication skills; show tolerance and respect for value differences among people; demonstrate a willingness to cooperate and collaborate with others in problem-solving activities; accept some responsibility for contemporary events; and evidence a willingness to fulfill the obligations of responsible citizenship in a democratic society.[59]

Against the background of disputes since the mid-1980s over a broadening of the curricular canon, for many reformers in recent years the paramount need has been to repudiate once and for all any lingering notion that the content of liberal learning can be bounded by Judeo-Christian, Greco-Roman, or Western society. As Richard A. Fredland of Indiana University has noted, "If ever a time was when liberal education could reasonably omit a substantial international component, that time has passed. It is now inconceivable that a sound education can ignore the international dimension of the lives graduates are ordained to live."[60] He added, "Virtually any imaginable form of interaction that we are likely to see in tomorrow's world will involve no less than a greater need for international understanding to be an effective participant much less an informed observer or decision maker. . . . Informed, responsive participation in the coming international system . . . will demand an international perspective."[61]

BASIC ISSUES RECONSIDERED:
THE CONTEMPORARY CONTEXT

Several years ago, in his book entitled *Higher Learning* (1986), Derek Bok astutely noted that all of the fundamental issues pertaining to the shape and substance of the college or university curriculum are perennial, that they endure as open-ended questions for each generation to ponder and wrestle with anew. Almost every important proposal already has been tried. No permanent or decisive victories are ever won. No serious arguments are defeated conclusively.[62] Nonetheless, he judged, even though new ideas are rarely if ever advanced, the ongoing discussion is still vital in every time, for contending positions must be adjudicated somehow and practical arrangements provided for in educating students.

One of the most basic of these questions, first, is about what sort of balance, if any, should be drawn between undergraduate liberal learning and preparatory training for a career. A second perennial question (provided some significant portion of the undergraduate experience *is* reserved for nonspecialized or general education) is how much of its content to prescribe and how much to leave to students' free election. Third, a major curricular issue has to do with the best means of achieving breadth in each student's education. Fourth, there is the enduring question about how to achieve some integration or synthesis, some pulling together of the whole.

Writing to the first issue, Linda Ray Pratt of the University of Nebraska has reiterated the basic question in the starkest of terms. "Are we educating good citizens, potential leaders, women and men with power over their own faculties and mental resources to question and discern?" she asks. "Or are we training a 'workforce'?"[63] As the interests of the market economy infiltrate and penetrate ever deeper into the academy, the pressure to focus the curriculum on vocational concerns increases. The time and space given over to liberal education correspondingly shrivels, and the value assigned to it is diminished. How far, she wonders, are colleges and universities willing to go in consigning general or liberal learning to what, in effect, amounts to a purely ceremonial or ornamental role? Exacerbating the problem is yet another trend, noted in a 1985 report by the Association of American Colleges—the tendency of undergraduates to devote half or more of their undergraduate work to a specialized major field of concentration, a percentage considerably higher than that obtaining only a decade earlier.[64] Hence the question assumes even greater force: How much room is left for general, non-specialized learning within a four-year undergraduate course of study?

It is virtually assured, as Paul Woodring has noted, that career-related training will be valiantly defended and stressed by state legislators, students, parents, and even a considerable number of illiberally educated academics themselves.[65] Predictably, if some proper balance is to be preserved, liberal education will need all the support it can get from those who appreciate the need for it and comprehend its importance. But in order to receive that support, the nature and function of such liberal learning needs to be clearly understood.

In its original sense, it is worth recalling, liberal education (from the Latin *librare,* to free; *liberalis,* liberal) meant the education of free human beings *(liberi),* in contradistinction to slaves and others engaged in menial tasks. To be free meant the opportunity to enjoy leisure—that is, to be absolved of the need or compulsion to engage in servile labor. Freedom in this sense entailed being one's own person, serving as no one else's tool or instrument. Freed from the imperatives of utility, the free learner could engage in activities as ends in themselves and not merely as means to further ends, most particularly in those activities thought conducive to the pursuit of wisdom and knowledge. (The Greek word for "leisure," *schole,* is, significantly, the root of the word "school" in Latin as well as in most Western vernacular languages. Leisure meant schooling; that is, the opportunity to learn.) Liberal education was thus understood as standing in contrast with vocational training.[66]

In this connection, Aristotle is credited with being among the first to set forth clearly the distinction between two different realms of human activity and the learning appropriate to each. "All of life," he wrote in the *Politics* (VII, 1333a-b), "is divided between work and leisure... and of our activities some are necessary and useful and others are noble. The same preference must be exercised in these matters as in regard to the parts of the soul and their activities. . . . For men must be capable of engaging in work and war, but still more capable of remaining at peace and at leisure. And they must be able to do necessary and useful things, but still more they must be able to do the noble things. Accordingly, it is with these aims in view that they should be educated." He concluded, "It is therefore not difficult to see that the young must be taught those useful arts that are indispensably necessary; but, those pursuits that are liberal having been distinguished from those that are illiberal, it is clear, then, that there are branches of learning and education which we must study with a view to the enjoyment of leisure, and these are to be valued for their own sake."

Divested of its historical association with the institution of chattel slavery and aristocratic privilege, liberal education as an idea has always lent itself to variant interpretations as to content or substance. Ancient writers distinguished seven liberal arts: the *trivium*—grammar, logic, and rhetoric (the arts of writing and speaking)—and the *quadrivium*— arithmetic, geometry, astronomy, and music (to which have been added countless other disciplines since). In one sense, however, the *artes liberales* did not designate fixed fields of study so much as they referred to activities or techniques; they were conceived of, broadly speaking, as ways of *doing* things: as, for example, the "arts" of engaging in grammatical, logical, and rhetorical analysis.

Collectively, the *enkylios paideia,* or "basic culture," of the liberal arts was the foundation of all education that was "general" (from the Latin *generalis,* "of or pertaining to the whole, not particular or specialized") as opposed to learning that was specialized and utilitarian. Cardinal Newman, it will be remembered, insisted that the distinction between the two hinged on the point that liberal learning was *désintéressant,* or "detached," self-sufficient unto itself and pursued chiefly for its own sake as an intrinsic good (although it might also be instrumental to some further good); whereas the character of "vocational" learning was "applied," and would always be valued relative to extrinsic ends beyond itself.

In modern times, the debate between those who would assign some specific content to liberal learning and those who resist the designation of any particular subjects as liberal has resurfaced many times over. On one side are those who want to argue that philosophy, speculative physics, the various branches of higher mathematics, music theory, and so forth rather obviously suggest themselves as suitable constituents of a liberal curriculum, whereas cooking, carpentry, book-binding, piano-playing, accounting, or neurosurgery, as applied arts, do not. Others affirm that chemistry, anatomy, and engineering as well as history or literature are matters of knowledge and that there is no reason a priori to decide that such knowledge cannot be pursued for its own sake.[67] The central consideration, always, is not mechanical acquaintance with any particular subject matter but, rather, the habits of mind and sensibility associated with intellectual and spiritual "liberation." They are fostered or nurtured, it is said, by the manner of thinking commonly developed by critical inquiry, aesthetic enjoyment, literary engagement, and philosophical reflection; and, arguably, almost any substance may be sufficient for the purpose.[68]

What unites the two sides is the conviction that liberal education, however it is construed, if it is to be efficacious must be aimed at freeing the learner not just from immediate considerations of utility but more broadly from the bondage of ignorance and received opinion. The goal, in Socratic terms, is the examined life, together with the sort of enlarged understanding critical reflection allows. "Liberal education," as Woodring puts it, "is the education that liberates [people] from the bondage of ignorance, prejudice and provincialism. It enables us to see the world whole and to see ourselves in perspective. It is the education appropriate for free men who must make wise independent decisions— in the home, on the job, in the voting booth, and on the jury panel."[69]

Jan Blits makes much the same point as follows: Liberal education, he claims, aims to prepare young people for an intelligent life. Its most important goal is to teach them "to become thoughtful about themselves and the world, about their actions and their thoughts, about what they do, what they say, what they want, and what they think." Further, "It seeks to illuminate life, and particularly to clarify the fundamental human alternatives, by delving into the roots of things. Liberal education is thus essentially a recovery or rediscovery of root issues and origins."[70]

Considering how many credit hours within the undergraduate course of study typically are given over to satisfying the requirements of an academic major, when all is said and done, in practical terms the question of a balance between general and specialized education nowadays tends to reduce to how much time and space are left over for liberal learning. For good or for ill, general education, as Rudolph Weingartner of the University of Pittsburgh correctly notes, may amount to little more than *the sum total of whatever the student did not specialize in*—including a retrospective conferral of that title, since the choice to specialize may come quite late in a student's college career.[71] Formerly, what was "left over" represented somewhere between 60 and 70 percent of a four-year program. In recent years, as specialty requirements have enlarged, the percentage of time available for students to take general courses has declined to half of a baccalaureate program or, in some cases, considerably less.

Although one might argue over how the precise balance ought to be struck, two or more years of study still leaves considerable scope for deciding what should be offered by way of general liberal learning. Here the second recurrent and enduring question is how much to prescribe and how much to leave to the free choice of students.[72]

Almost no one is prepared to go as far as President Eliot of Harvard did in the mid-nineteenth century in advocating unlimited electives—which is not to deny that some undergraduate students still would prefer unrestricted choice ("It's my time and money, so I should be allowed to take any courses I want"). But those who favor electives tend to fall back on Eliot's argument that students are much too diverse in their interests and abilities, too varied in their aspirations and goals, to be forced into a one-curriculum-fits-all mold. Those who would prescribe require-ments in extensive detail, on the other hand, argue—much as did McCosh and others of Eliot's original critics—that young collegians are too inexperienced and immature to make wise choices when left to their own devices. Either way, imbedded in the debates that continue to surround the controversy of choice versus prescription are two elements that frequently go unacknowledged, a strategic consideration and a philosophical stance.

The *strategic* consideration turns on the distinction between ful-filling an educational goal and completing a formal course. Character-istically, the tendency of the respective protagonists is to equate prescribed requirements with the completing of discrete courses, in which case the focus becomes one of deciding in specific cases whether some particular course should or should not be required. Most such disputes prove fruitless, apart from the fact that very little consideration is given over to how the course in question is taught and whether it succeeds in achieving its intended purpose. Faculty-generated curricular requirements rarely fasten on a specification of goals and objectives, as distinct from lists of courses to be completed. Nor do they allow for a multiplicity of means of achieving them. More commonly, prescription translates into lists of courses (or alternatives among courses) to be completed in order for students to satisfy general education require-ments. And, again, still less attention is paid to how the courses are organized and whether they are well taught.

The *philosophic* difference between advocates of free elective choice and curricular prescription amounts basically to that between what Weingartner and others have termed an a priori conception of the educated person, perceived as the goal of liberal learning, and an a posteriori notion of what may reasonably be anticipated as an outcome. That is, the a priori view begins with a specification of the attributes or defining characteristics of the well-educated person cast as a pedagogical ideal. Teaching and learning, in this view, are means or instrumentalities intended to bring students to that predefined state or condition. One cannot decide what is to be taught, it is assumed, unless one holds in mind some definite idea of what it means to be a liberally educated, well-rounded person, some perspective on what, ideally, a graduate should know and be able to do. Those who favor this approach tend to support explicit requirements and prescriptions adapted to the end in view.

Apologists for the a posteriori view, in contrast, argue that it is impossible to define the jointly necessary and sufficient attributes of the educated person, considered as a unitary ideal. On the contrary, there can be no single definition of the well-educated person, it is alleged. Hence, the focus should be on what is learned, on the *increments* achieved by a multiplicity of pedagogic means, without any presumption that all learners share a common destination or eventually will achieve the same end. And because there can be many different types of educated people, taking into account their differences means making adequate provision for student choice throughout the undergraduate experience. While many contemporary writers return repeatedly to the first alternative, it would seem that, either by reason of principled conviction or simply by default in the absence of agreement or consensus, popular opinion today more heavily favors the second pluralistic choice.

A third fundamental concern speaks to the issue of how to achieve scope or "breadth" of content in each student's education. Thanks to literally decades of discussion during which rival groups have advanced their claims, the issues involved have become quite familiar. Oversimplifying somewhat, at least three, possibly four, different points of view contend for acceptance.

The first emphasizes the importance of transmitting a defined body of learning, often reduced to a specific list of the great works of human thought (illustrated in part by E. D. Hirsch's work *Cultural Literacy* and exemplified also in the Great Books program at Chicago under Robert Maynard Hutchins).

A second school of thought stresses acquaintance with the modes of inquiry and forms of understanding distinctive of different disciplines, the "knowledge domains" represented by literature, mathematics, history, the fine arts, the social sciences, and the biological and physical sciences (illustrated in Daniel Bell's *The Reforming of General Education* and incorporated also in Richard McKeon's discussion of knowledge "structures" and "principles").

A third position proposes to achieve breadth simply by requiring students to take a minimum number of courses in each of several disciplinary categories: so many hours in the humanities and fine arts, a course or two in mathematics, a fixed number of courses in the sciences, and so forth—the well-known "distribution" requirement (exemplified partly in Harvard's program of the late 1970s).

To these might be added a fourth approach now very much out of favor, namely, a course of general studies built around synoptic, interdisciplinary survey courses.

Each approach attracts adherents today. Those who would stipulate a central body of knowledge or a list of great books are prone to complain that without some fixed content to general education students may graduate without ever having become acquainted with the works of Plato, Aristotle, Shakespeare, Aquinas, or other great minds of the past. To such partisans, distribution requirements amount to little more than formless choices from a cafeteria-like menu of options, while approaches emphasizing modes of thought represent nothing more than crude political compromises hammered out among competing academic departments.

Advocates of general learning based on initiation into different modes of knowing may concur that distribution requirements are insufficient, but lists of great books are judged to be too arbitrary and static to be of much utility either.[73] Those who support distribution requirements point out that the arrangement offers at least one indisputable advantage in that it avoids futile debate over specific courses, while still blending student choice with an element of compulsion.[74] The goal of breadth, moreover, can be achieved without the need for faculty to design and offer special courses.

Parenthetically, over the past decade or so (as previously noted) much attention has been given to the question of a curricular "canon."[75] Traditionalists argue that undergraduates are poorly served when they are allowed to pass through college without ever having been afforded in-depth exposure to "classical" works that treat in some exemplary way the most profound issues of the human condition. Hallowed by time, revered by thoughtful readers down through the centuries, such works collectively supply the intellectual and aesthetic foundation for liberal learning, a base for which there is allegedly no satisfactory substitute or alternative.

Anti-traditionalists, for their part, respond by pointing out that the so-called canon is comprised mainly of artifacts produced by White, upper-class males; that there is no one authoritative and changeless list of canonical texts accepted by all; that the usual lists of such works are confined to the Western intellectual tradition, thereby leaving out the rest of the world; and that the achievements of women and minorities, many of them heretofore downtrodden and oppressed, have not been represented adequately.

A number of quite different issues appear to have become entangled throughout the course of the various debates over the canon. Oftentimes, for example, disputes over which authors or thinkers deserve canonical status shift to derivative—and generally futile—questions about specific works and titles. If it is agreed that Plato should be included, does it really matter whether students are set to reading the *Apology* or the *Phaedo* or the *Laws?* Should Aristotle's *Ethics* or his *Posterior Analytics* be commended to undergraduates, if room is lacking for both? Would the reasons for including Karl Marx be the same as, or isomorphic to, those dictating the inclusion of Thomas Hobbes or Dante? Is it important to read and be intimately conversant with works of purely historical significance in mathematics or the natural sciences, say, Ptolemy's *Amalgest* or Aristarchus' *On the Distance of the Sun and the Moon?* Is it essential for everyone to have read Darwin's *Origin of the Species* or Newton's *Principia?* What mathematical "classics" should be mandated for inclusion?

Further, if acquainting students with the main ligaments of the Western cultural heritage poses a major pedagogical challenge, yet simultaneously it is thought necessary to include works drawn from other cultures, can someone peruse Wang Ch'ung's *Lun-Heng* or the *Vaisesikasutras* of Kanada and make much of either work without a sense of historical perspective or a feeling for its particular cultural context? Does the inclusion of, say, the poetry of an otherwise-obscure Hispanic peasant woman represent a bona fide effort at curricular "balance," or is it simply a political expedient designed to confer prestige and visibility upon its author and the entire social class she is made to symbolize? What is one to make of a list of authors encompassing so diverse a group as, for example, Augustine, Homer, Cicero, Spinoza, Voltaire, and William Blake? Furthermore, must "great works" be limited to *printed books*—should liberal learning, for example, include the study of outstanding architectural exemplars, masterpieces of painting, and great works of music? Might not the performing arts have a place as well? Is it not true that there are "classics" in the world of opera and dance with which almost everyone ought to be familiar?

Is it the case, further, that a fixed canon is capable of furnishing what Hirsch has called "the basic information necessary to thrive in the modern world," the "network of information a competent reader possesses"?[76] Would any single list, as Allan Bloom contends, supply "the treasury of great deeds, great men [sic] and great thoughts" considered essential for a well-educated person to know?[77] Or, alternatively, as still another critic has alleged, Is the quest for an authoritative curricular canon simply an intellectualist exercise conducted "for a restricted class of potential connoisseurs of certain rare and marvelous objects . . . deserving appreciation"?[78]

A fourth question that forever dominates discussions about the liberal arts curriculum is how to achieve a synthesis or integration of all the constituent elements of the whole. Many ingenious proposals for solving the problem have been put forth; quite a few have found application in specific colleges and universities willing to experiment with various alternatives. Sensitive to charges that today's students are encouraged to amass courses and then turn them in like so many coupons in exchange for a degree, advocates for a more integrated liberal arts curriculum continue to seek ways of encouraging students to draw connections among what they have learned, to link different bodies of content, to discern important relationships among otherwise disparate subjects.

Sometimes it is proposed that seniors complete integrative courses designed to help them pull things together in their final year. Other times the effort is to identify large themes and to "cluster" courses around them. Again, a "capstone" experience has been tried, whereby students are afforded opportunities to apply what they have learned in producing some creative project or in the drafting of a senior thesis paper. Overall, no one approach has proven itself demonstrably superior to any others.

The specific objectives and goals of general learning or of a liberal "core" curriculum have always been a topic of disputation. They continue to provoke debate today. A survey of chief academic officers conducted by Vassar's Virginia Smith a few years ago, however, yielded a quite conventional if abstract enumeration of perceived purposes: (1) *heritage:* providing a common core of great ideas and books, passing on the cultural heritage; (2) *counterpoint:* assisting students to broaden their patterns of course work, to achieve curricular breadth; (3) *instrumental:* developing particular skills, such as writing, speaking, and critical thinking; (4) *development* or *empowerment:* development of the whole person; (5) *valuing:* inculcating certain values; and (6) *social agenda:* infusing the general education component with some specific social purpose, such as global awareness, environmental sensitivity, or preparation for responsible citizenship in a democratic society.[79]

What seems distinctive about the contemporary phase of this debate is the extent to which some "social agenda" or set of external political considerations is construed as wholly and exclusively determinative of the discourse. "I do not think that educational issues are in fact exclusively educational issues; rather, they are . . . a reflection of problems that occur on the economic, political, social and ethical levels as well," declares television commentator and columnist Martin Kaplan. "And thus, the problem to which a core curriculum is a solution is not an educational problem but is a political, moral, ethical, and social problem."[80] The peculiar feature of this argument, however, is the degree to which it seems to confuse the part with the whole. Granting that the aims of liberal learning are multiple, intertwined, and often jumbled together, that they have been thought to range from promoting civic responsibility to cultivating aesthetic sensibilities, from compensating for the crass commercialism of society to strengthening critical reflection—it does not necessarily follow that each and every one of them is exclusively the expression of some partisan political imperative.

It is one thing to claim that societal concerns help shape the collegiate curriculum, or that decisions about general education tend to be responsive to broader social concerns. It is quite another to assume, as do some reductionist analyses, that the curriculum is wholly and exclusively a political construction, or that any putatively objective educational proposal is nothing more than a rationalization for some particular cultural bias, a given economic structure, or a class interest.[81] The chilling effect of any such analysis on anyone's willingness to advance proposals for reform in good faith or to defend any particular stance about the nature of the educated person can hardly be overestimated. A charge, for example, that the impulse for curricular reform arises from class interests and "does not originate in ivy-wreathed missions of universities, faculty ideals of the educated person, or the irrefutable logic of ivory tower knowledge" may have a way of becoming a self-fulfilling proposition.[82]

Part of the modern problem perhaps is that society's internal divisions seem larger and more pronounced than ever before in living memory. With regard to liberal learning, as David Saxon has commented, up until recently there was always at least one continuing thread that provided a constant over the years. "Liberal education," he observes, "has always attempted to reflect what a particular society thought was important to know and to understand at a particular time. It represented society's collective wisdom about the skills and knowledge a person needed in order to be at home in the world and to make the best use of and derive the greatest pleasure from whatever talents he or she possessed."[83] The question today is whether any such consensus still exists or can be forged anew. Martin Trow, for example, speaks for many observers in judging that contemporary society is witness to nothing less than "a complete collapse of any generally shared conception of what students ought to learn."[84]

When a culture or a society institutionalizes its learning, Martin Kaplan argues, it projects and reifies a particular myth and vision of itself. When it stipulates (or refrains from declaring) what it is that people ought most to know, when it defines (or avoids defining) basic skills and information, when it establishes (or skirts establishing) the rudiments of competence without which a person is thought unable to function in the society, it has thereby revealed much about itself. If nothing else, it gives evidence it is hopelessly divided against itself. "A culture's educational ideals for its citizens, and the de facto ideals that its educational institutions carry," he asserts, "are the products of a vision of the good society, of what ought to be....If we have substituted an open curriculum free of requirements for patterned and limited options, if we promote diversity over control, then in our way we, too, have offered moral and political answers to educational—that is, moral and political—questions."[85]

Ultimately, there must be a standard of achievement that can be used to measure and compare the goals even of diverse educational schemes, Kaplan insists. There must be some skills, values, and a body of knowledge that all people—no matter what their autonomy and particular interests—ought to acquire, if they are to be considered educated. But to the question, "What is an educated person?" few seem prepared to offer a blunt declarative answer. The *least* likely response nowadays is "An educated person is..." followed by a list of qualities or attributes and a set of required educational experiences designed to produce them. Yet to abandon the effort to supply an intelligible answer, in effect surrendering the university to market interests—to whatever people claim to want—in the name of pluralism or diversity, is a relativism, Kaplan added, "that slides quite effortlessly into nihilism."[86]

PROPOSALS FOR A REFORM AGENDA

In academe as elsewhere, it has been said, the merits of any particular proposal sometimes seem inversely proportional to the likelihood the idea in question will win widespread acceptance. Bad ideas, if they are capable of helping effect economies of time, energy, resources, personnel and thought, tend to drive out the good ones. If indeed some such perverse rule holds, prospects for revivifying general learning of a liberal character are not good. For restoring the liberating arts to a place of primacy within the undergraduate curriculum in contemporary American colleges and universities—especially within the larger graduate universities now stressing research and graduate training—will require no small effort. Smaller liberal arts college already committed to general learning may effect the changes needed with relatively moderate strain. Larger schools (where most of today's college students are enrolled) might find the task nearly impossible.

Academic leaders who currently guide the fortunes of the nation's trend-setting universities are well aware that popular pressures for reform have been mounting. And in the main, as George C. Douglas of the University of Illinois noted in a 1992 work entitled *Education Without Impact,* they do grasp the main thrust of the complaints. They are well aware that undergraduate education has suffered neglect in recent decades; and many are willing to acknowledge the very real disorder and incoherence exhibited by the curriculum. But the major universities have been so long paralyzed by institutional inertia, so long dominated by the imperatives of graduate training and by popular pressures for direct job-training, by research priorities, and by the publication treadmill, they would find it nearly impossible to make the massive shifts in ways of "doing business" required to bring about changes on the scale needed. The typical approach is to put up some window-dressing and then revert to business as usual.[87] The task ahead will require much more than window-dressing.

First and foremost must come widespread acknowledgment that most four-year colleges and universities have mindlessly mixed vocational training and academic education, and have done so bereft of any guiding vision of the whole. As William Schaefer of the University of California has observed, it simply is not true that within the constraints of a four-year undergraduate degree program, students are both trained effectively for a career and supplied with a broadly-based liberal education. In attempting to do both, they in fact succeed in doing neither.[88]

The first step then, as an exercise in "truth-in-advertising," would be for institutions of higher education to incorporate a disclaimer in their mission statements. They should explicitly disavow any intent to prepare students directly for employment at the baccalaureate level, thereby disabusing prospective applicants and their parents of the mistaken notion that the primary purpose of coming to college is to enable a graduate "to get a better job." Postsecondary education has a great deal to do with preparing for employment, of course, but the contribution of undergraduate training to that important task should be seen for what it is: a broad albeit indirect mode of preparation involving the acquisition of basic knowledge and skills, most of which are not closely linked with specific, occupationally-relevant competencies. Students interested solely or primarily in securing a job, of course, would be better advised to attend a two-year vocational school.

Second, new administrative configurations will be needed within some colleges and most universities. As matters now stand, whereas post-baccalaureate education usually is placed under a graduate school headed by a designated academic administrator, general studies lack the management structure and coordination of resources needed for developing coherent programs at the undergraduate level. Prevailing practice assigns the task to the dean of the arts and sciences college, who, juggling the demands of scores of rival departments, must then compete for institutional support with the heads of professional schools or colleges offering their own undergraduate majors and degrees, each of them determined to maintain its own share of scarce resources. A more rational approach would be to establish an undergraduate college equivalent to the Graduate School and charge the former with the coordination and design of *all* undergraduate courses of instruction, much as the latter presides over graduate instruction.

Third, academic departments as separate and distinct administrative units need to be dismantled, at least so far as undergraduate programming is concerned. (The anguished howls of protest from faculty greeting any such initiative can only be imagined.) Departments serve chiefly to accentuate the quite natural and understandable tendency of faculty scholars to retreat into their respective academic specializations. They polarize and intensify the competition for resources and student majors among the disciplines. Departmental structures further render genuine interdisciplinary collaboration less likely. Most of the useful purposes of departmentalization at the undergraduate level could as easily be preserved if faculty were grouped loosely into overlapping "clusters" or programmatic "teaching areas," which is to say, more informal units not always precisely aligned along the boundaries of the established academic disciplines.

Extensive experimentation with different structures and configurations probably would be helpful, as some schools currently are discovering. But the basic goal of reducing intellectual fragmentation and splintering in the interest of developing more integrative undergraduate courses of study should always be held uppermost in mind. At an absolute minimum, if liberal learning is to be revived in some meaningful way, the department as an autonomous unit for resource allocations and programs must be abandoned. Not only has it outlived its usefulness; it has become a positive obstruction to the work of creating an institutional environment in which liberal learning can flourish.

Fourth, in spite of a current bias that works strongly against any such attempt, faculties (perhaps in concert with representatives of external constituencies) must once again be set to the task of stipulating what knowledge, abilities, skills and values students will be expected to have acquired after three or four years of undergraduate education—attributes and characteristics which will have made them educated in ways different from (and implicitly better than) those who did not elect to attend college or who attended a different type of institution.[89]

Here the logic seems inexorable: If the incoherence of a curricular "smorgasbord" is to be avoided, if the pick-and-choose, hit-and-miss approach is deemed undesirable and ultimately counterproductive, some working agreement on basic goals is essential. Not until some consensus is reached respecting pedagogical outcomes can curricula and instructional strategies be devised (much less ways of assessing their effectiveness) that are demonstrably adapted to achieving the ends identified. Protestations on behalf of "pluralism" and "diversity," it needs to be said, in this connection appear to serve mainly as rhetorical camouflage for avoiding the difficult task of building agreement over objectives.

Mindful that many formal lists of desired student attributes have been generated over the years and then promptly forgotten, the initial step—but only a first step—would be some enumeration of the proficiencies or skills students might reasonably be expected to acquire: discrete performative abilities such as using a computer for word-processing, conversing in a foreign language, solving simple linear equations in mathematics, communicating ideas lucidly and clearly in written form or oral discourse, and so on. The prudent course would be to limit the list to those specific proficiencies for which testing procedures can be devised. The proof of the pudding, so to speak, would be students' ability to demonstrate that the skills in question had been mastered at an acceptable level.

Some skills of course are best acquired by requiring students to enroll in particular courses. Nonetheless, means and ends ought not to be confused with one another, as is now often the case. At the risk of stating what should be obvious, if a faculty body were to demand a specified level of proficiency in some language other than English in order to satisfy the requirements of the baccalaureate degree, for example, a rather brief and informal interrogation of a student by a native speaker of the foreign language involved (or someone who had acquired mastery) would better serve as confirmation that the goal had been attained than a transcript attesting to the student's satisfactory completion of a sequence of language courses. The test for computer literacy would be a demonstration that the learner could work with a data base, a spreadsheet or some other appropriate document. An "A" received as a final grade from an English composition class is meaningless unless the student can produce a well-written paper; and so on.

Likewise needed in a specification of hoped-for outcomes would be some general identification of "conversancies," that is, familiarity with the generative concepts, motive ideas, central themes and important terms and names particular to a given knowledge domain—in other words, the basic information and modes of inquiry peculiar to a discipline (or some linked array of similar disciplines).[90] Finally, the list might include values and habits of mind considered integral to the academic enterprise, for example, tolerance and respect for honest differences of opinion; a sense of style; the importance of critical analysis and logic; respect for the role of evidence in argumentation; intellectual honesty; awareness of the differences among opinions, beliefs, normative judgments and empirical facts; aesthetic appreciation of creative works; and so on.

The meaning and significance of a baccalaureate degree, it would seem, are virtually impossible to assess in a vacuum, without some specification of the distinguishing marks of the college graduate to whom it is awarded. Hence, once again, the point needs to be emphasized that institutions may tinker endlessly with their breadth requirements, fiddle with the specifics of a curricular core, or modify existing courses and devise new ones, as colleges and universities are indeed prone to do from time to time. But without some identification of the larger purposes served, all such exercises would seem largely futile and self-defeating.

Fifth, faculties need to be regrouped. There is little reason to suppose there might not be many alternative patterns deserving exploration. One configuration worth considering would involve five different undergraduate "divisions" or schools: *Physical Sciences and Technologies* (mathematics, computer science, inorganic chemistry, physics, astronomy, geology, and so on); *Biological Sciences and Technologies* (microbiology, botany, zoology, genetics, organic chemistry perhaps, paleontology and some few others); *Social and Human Studies* (to include psychology, sociology, anthropology, economics, history, political science, possibly geography, archaeology, and comparative religion); *Fine Arts* (theater, dance, art, music); and *Arts and Letters* (English, comparative and world literature, philosophy, classical studies, languages, speech and communication). Details as to the number of groupings and which disciplines belonged where could be left to trial and error as well as local preference. Some institutions, for example, might decide to assemble only three aggregations, organized respectively around science and technology, the social sciences, and the arts and humanities.

Sixth, to each faculty grouping would be assigned responsibility for developing a two-year sequence of courses, each of whose major elements or "modules" would be required of all students throughout the second half of the freshman year, extending throughout the sophomore year, and into the first half of the junior year. (The first half of the initial year of college, or some of it at least, probably should be given over to intensive work in written and oral communication, mathematics, and other skill-oriented subjects.) Inaugurating interdisciplinary course sequences of a general nature would not inevitably signal a return to the now-discredited fixed and uniform curriculum of yesteryear. A limited number of options and alternatives within each sequence might prove unobjectionable, so long as the scope of elective choice did not serve simply to revive conventional "distribution" requirements. (Flexibility would be important throughout, especially if special provision had to be made for those in the performing arts, where intensity and continuity of training are essential.)

Some elements within each sequence—not necessarily freestanding courses—might be varied to take into account differences in students' aptitudes and interests. The range of possibilities, extending from "remedial" to "intensive," from "standard" to "enriched" to "honors" would be limited only by the ingenuity and imagination of curriculum planners. The point would be to ensure that all students completing each sequence would have been afforded opportunities for "initiation" into the several universes of discourse thereby represented.

Care would be needed to prevent such courses of study—the phrase is used advisedly—from degenerating into mere surveys of a superficial character, or simplistic "introductions" to the disciplines, or watered-down versions of more advanced courses, or as hurdles to be surmounted en route to more specialized studies. Nor, of course, would the sequences proposed be adapted to recruiting prospective student majors for any given field. The overall objective, always, would be to induct learners into ways of knowing, assisting students to "pass into" and "walk around" inside varying fields of study, to explore, as it were, the several worlds of humankind's physical and biological environment, of contemporary civilization and its historical antecedents, and the "inner space" of the human mind, its workings, and the products of its creative imagination. Or, to adapt a somewhat different metaphor, the purpose would be to lead students into a array of conceptual and thematic landscapes, pointing out significant features of the topography along the way, and teaching them how best to investigate and become familiar with the terrain. The same point is served by reference to the "syntactical" structure of the various academic disciplines or fields of knowledge.

Designing course sequences of an appropriate character would amount to a major intellectual challenge for faculty. Much time and energy would be needed to think things through afresh, to identify the basic organizing conceptual structures latent in each disciplinary combination, to find ways of linking ideas together to form intelligible wholes, to exhibit the modes of inquiry and of knowing specific to and distinctive of different subject matters, to draw out integrative themes and continuities, and to sequence information in ways most likely to be helpful to student novices. Only scholarly experts in the various fields would be equal to the task. Unfortunately, the more specialized their own training, the more difficult it might be for them to "step back" and plot out the routes along which the uninitiated need to be led.

The logistical and pedagogical challenges also would be daunting. It should be emphasized, however, that faculty would not have to rely solely upon standard three-credit-hour courses as the only constituent building block for each interdisciplinary sequence. Provided there were sufficient planning and foresight, and a careful husbanding of resources, institutions might want to experiment with a combination of learning experiences and activities, employing differing instructional formats and "segments" of varying duration: standard courses of a conventional sort,

certainly, but also so-called "minicourses," short courses, special conferences, workshops, seminars, colloquia, tutorials, independent study,
study-abroad experiences, internships and practica—the list of worthwhile possibilities could be quite extensive. As for "skill-building"
courses such as written composition, finite mathematics, computers, and
so forth, adequate arrangements could be made to allow students already
proficient in those areas to "test out" of certain elements in each sequence
through some type of competency assessment.

Seventh, some version of a "pass-fail" system should replace letter
grading in individual courses. Alternatively, the number of assessment
categories (typically ranging from "F" to "A") should be reduced from
five to no more than four: "fail," "marginal pass," "pass," and "pass with
distinction," thereby discouraging if not precluding the calculation of
that most dubious of American contributions to higher learning, the
cumulative grade-point average. (To counter grade inflation, faculties
might further consider instituting a policy forbidding any teacher from
awarding more than a fixed percentage of grades designated as "pass
with distinction.") Whatever the merits of different grading scales, to
the extent that the current system reinforces the idea that a college
education is no more than the sum of individual courses completed and
grades awarded, it deserves abolition. Hardly anything could be more
antithetical to the idea of liberal education.

Eighth, comprehensive or general examinations, both written and
oral, positioned halfway through the junior year ought to be instituted
prior to allowing students to select their major concentrations. The
practice would serve to shift the focus of effort and attention away from
student achievement in individual courses, as they are now, and place
them where they belong, on global learning outcomes. To the usual
objection that professors would be tempted to "teach to the tests," the
best rejoinder is to ask, "Why not?" If comprehensive examinations
were assembled such that student performances on them were valid and
reliable indicators of what had been learned (or a reasonable sampling
thereof), the testing process itself should be considered unobjectionable.

From a teaching perspective, possibly the most corrosive and
debilitating practice to be found in academe is its traditional reliance
upon large lectures (sometimes taught by inexperienced graduate assistants) as a vehicle for delivering lower-level "service" courses. The
problem is not that students fail to learn, it is that (with rare exceptions)
they learn all the wrong lessons: how to be a receptacle of data, a passive
learner, a consumer and processor of pre-packaged information. Ironi-

cally, those beginning students most in need of individualized attention, of the intellectual give-and-take of the tutorial or seminar, are those who, massed together, are least likely to be afforded opportunities to participate in the most fruitful sort of teaching and learning exchanges a college or university is capable of offering. Meanwhile, more advanced students who are—or should be—better able to make their own way through the curriculum, stand a far greater chance of direct, firsthand exposure to the faculty members with the most to offer in the way of academic knowledge and experience. No one should nurture the illusion that authentic liberal learning can be had "on the cheap" via mass lectures.

Ninth, the last year and a half of the undergraduate experience ought to be reserved for a "concentration" in an academic major—though not quite in the traditional mold. (Successful performance on comprehensive examinations at the mid-point of the junior year, of course, would be prerequisite to admission for specialized study.) Three semesters' worth of full-time course work or its equivalent, culminating in some appropriate sort of integrative "capstone" experience, would represent close to 40 percent of all academic work completed. This seems a reasonable portion to reserve for the in-depth study of a particular discipline or, better yet, a linked array of similar disciplines

Once again, the armature might be supplied by the tripartite or fivefold clustering of fields alluded to previously. Thus, a student would "major" in the sciences, or the social sciences, or the arts and humanities, selecting electives from among a sequenced array of advanced-level specialized courses. Alternatively, under certain circumstances the practice of allowing a student to pick a specific discipline (psychology, physics, drama, chemistry, or whatever) in which to concentrate might be retained. Finally, if it were found essential to do so, it should be possible to allow graduate units to offer a very limited number of pre-professional courses at the undergraduate level in such fields as journalism, nursing, pharmacy, engineering, business and public administration, education, and so forth. Otherwise, "applied" courses would be reserved exclusively for graduate-level training, instead of being allowed to encroach progressively upon the time and space available for general education as now seems the case.

Would the time intervening between high-school graduation and the onset of pre-professional training be increased? In some cases, probably so, unless the baccalaureate-degree program was cut back to three years. But it is worth noting that under current conditions many undergraduates do in fact change majors several times, resulting in an almost-inevitable lengthening of the time needed to satisfy all of the requirements for the baccalaureate degree. It could be argued that the gains registered by having all college graduates broadly educated would far outweigh the disadvantage of postponing pre-professional training to the post-baccalaureate level, the cost of attending college nowadays notwithstanding. Moreover, it seems reasonable to assume that systematic exposure throughout the first two and a half years of collegiate study to the knowledge-domains underlying applied fields would help facilitate students' choices of majors and possible future careers at the halfway point of the third year.

It should be recalled, too, that the unbroken progression from a degree in some job-related field such as engineering or nursing to professional employment is far from being a universal norm. Most arts and sciences concentrations, for instance, do not lead directly to related careers without some intervening graduate-level instruction. Furthermore, many students enter—or end up in—positions wholly unrelated to the fields in which they majored as undergraduates. In any case, it is increasingly the trend in some fields, such as teaching, to require completion of a graduate degree prior to entry into the trade or profession in question. Hence, thoroughgoing reform needs to take into account the intrinsic pedagogical purposes of an undergraduate major at least as much as the extrinsic purposes it sometimes—but not always—serves.

Tenth, liberal and general education must be recognized as something more than the product of formal classroom learning alone. The institutional environment, and the totality of experiences that contribute to undergraduate life as a whole, may serve to impede or to encourage the intellectual, moral, spiritual, and aesthetic development institutions of higher learning ostensibly encourage and foster. If the climate is cold, uninviting, and impersonal; if bureaucratic routines serve chiefly to alienate students; if faculty-student interaction outside the classroom is infrequent or perfunctory; and if cocurricular involvements are not actively encouraged, authentic learning suffers.

If the college or university functions as though it was a giant emporium or bazaar where students come to purchase prepackaged learning doled out in the form of courses, students as customers will most certainly come to regard it as such and behave accordingly. As Douglas rightly notes, our universities are presently not well adapted to providing the type of setting truly supportive of general education. Typically, they are "too big, too full of hustle and bustle, too busy doing society's work, to be the sort of places where a vital human transaction can take place." Insofar as they are merely knowledge factories, or places operating on a "trickle-down" theory of undergraduate education where the bulk of attention is paid to graduate training, to just that extent they are unlikely to nurture liberal learning.[91]

On the basis of an exhaustive review of relevant literature, Patrick T. Terenzini of Penn State University and Ernest T. Pascarelli of the University of Illinois conclude that genuine quality in undergraduate education resides more in the climate the institution provides and what it does programmatically than in its stock of resources. The most important determining factors, they avow, are those having to do with the nature and cohesiveness of students' curricular experiences; the patterns of course work they complete; the quality of teaching they receive; and the extent to which faculty members involve students as active participants in the teaching-learning process. The same evidence suggests that the changes students undergo are most probably the cumulative result of a set of interrelated and mutually supporting experiences, in class and out, sustained over an extended period of time.[92]

Among the most important considerations, Terenzini and Pascarelli claim, is the quality of interaction sustained between faculty and students. "Many faculty members and more than a few administrators," they observe, "appear to believe that faculty obligations to contribute to the education of undergraduate students begin and end at the classroom or laboratory door. If these obligations extend beyond the classroom at all, it is only to the faculty member's office, to class-related questions or academic advising. Faculty workload policies and reward systems implicitly support this narrow conception of the faculty member's sphere of influence. The research literature does not."[93]

What empirical research does indicate, they point out, is that faculty exert much influence in their out-of-class contacts with students during the 85 percent of the waking hours they spend outside the classroom. "A large part of the impact of college," they point out, "is determined by the extent and content of students' interactions with the major agents of socialization on campus: [including] faculty members. . . . Further, faculty members' educational influence appears to be significantly enhanced when their contacts with students extend *beyond* the formal classroom to informal non-classroom settings."[94]

All things considered, the work of turning matters around, transforming the academic culture and pointing it in the direction needed, will be no small undertaking. Universities especially will not be easily diverted from their preoccupation with prestigious research projects and graduate-level career preparation. Persuading faculty members to cease regarding undergraduate teaching assignments as a form of penal servitude, drudge work unworthy of their talent and time, will be difficult.[95] The entrenched professorial reward system will not change until the real costs of the publish-or-perish syndrome afflicting so many campuses are frankly acknowledged and addressed. The work of rethinking and reshaping curricula with a view toward the rehabilitation of liberal learning has hardly begun. Creating a climate in which good teaching is strongly valued—all of these are imperatives contributing to the formidable reform agenda lying ahead.

America's colleges and universities, the best among them at any rate, exhibit many significant and undeniable strengths. More than a mere handful are distinguished centers of scholarship and instruction. They perform useful services valued by society at large; and they do so on a scale undreamt of scant decades ago. Most of the nation's institutions of higher learning are efficient processors of information. They are unexcelled purveyors of professional credentials. The flood of technical reports, studies, books, articles and monographs that issues from within their precincts likewise has no equal anywhere else in the world. What they do least well is educate undergraduates.

If the goal celebrated in the lofty rhetoric of commencement speeches and college catalogues is truly to educate human beings in ways that matter, if the aim is one of preparing literate and informed citizens for participation in a democratic social order, and not simply one of training people to serve as cogs within the social machinery, then something akin to a paradigmatic shift in thinking must occur. Piecemeal reform of the traditional sort has proven itself insufficient to the challenge of reclaiming liberal learning and making it whole. Something more thoroughgoing and systematic in the way of fundamental change is needed. Whether colleges and universities are equal to the task remains to be discovered.

V.

ACADEMIC PRIORITIES AND THE PROFESSORIATE: WHO SHALL TEACH?

REFORMING ACADEMIC CULTURE

If American institutions of higher learning are to survive and flourish in the twenty-first century, a great deal of systematic thinking about their multiple purposes, diverse programs, and services to external constituencies will be required. The university especially, as Cameron Fincher of the University of Georgia has argued, "cannot be all things to all people, and we must leave to other public or private institutions the educational services they can best provide."[1] In any pending rearrangement of institutional priorities, four-year colleges and universities would be well advised to reaffirm the enhancement of learning and teaching as their fundamental commitment.

Making instruction and students central to the life of institutions of higher learning seems an unexceptional aim—indeed, most of the lay public might find it odd that this goal needs any explicit reiteration whatsoever. One might safely assume there are thousands of dedicated classroom teachers in academe—tens of thousands, even—whose life work is focused on teaching and learning. They care deeply about students. They work long and hard. And by and large, they help make a difference. The point is not that inspired teachers are lacking or that most professors are ineffectual. Neither claim is even close to being true.

Rather, it is that in many larger institutions especially, dedication to the work of teaching runs counter to, or at least does not find strong support from, the underlying academic culture. A 1991 survey of over 35,000 faculty members conducted by the Higher Education Research Institute, for example, was typical in finding that only 10 percent believed their institution valued and rewarded good teaching. Eighty percent reported that research was the top institutional priority.

Much eloquent rhetoric to the contrary notwithstanding, instruction and student mentoring tend to be taken for granted or relegated to the periphery of academe, at least within larger institutions. Significantly, nowhere is the attitude of relative indifference more pronounced than in the most prestigious, research-oriented universities whose combined student enrollments account for the great majority of students now pursuing higher education. Center stage there tends to be occupied by other professorial activities (research, consulting, publishing) having little to do with undergraduate instruction. Paradoxically, most large graduate research institutions are built on an undergraduate infrastructure and would not be economically viable without it. Yet relatively low priority is paid to undergraduate teaching.

Renewing the institutional commitment to meaningful teaching and learning will demand a fundamental shift in thinking. While they may deny it emphatically (assuming they have given it much thought at all), far too many professors implicitly treat teaching as a simple, linear "information-transfer" process, a straightforward matter of getting information or knowledge directly into students' heads—witness the ubiquity of the didactic lecture as the single most common instructional format employed in higher education, as countless studies attest.[2] The attitude seems to predominate, interestingly, regardless of whether a faculty member values teaching or not.

Contrary to present thinking, classroom instruction must come to be redefined in future years as the *re*-creation of knowledge for its effective dissemination to learners. At its best, it will involve, among other things, the employment and refinement of instructional methods that encourage *active* and *participatory* learning; innovative uses of technology to facilitate teaching and learning as *independent* and *interactive* processes; and the engagement of open, searching, inquiring minds in the pursuit of competence and understanding.[3] Correlatively, learning will come to be thought of as the product of experiences that take place in many different settings, not simply something that occurs solely or exclusively in classrooms, libraries, laboratories, and computer centers.

The reformulation of teaching and learning will necessitate a restructuring of courses, programs, and academic units at multiple levels. Unshackling learning from the time constraints of the traditional three-credit-hour course or seminar, where possible, poses just one initiative worth pursuing. Helping students to understand they ultimately are responsible for their own learning is more important still. Undergraduates no less than graduate students must be brought to appreciate the very profound truth that a college education is not something done "to" or "for" them as passive recipients. Nor can an education be directed "at" them with much hope for success either. Quite the contrary, it must be conducted "with" them as active collaborators in a shared enterprise. Above all, administrative and structural reorganization (at the undergraduate level at least) will need to be made more functional, in the special sense that their forms reflect purpose and experience more than simply the outmoded traditions of the past.

It should be recalled in this connection that universities have long been dominated by professional and academic fields of specialization established at the turn of the century whose internal organization has changed but little ever since. Seeking to gain a place within the curriculum, each academic discipline fought a bitter battle with its established predecessors. Now trying to hold their positions, many practitioners in today's entrenched disciplines continue on academic grounds to oppose efforts aimed at reorganizing knowledge in ways optimally adapted for its dissemination and use.[4] Internal academic struggles, in other words, are often about position and prestige and competition for resources, not about functional effectiveness. Recurrent squabbles have more to do with obsession over disciplinary autonomy than with the work of deciding how teaching and learning can best be facilitated for the intended beneficiaries—students.

Structural change, however, will be of little avail unless it is linked to clearly articulated goals and the garnering of broad support for a coherent system of institutional priorities. Rehabilitating the ideal of providing undergraduates with a first-rate liberal arts education surely must count among the most urgent items to be addressed. A baccalaureate-level course of studies organized around the liberal arts, affirms Richard Hersh, president of Hobart and William Smith colleges, "represents the best kind of education for meeting the complex demands of the twenty-first century." Yet, as he also notes, in recent years the public has come to see little relative value in the liberal arts compared with what passes for "professional" education. Facing up to the root causes of society's disaffection, he believes, is a key to the survival of liberal education in the years ahead.[5]

With funding from the AT&T Foundation, in 1993 Hersh commissioned a major opinion research firm to undertake a pilot study of public attitudes toward the liberal arts. So-called focus groups of consumers of higher education were assembled. They included college-bound students, their parents, current college students, and recent graduates. Also polled were academic administrators and business executives in a wide range of industries. Hersh's study found that corporate leaders, educators, parents and students alike all professed to see great value in the *concept* of a liberal arts education. However, at the same time they reportedly felt that today's fragmented college curriculum fails to deliver on the promise latent within the ideal.

Business executives reported strong interest in hiring liberally educated generalists rather than narrowly trained specialists, believing that the former are better adapted to the changing needs of an extremely competitive business environment. The liberal arts, they claimed, are well suited to engendering the attributes most needed by employees in today's corporate world: (1) excellent reading, writing, and oral communication abilities; (2) foreign language proficiency and understanding of foreign cultures; (3) critical judgment and problem-solving skills; (4) flexibility in dealing with people, taking on new tasks, and switching gears quickly; and (5) a highly developed sense of personal responsibility and ethics.[6]

At the same time, respondents in the study repeatedly cited much the same criticisms of institutions of higher learning. Academic standards were perceived to have declined. The same was reported about canons of decorum and personal conduct. Colleges were viewed as "disconnected" from real-world concerns, tending to be preoccupied with such allegedly sterile and irrelevant controversies as "political correctness" and the like.[7] Common complaints heard were that colleges and universities are failing to help develop such good work habits in students as perseverance and attention to detail; that they fail to encourage maturity, responsibility, and independence; that curricular requirements are not sufficiently demanding; and that not nearly enough attention is paid to students' ethical behavior.

Critics frequently allege that the relatively more frenetic pace of academic pursuits nowadays forms part of the problem as well. On the plus side, the flurry of activities and ongoing events, the presence of so many interesting people on campus, certainly makes academic life rich and varied.[8] The converse side of the coin, the negative aspect of all the activity, as philosophy professor Raphael Sassower of the University of Colorado at Colorado Springs points out, is that the academy is so full of distractions and constraints that its milieu has come to differ but little from that of any other governmental or corporate business institution.[9] There is a bureaucratic hierarchy and an accountability system; there are policies and procedures and budgets to worry over; there are endless committee meetings and proceedings; countless evaluations; and various and sundry other obligations to which faculty must attend.[10] The climate is so all-consuming that to avoid becoming embroiled in the trappings rather than the substance of useful work is oftentimes nearly impossible. The environment is burdensome, sometimes overpowering, and it conduces to a neglect of just those activities that genuinely matter most of all.

As some critics now increasingly argue, the root of the problem, however, is that for a variety of reasons, institutions of higher learning appear to have lost sight of their primary obligation to educate undergraduates and to put that obligation before all else.[11] Reordering priorities in order to restore baccalaureate-level teaching and learning to its deserved place at top of the pyramid of functions and involvements will require more than good intentions, pious rhetoric, or piecemeal adaptation of existing policies and procedures. What is needed, at an absolute minimum, is a thoroughgoing reexamination of academic culture as a whole, the total institutional environment inhabited by the professoriate. Practices seemingly unrelated to issues of teaching and learning, certain customs long hallowed by tradition and historical precedent, many well-entrenched attitudes and values, will all require closer scrutiny than is customary in most discussions of collegiate teaching and curricula. The practice of granting something close to absolute job security for tenured academics affords a case in point.

ABOLISHING FACULTY TENURE

One of the most prominent and visible features of academic life known to outsiders is the institution of faculty tenure. Once a new faculty member has concluded a probationary period of upward of six or seven consecutive years of service, it is noted, provided his or her professional performance has been judged worthy by colleagues, he or she is awarded tenure. Thereafter (or so it is claimed), the fortunate recipient enjoys what amounts to a guarantee of lifetime career security and to a degree practically unknown in other walks of life. Once tenured, the faculty member cannot be fired except under extraordinary circumstances, or for the most egregious sort of misconduct or malfeasance imaginable—and conceivably not even then. Possibly no other academic convention has been more controversial or so frequently criticized by the lay public.

What critics have in mind, of course, is the image of that small minority of professors who shamelessly neglect students while devoting too much time and energy to their own esoteric research projects or to lucrative outside consulting. Even worse, according to popular stereotypes, are those who, as the saying has it, are simply "burned out." They may once have been productive and contributing members of the academic fraternity, but as the years took their toll, they lost touch with academic life or were simply overtaken by developments in their field. Not having had a fresh idea of their own in years, they now do little more than go through the motions. They teach from faded notes unchanged for a decade or more; most have given up even the pretense of keeping current in their specialties. They are academic "deadwood." Yet because they are tenured, little if anything can be done. They are rarely dismissed, not even for gross incompetence. Nor can they lose their appointments for dereliction of duty. For all practical purposes, these professors are forever immune from pressures to rectify their ways.[12] Privileged status as tenured faculty, together with the abolition of mandatory retirement at a specified age, assures them a comfortable academic sinecure until they retire or drop in their tracks.

As with many stereotypes, there is at least a modicum of truth in the folklore of lazy, irresponsible academics hiding behind tenure. Almost everyone familiar with academe, after all, has at least one or two horror stories to share recounting instances of professorial arrogance and irresponsibility. But there is little hard evidence to suggest that these occurrences are nearly as widespread as some critics would have the public believe. "Do I really live a cushy life, luxuriating in generous fringe benefits?" James Perley, professor of biology at the College of Wooster, asks somewhat plaintively. Is tenure the unmitigated evil it is sometimes alleged to be, and does it confer unlimited leisure? "Do I teach three hours a week and then mow my lawn the rest of the time? Do I really spend my time drinking cappuccino with my friends, only condescending to meet students when I choose to?"[13] The scenario, he asserts, scarcely conforms to the reality of what he has known in the academic world; and it hardly does justice to the lives most other professors live either.

Tenured or not, the vast majority of college teachers are conscientious, diligent, and genuinely interested in their work. To this needs to be added the point that evidence abounds showing that productive scholars who are "self-starters" and somewhat inner-directed are inclined to remain productive in research and publishing throughout their careers, regardless of tenure status, just as outstanding or exemplary teachers usually continue striving for proficiency in the classroom from the time they first embark upon their academic careers until their conclusion. Contrariwise, indifferent or mediocre young academics whose performance may have left something to be desired at the outset (or whose minimal achievements seem to have been prompted mainly by external pressures imposed upon them) rarely register subsequent improvements in scholarship or instruction throughout the later phases of their careers.

But popular myths die hard. As Harvard economist Henry Rosovsky notes, suspicion persists that academics somehow are "getting away" with something, that lifetime tenure encourages indolence, stifles professorial initiative, and otherwise contributes to lack of on-the-job performance[14] A 1994 article in *The Wall Street Journal* was typical in blaming tenure for the glut of young academics today who must settle for marginal appointments as adjuncts in colleges and universities, while full-time slots are monopolized by senior faculty who, as the editorialist put it, are "privileged, enjoy lifetime jobs, with comfortable benefits accrued during decades of academic expansion."[15] Justified or not, the notion that academic mandarins enjoy near-total and complete job security, independent of performance, is unsettling to many.

Even within the ranks of the professoriate, voices are raised casting doubts on the tenure system and the way it is deployed. "Instead of protecting the tenure system as the safeguard of academic freedom, have we not helped administrators make it a whip with which to beat out of untenured faculty every last measure of a specious 'productivity'?" wonders Linda Ray Pratt, past president of the American Association of University Professors. "We've used, and abused, the tenure process as a budget tool and instrument of social control."[16] Concedes Paul Nuchims of West Virginia State College, "The letting go (firing) of good candidates for tenure in their sixth year ostensibly because they didn't quite measure up, but really because there is a sense that there are thousands of replacements waiting to take their place and they will be more malleable, this makes me sick at heart. . . ."[17]

Before attempting to assess the cogency of arguments brought by critics, however, the affirmative case for tenure as one of the essential aspects of academic life also needs to be restated. The standard defense is the claim that tenure serves as the principal guarantor of academic freedom, ensuring that faculty members continue to enjoy the right to teach and publish what they believe, to espouse unpopular causes, and otherwise to follow wherever their scholarly investigations take them. All this they must be able to do so without fear of retribution or summary dismissal by those who might be offended or outraged by heterodox opinion. Given a long and unsavory history in the United States of attacks upon academic freedom and the bitter struggle to protect professors from the arbitrary or capricious machinations of high-handed administrators, trustees, or college presidents, the security afforded by tenure certainly ought not to be dismissed lightly.[18]

Throughout most of the nineteenth century, for example, it was taken for granted that trustees or college presidents could dismiss members of the faculty at will, without due process and without explanation. The operative analogy drawn was to business corporations where management's right to fire employees always had been an unquestioned prerogative. Professors, too, it was widely assumed, were mere hirelings with no more rights than ordinary shop or factory employees. In 1810 the New York State legislature declared unequivocally that faculty held their academic positions solely "at the pleasure of the trustees" and could be dismissed at any time, for any reason.[19] The tendency of businessmen on governing boards for decades on end was to treat institutions of higher learning very much like business corporations, vividly illustrated on more than a few occasions by their readiness to get rid of professors whose opinions they disliked. Also reflective of prevailing attitudes was a proposal from Cornell's president Andrew White in 1867 that every professor should be scrutinized annually by the trustees, "with dismissal to follow upon a sufficient number of unsatisfactory ballots."[20]

When Cornell's governing body saw fit to fire William C. Russell from the university's vice-presidency in the late 1800s, its members did not so much as assign a cause; and when questioned, a trustee told a reporter from *The New York Times* that the governing board did not think it necessary or appropriate to defend themselves publicly in such a case.[21] In 1900, when the wife of Leland Stanford, founder of the university bearing his name, insisted that the president fire economist

Edward Ross because of his campaign for public scrutiny of the railroads and for the municipal ownership of public utilities, she clearly entertained no doubts about her right to dictate hiring and firing decisions.[22] Elsewhere, few were prepared to challenge the right of governing boards to act as they saw fit, without benefit of any public hearing whatsoever. In 1894 the Wisconsin courts upheld the regents' aversion to an open tribunal, claiming that "with its delays and publicity and the excitement it would produce and the feelings it would engender," a hearing could be prudently avoided.[23] Again in 1901 when the West Virginia court pondered whether a university's board of regents might act as it pleased, "without control, erroneous as its action may be," the high court responded unconditionally in the affirmative.[24]

Suggestions advanced around the turn of the century that professors deserved some of the same job protection coming to be enjoyed by civil servants, that academics were not simply "hired hands" and should be dealt with more as members of a self-governing guild than as corporate employees, or that faculty appointees should be likened to appointed magistrates with judicial immunity from arbitrary dismissal were uniformly rejected by those in positions of power. Commenting on the firing of two professors from Columbia University in 1917, a writer in *The Nation* complained, "The Board looked upon the point as one between themselves and their employees; and are in amazement that anyone should doubt their right to do what they will with their own. That the thing upon which they have laid their hand is not 'their own,' that they are trustees and not proprietors . . . have never entered into their field of vision."[25]

In 1915 the fledgling American Association of University Professors issued a report arguing that whereas professors are the appointees of university trustees, they are not in any proper sense their employees. Reaction was swift. "It is well to note the strange tendency to ignore the fact that, speaking legally, all persons receiving salary from a corporation are employees," declared one editorialist.[26] "This assertion has been resented bitterly by some writers who hold that college teachers are appointees, not employees, and that the corporation, having confirmed an appointment, has no authority to remove the appointee. . . . The claim is without basis."[27] Considering the climate of the times, perhaps it is not surprising that not only did trustees feel free to hire and fire professors at will, they likewise did not hesitate to dictate curricula. As a trustee of Northwestern University declared in 1903, "As to what should be taught in political science and social science, the professors should promptly and gracefully submit to the determination of the trustees."[28]

Coupled with professors' demands for academic freedom throughout the first half of the twentieth century were pleas for job security. As Henry Seidel Canby recalled, "Our strongest desire was to be made safe, to stay where we were on a living wage, to be secure while we worked. . . . No scrimping, no outside earning, could safeguard us. We were dependent upon the college, which itself was always pressed for money, and could not be counted upon to be either judicious or just."[29] Professors' motives here were no more exalted or lofty, of course, than those of steelworkers or miners or any other type of laborer: Their quite legitimate concerns were over wages, job security, and the need for some procedural system to provide due process. As historian Page Smith observes with some justification, the long struggle for tenure "was far less a fight for the right to express unpopular opinions than against an imperious and autocratic administration." What faculty needed and deserved to have were review procedures that protected them from arbitrary actions by administrators or trustees. Ultimately, he adds, "What they got was much more. . . ."[30]

Not until 1940, following nearly a half century of debate, did there appear anything approximating an "authoritative" definition and rationale for academic tenure. "After the expiration of a probationary period, teachers or investigators should have permanent or continuous tenure," announced the American Association of University Professors (AAUP) in a widely publicized *Statement of Principles,* "and their service should be terminated only for adequate cause, except in the case of retirement for age, or under extraordinary circumstances because of financial exigencies."[31] (The retirement part of the stipulation has since been modified by the 1986 amendments to the Age Discrimination in Employment Act—PL 99-592—which, as of 1993, uncapped mandatory faculty retirement at age seventy.[32])

The dismissal procedure ensuring due process, according to AAUP guidelines, must include a written notice of the grounds for termination of an appointment, full and complete disclosure of the evidence supporting a faculty member's termination of employment, the right to confront and cross-examine adverse witnesses and to challenge documentary evidence, an opportunity to be heard in person and to present witnesses and evidence, a neutral and detached hearing body, and a written statement by the fact finders as to the evidence relied on in drawing conclusions.[33]

Grounds for dismissal include personal conduct that discredits the institution, immorality or moral turpitude (for example, a pattern of sexual harassment of students), neglect of professional responsibilities, bona fide financial exigency, and pending program discontinuance.[34] Always the burden of proof that sufficient cause for dismissal exists rests with the institution.

Subsequent litigation in the courts since the AAUP's original 1940 pronouncement on tenure has confirmed the principle in law that tenure, once secured, is a property right subject to constitutional protection. Further, the granting of tenure, it has been held, amounts to a contractual agreement between an individual faculty member and the academic institution, an agreement whose particulars are to be interpreted and governed in accordance with the published policies and procedures of the granting institution. Dismissal must be conducted, courts have affirmed, in conformity with explicitly stated institutional policies and procedures. In effect (and appropriately so), procedural safeguards make it extremely difficult—though not altogether impossible—to fire a tenured professor.

On historical grounds and otherwise, the claim that tenure safeguards academic freedom is a very powerful argument, one difficult to resist. Affirmations on the part of a college or university administration that it subscribes to the principle of freedom for academics to speak out as they so choose would ring hollow indeed if there were no correlative provision for protecting faculty members from dismissal once they exercise their rights. Something more than a simple presumption of continuing employment is needed, or so it is argued, in order to offer adequate protection for those who challenge established wisdom, advance unorthodox theories, or otherwise somehow end up offending and outraging those constituencies on which the college or university necessarily depends for its support. History is replete with pious protestations of support from officialdom for academic freedom in the abstract, linked with specific instances where those who dared to speak out were fired for their trouble. And without academic freedom for its members, a college or university is little more than a hollow shell, a mockery of what an institution of higher learning must be.

There are, nonetheless, several legitimate questions worth asking about tenure. The first is whether academic freedom is now so firmly established that tenure is no longer necessary. One might argue, for example, that the United States is a considerably more tolerant nation than it was a scant few generations ago.[35] The range of socially accepted behavior and speech is much broader; courts have become more vigilant about protecting individual liberties than they once were; and society in general seems to exhibit more permissiveness than ever before. While not discounting entirely the possibility of spasms of repression, some would claim that prospects for a return to the "bad old days" when abridgments of academic freedom were commonplace are most unlikely.

More to the point, some allege, professors nowadays are rarely threatened for the substance of what they have to say. Only a tiny fraction of faculty write or publicly make pronouncements so controversial or explosive as to place their jobs at risk. Academic freedom as such is therefore hardly ever the issue.[36] When faculty members get into trouble, it is because they have acted unreasonably or made nuisances of themselves, they have alienated colleagues, irritated a powerful superior, ended up on the losing side of some heated internal debate, refused to take no for an answer to some request, or persisted beyond the bounds of collegiality in challenging some hallowed institutional policy.

The claim that academic freedom (not to mention the freedom to be obnoxious, obstructive, or cantankerous) demands job protection has undeniable force. In fact, only the hopelessly optimistic would be willing to believe that academic freedom is now and forever so secure that it can be taken for granted. Where the argument falls short, however, is in demonstrating that *nothing less than* tenure is sufficient to protect academic freedom. As now constituted, in other words, tenure may very well be looked upon as a species of overkill—it affords *more* protection (lifetime job security) than any likely set of circumstances is apt to warrant.

Provided an academic institution has committed itself to a lengthy and involved system of safeguards against arbitrary dismissal, and *if* adequate provision has been made to preserve each individual's due process rights, the very complexity and cumbersomeness of the arrangements required should suffice to satisfy any legitimate concern for the protection of academic freedom. Hearings conducted by and in the presence of all interested parties (including faculty peers vested with a controlling power) virtually assure that all of the various protagonists' views will be brought out into the light of day and held up for close scrutiny, that motives will be carefully examined and assessed, and, ultimately, that justice will prevail.

Formerly the employing institution held all the power. The individual faculty member was treated as little more than a pawn to be disposed of capriciously or at will. Arguably, however, under present circumstances, the balance of power has since shifted to the opposite extreme. The ways in which an academic institution can intervene to correct a faculty member's irresponsible behavior, to challenge unsatisfactory performance, or otherwise to act decisively to resolve all but the most serious problems are patently inadequate. Assuming there is sufficient provocation and justification, a faculty member's administrative superordinate could withhold discretionary salary increments or a promotion in rank, for instance, as a way of sending a message. The department chair or the dean might try reducing resource allocations in the form of office or laboratory space, travel stipends, help from graduate assistants, or equipment monies. The faculty member could be saddled with the least desirable teaching or committee assignments. But otherwise, there is little to be done, most particularly if the culprit involved knows that he or she cannot be fired except under limited and extraordinary circumstances because of tenure. In fact, the typical response whenever a college or university attempts to discipline one of its own is the prompt filing of a formal counter-grievance by the putative offender. All things considered, it is not a system conducive to personal accountability.

Some defenders argue that tenure offers no more job security than that afforded senior employees in the federal civil service system where, as is well known, it is nearly impossible to fire someone no matter what his or her transgressions. What tenure bolsters, or so the argument runs, is essentially no more than the same presumption of continuing employment typical among other professionals, a security akin to that enjoyed by attorneys in a legal firm, physicians sharing a medical practice, or partners in a business undertaking. Whether a salaried, tenured faculty member's situation is really analogous in the manner suggested is open to debate. But, again, the issue is *not* whether faculty members should enjoy a high degree of job security and protection from arbitrary dismissal. These imperatives should be accepted as a given. The real question is whether due-process guarantees rooted in institutional practices governing termination of employment are sufficient for accomplishing those quite legitimate purposes.

Were there nothing else to consider, the distinction between *due process* in determining adequate cause for dismissal and the more stringent safeguards afforded by *tenure* would be, indeed, purely "academic." But tenure as an absolute carries with it certain other liabilities and disadvantages that ought to be taken into account in deciding whether it is worth retaining. On balance, a good case *can* be made for abolishing tenure—both for reasons commonly adduced and on grounds less frequently considered.

In the first place, tenure advocates have not always been completely forthright in acknowledging the problem of academic "deadwood." In some cases at least (fewer than critics of tenure allow, but considerably more than defenders typically concede) near-total job security *does* seem to offer "excessive" protection to those who do not deserve it and may even encourage irresponsibility on the part of some. Many professors nowadays enjoy careers extending over several decades. A few—not many perhaps—grow lazy or incompetent with the passage of time. Proponents of tenure are quick to point out that, in theory, the system does make provision for getting rid of deadwood. But when the great difficulties of doing so are pointed out, when it is noted that in fact hardly any tenured professor is actually ever let go, the somewhat disingenuous response is to say that this is as it should be, that it *ought* to be difficult to terminate someone's employment. Less well considered is the obverse side of the coin: *that job security should have some connection with continuing competence and that it should not be allowed to depend on a single, one-time personnel decision made years ago.*

Second, tenure protects not only deadwood but also a small segment of the professoriate whose members are instantly recognizable to almost all other faculty members and most academic administrators—those few individuals some have aptly dubbed "rotten wood."[37] As distinct from faculty members who are lackadaisical about performing their duties, there seems to exist in every institution, within almost every college or department, one or two otherwise competent individuals who, for varying reasons, turn out to be chronic "troublemakers" in the most offensive and counterproductive manner imaginable.

Reference here is most emphatically *not* to individuals who are benignly eccentric, nor to intellectual dissidents of strong principled convictions, nor to the courageous minority who are unafraid to challenge a reigning orthodoxy, nor to those of whom it may be said simply that they "march to a different drummer." "Rotten wood," rather, serves to designate an altogether different class of individuals: the aggressively disgruntled, the chronically disaffected, the angry malcontents who, in reckless disregard for the ordinary canons of decorum and collegiality that make organizational life possible, pursue their own narcissistic ends regardless of the cost to others.

For whatever specific reasons, having grown deeply alienated from their colleagues and the institution that employs them, a good portion of their time and energy is spent making life miserable for everyone else—by flouting or opposing all rules and regulations that happen to inconvenience them in the slightest, by constantly assailing the institution's administration for its alleged incompetence, by attacking or quarreling with colleagues over the most trivial matters, by issuing lengthy and frequent diatribes against students, by constantly seeking redress for imagined slights and inequities.

Ostensibly their machinations are prompted only by the loftiest of motives and principles; in fact, their behavior typically is wholly unprincipled. They flourish, in the final analysis, because academics on the whole tend to be very tolerant of eccentricity and personal differences, even when the power of the few over the many threatens major disruption and paralysis. But if the individuals concerned are tenured, this species of faculty can continue to exert a malign influence vastly disproportionate to their numbers. Unchallenged, they are apt to spread discord with impunity, sometimes for years on end. Once again, in the absence of viable alternatives, the capacity of the institution to protect itself against rotten wood remains limited.

Third, the full cost of tenure must be reckoned by taking into account yet another class of faculty members who abuse the system. In a perfect world, each and every faculty member would be a responsible, contributing member to the total community. Quite clearly, this is never the case. Here critics of tenure as an absolute right register a valid point. In every institution there appear to be some few individuals who defy or bend the rules for their own selfish purposes, who neglect their duties or perform them perfunctorily at best, secure in the knowledge that the power of the employing institution to intervene is exceedingly limited. Examples are well known: professors who occupy themselves more with their own projects than in fulfilling their assignments, who form their own consulting agencies and absent themselves from campus while continuing to draw a full-time salary from the college or university, who miss classes or show up unprepared, who are inaccessible to students or treat them peremptorily.

Their numbers, it should be emphasized once again, are proportionately few. And in any given case, the individual may not necessarily deserve to be fired for a specific offense. But the real question that must be asked is whether protection for the undeserving few is the necessary, inevitable, and unavoidable cost of affording protection for the deserving many. Are there no alternatives? Where else, for example, besides academe would a recurrent and chronic pattern of misbehavior *having nothing whatsoever to do with the legitimate expression of free speech* be tolerated indefinitely without meaningful sanctions or consequences?

There is, however, a still more compelling set of reasons for abolishing tenure. It has to do with what an increasing number of observers, both inside academe and without, judge to be the fundamental imbalance, the unfavorable trade-off between the job security afforded those who have attained tenure and the terrible psychological insecurity imposed on those still seeking it.

Two or three decades ago when academic positions were still relatively plentiful, securing tenure was a more casual and informal affair than it is today. Now that academic jobs are scarcer relative to the number of prospective applicants seeking academic employment, circumstances have changed drastically. Attaining tenure at some institutions has come to symbolize a major milestone in one's academic career. For perfectly understandable and justifiable reasons, it looms in the minds of many faculty as a formidable hurdle to be surmounted; and both the criteria and the processes governing its conferral are more stringent than may have been the case in the past. For those who ultimately attain tenured status, the prospect is one of steady career advancement. For those who fail, provided they still intend to remain in academia, the likelihood is one of starting over on the treadmill somewhere else (assuming they can find jobs) or accepting short-term, part-time adjunct appointments wherever they can be found. In short, whatever the outcome, the stakes are high.

The system can be brutal. The formal probationary period applicable to entering faculty varies from school to school, ranging from as little as two or three years, commonplace at about half of all two-year community colleges, to around four years at two-thirds of all four-year colleges. About 65 percent of the nation's private universities and almost 40 percent of all public universities set the tenure limit a bit higher, typically at six or seven years.[38] Thus, by the time a faculty member reaches the fatal decision point ("up or out," as it is called), he or she has expended upward of twelve to fifteen years in preparation for the all-important tenure review—five or six years in graduate school, plus another half dozen or so laboring in a year-to-year tenure-track position. The metaphor is an apt one, because great care must be taken to avoid having a career "derailed" prior to receiving tenure.

Page Smith exaggerates only slightly in alleging how difficult it is to imagine "the strain that this barbarous system places on the psyches of the young men and women subjected to it," not to mention the stress upon their families. Young faculty live for years, as he puts it, "in a state of suspended animation, not knowing whether they are to be turned out in disgrace by their friends and colleagues or retained." Ostensibly, the review, when it finally takes place, will be fair and impartial. Yet practically anyone who has spent time in the academic world in recent years can offer testimony to how grueling and lonely is the ordeal of awaiting final judgment.

For Smith, the tenure ritual is comparable to the ancient rites of human sacrifice found in preliterate societies, where, just as the number of human offerings was taken as a measure of sacral piety, the numbers of those sacrificed on the altar of tenure review is esteemed as evidence of the institution's having upheld rigorous academic standards.[39] It may be no coincidence that at a time when higher education is being subjected to closer public scrutiny than ever before, the tendency at some schools has been to lengthen the pretenure probationary period for entering faculty. Though difficult to document, it similarly appears that the standards by which supplicants are judged worthy of tenure have changed too—though, perhaps, in quite the wrong way.

What tenure has done, in effect, is to create two distinct classes of regular, full-time faculty. One group consists of all of the so-called senior faculty members, professors whose job security is virtually assured by tenure. Untenured academics constitute a separate underclass, the so-called junior faculty. Differences between the two in terms of status and social standing are often pronounced. Junior faculty frequently are made to feel they must take special care not to offend. One political misstep can ruin an entire career or at least place it at risk. Those who do not "fit in" or who are disliked, those who are perceived to be uncooperative or insubordinate—these are the unfortunates who must live every day with the knowledge they can be cashiered out at any time.

Most deserving faculty members eventually do attain tenured status. Unfortunately, because human judgment is fallible, some who are undeserving obtain it as well. But at some few schools, it has been alleged, an insidious sort of revolving-door phenomenon operates whereby a probationary faculty member is kept on for a few years and then dismissed prior to tenure review, not for any particular failing but because senior colleagues want to keep the position "open" on the off-chance someone even better can be found. That such instances are rare is undoubted. That it does happen sometimes, and that it is cruel and manipulative, is equally beyond questioning.

Whether tenure in fact serves as a deliberate mechanism of social control, whether it is misused as a sword held over the heads of the untenured in order to ensure their ideological conformity, would be difficult to confirm empirically one way or the other. Critics neverthe-less harbor strong suspicions. "Tenure corrupts, enervates and dulls higher education," claims Charles J. Sykes, author of *Profscam: Profes-sors and the Demise of Higher Education* (1988). "It is . . . the academic culture's ultimate control mechanism . . . [of] the creative, the noncon-formist" and "it is used often ruthlessly to snuff out dissent among uppity junior professors who deviate from the standard line."[40]

Sykes is probably guilty of overstatement. Nonetheless, it would be naive to assume that his allegations are universally unfounded, or that some "self-policing" never goes on among the ranks of the untenured. Weighing all of the evidence, two critics bluntly draw their own conclu-sion. "Tenure should be eliminated," they state flatly. "It has become a brutal rather than benign institution. It has resulted not in job security but in greatly increased insecurity. It has exaggerated differences in power and status and led to all sorts of abuses."[41]

Abuses notwithstanding, a plausible case for retaining tenure still might be viable—were it not for the process academics must undergo in order to achieve it. Nothing could be more fundamentally injurious to the cause of good teaching. Among some smaller institutions, tenure is still based mainly on instructional performance. But at an ever-increasing number of major universities, the major criterion by which a tenure applicant is judged is research productivity—or, rather, the frequency with which the faculty member has successfully published in the professional literature. Administrators—with little more than equivocal evidence to buttress either claim—are prone to asserting confidently that good researchers make for good teachers and vice versa, and that both good teaching and good research are needed. But as Benjamin R. Barber of Rutgers bluntly observes, "To talk about the 'balance' needed between research and teaching is, at best, an exercise in wishful thinking. At worst, it is a lie. The dirty little open secret of American higher education," he continues, "known to every faculty member who manages to gain tenure is this: No one ever was tenured at a major college or university on the basis of great teaching alone; and no one with a great record of research and publication was ever denied tenure because of a poor teaching record."[42]

Barber speaks of "the vast apathetic mass of faculty" in higher education today "who do not much give a damn one way or another" about what goes on in classrooms. Too many faculty members on too many campuses, he claims, do not care—or, more probably, cannot afford to care. (It may be significant too, that when asked to define themselves professionally, many professors refer to themselves as disciplinary specialists—as physicists, sociologists, historians—without calling themselves *teachers* of respectively, physics, sociology, history.) If teaching is more or less taken for granted and a faculty member's publishing record is what counts the most toward tenure eligibility, it is small wonder then that the dominant academic culture reinforces what is required for success and ignores what is not.[43] Rendering qualitative judgments about someone's performance in the classroom is an extraordinarily problematic undertaking. Counting publications is easy.

The result is as predictable as it is perversely rational. A great pall of cynicism descends on the untenured. The talk in offices and in the hallways is not about classes or curricula or students. It is instead about the need to "get something into the pipeline," to "turn out" an article or two each year—an imperative utterly divorced from the question as to whether the faculty member actually has something worth sharing with the world. Long-term research projects are tacitly discouraged; what matters is success in generating a succession of reports and articles, provided they can be placed in "refereed" (that is, peer-reviewed) journals or accepted for presentation at the "right" national conventions. Much attention is given over to what "counts" in the elaborate calculus that ultimately confers tenure: Is shared authorship of an article acceptable? How important is it to be listed as first rather than as second or third author? How much will a monograph or a chapter contributed to someone else's book count for something?

The first few years of a faculty member's professional life are thus spent in a frenzied paroxysm of activity whose basic purpose is not to advance scholarship in a field so much as it is to generate a record of individual "productivity." All the while, great piles of unsolicited manuscripts collect on the desks of journal editors. A distressingly high number of submissions, as it turns out, are poorly conceived, trivial in content, or badly written. University libraries, already hard-pressed to keep up with the cost of maintaining literally thousands of periodicals, nevertheless remain under relentless faculty pressure not to reduce their holdings. The point after all is not to have the journals to read; it is to maintain them as publishing outlets.

All things considered, if for no other reason than because tenure marginalizes teaching and places an undue—some would say absurd—emphasis on publishing, it should be done away with at the earliest opportunity possible. Proposals for alternatives abound. One quite unoriginal suggestion is that tenure be replaced by a succession of at least three renewable one-year contracts following a faculty member's initial appointment. Thereafter, longer contracts of some stipulated length (somewhere between three and five years) would become the norm. The presumption in the overwhelming majority of cases would be of near-automatic renewal, provided there were no counter-indications of unsatisfactory performance. In the event of a dispute or divided opinion, the issue would be subject to full-scale peer review. All due process guarantees would remain in place in any instance where termination of appointment was contemplated. Procedures for recommending promotions in academic rank would be maintained entirely separate and apart from normal contract reviews.

Productive faculty members with nothing to fear from periodic performance assessments would hardly note the difference. It seems fair and realistic to imagine that only the incompetent, the unproductive, and the deliberately obstructive might feel threatened without the illegitimate and unwarranted security that tenure now affords. Very few faculty members might lose their jobs (though, significantly, even the hypothetical possibility of that contingency might be sufficient to galvanize improvement in faculty performance where it was genuinely needed). Presumably, academic freedom in its fullest sense would flourish and continue to be steadfastly protected. Faculty members might feel freer to take intellectual chances, to exercise greater creativity and originality; they might be more inclined to initiate long-term research projects of great potential significance without having to worry about the short term, for example, or to tackle unconventional and unorthodox topics. They might even publish less frequently.

More important, the real change would lie in the enhanced power enjoyed by faculty to reshape curricula and programs, in the enlarged capacity of academic administrators to engage in meaningful strategic planning, and in the greater accountability colleges and universities might be able to display in response to changing environmental conditions or institutional circumstances. Above all else, if abolishing tenure accomplished nothing more than to encourage reform within the academic culture of American higher education, moving teaching back into the forefront and minimizing the deleterious effects of the publish-or-perish syndrome so prevalent throughout academe, this alone should commend the proposal for favorable consideration.

SCHOLARSHIP AT GUNPOINT

Debate over faculty priorities—about publishing or perishing, about teaching versus research—extend well beyond the tenure arena. The issues involved are much broader; and they have become a source of acrimonious disputation both within the academy and off campus. Allegations of a flight from the classroom by "absentee" faculty members, for example, have become a regular refrain from critics, as have claims that the securing of external funding through grants has become almost an end in itself, a way of "counting coup" in the competition for promotion and salary increases. Charges that undergraduate education as a whole still suffers from neglect despite repeated denials and academic leaders' protestations to the contrary, popular suspicion that the caliber of academic instruction offered by many colleges and universities has declined seriously or is not nearly as high in quality as it could or should be, and that students' interests are regularly ignored as the "by-product of an excessive emphasis on research" are by now more than slightly familiar.[44]

Jacques Barzun, one among many, claims that the publish-or-perish syndrome reinforced by the policies and practices of so many institutions of higher learning, beginning with the requirement of a doctoral dissertation imposed upon future professors during graduate training and continuing with an imperative to publish throughout the initiation rites of tenure and beyond, has led to a marked overemphasis on research and grantsmanship and a corollary distaste for teaching. What it all amounts to, he argues, is a fundamental betrayal of the educational and intellectual mission of the college and university. Part of the remedy, he further alleges, will require a movement toward deemphasizing the importance placed on "scholarship at gunpoint." The result of not having done so long ago is apparent to all: a veritable tsunami of professorial writing authored by those who cannot afford not to publish.[45] A faculty member's ability to generate publications ought not to weigh nearly so heavily in the tenure decision as it now does, Barzun insists. Nor should the number of research articles churned out figure so prominently in other decisions about an individual's salary increments or promotions in academic rank.

Curiously, for all the newspaper op-ed pieces lamenting the excessive emphasis placed on academic research and the unseemly scrambling for external grants emphasized by many institutions, despite complaints over misplaced priorities from legislators, dissatisfaction registered by disgruntled college students and their parents, and demurrals surfacing in the academic and professional literature, the institutional response to date has been lethargic at best.[46] In ways that matter—for example, actually trying to change the faculty reward structure—colleges and universities for the most part have remained quiescent, seemingly complacent despite the growing barrage of criticism. With very few notable exceptions, the academy has continued in a business-as-usual manner—indeed, sometimes acting in ways to accentuate the trend toward still more research. Orthodox opinion still holds that there exists an important interrelationship between teaching and faculty publishing, that the two activities are mutually enriching and convergent, and that excellence in both can be achieved.[47] Academic administrators continue to affirm the need for a judicious "balance" among teaching, research, and service, and insist on retaining the hallowed trilogy as the basis for making judgments about faculty performance.[48]

Thus, lip service is paid to the principle that classroom performance and service are to be accorded about the same weight as publications. But so far as many faculty are concerned, the common perception is that the three are rarely assigned equal merit. As one young professor lamented, reported in a 1993 study, "As a new junior professor, I have come into the profession with a strong interest in research but an equally strong interest in serving students by helping them learn both in and outside of the classroom. The attitude I'm receiving from all levels . . . is that research is what counts. If the other areas of service and teaching are lacking but research is strong, then promotions will follow. Unfortunately, I think this is the wrong message to be sending faculty."[49]

Proposals to redress the perceived imbalance in academe between teaching and scholarship have not been lacking. But what various surveys and polls have shown consistently is that faculty and administrators across the entire spectrum of institutions of higher learning continue to believe that grantsmanship and research productivity are still the principal factors in achieving tenure, promotion and salary increases. A recent study involving a nationally representative sample of 11,071 faculty from 480 colleges and universities, for instance, examined the relationship between remuneration and faculty activities—teaching, research, administration, and public service—in order to determine what messages academic institutions convey to faculty about priorities. Despite assurances from institutional representatives that teaching quality was valued most, the perception of faculty members surveyed was that rewards remain dependent on research activity and the degree to which a faculty member brings in funding from outside sources to support various projects, not on classroom performance.[50]

What faculty also report is a strong sense of conflict between teaching and research imperatives.[51] Those committed to teaching find themselves torn between their concern for supplying high-quality instruction in the classroom (always a time-consuming undertaking if done well) and the demands of grant-writing and project management, of research and publication that are viewed as essential for professional advancement within their home institution and within their discipline. Ernest Boyer in his 1987 study *College: The Undergraduate Experience in America,* for example, reported that divided professional loyalties and competing career concerns were major points of tension among faculty. They "appeared with regularity and seemed consistently to sap the vitality of the baccalaureate experience," he observed.[52]

Most faculty members remain skeptical about prospects for changing an academic ethos that was begun more than a century ago when Johns Hopkins University adopted the German research university model and set a pattern widely adopted elsewhere ever since.[53] Despite declarations that teaching and research are "inescapably incompatible," as two recent contributors to the faculty priorities debate avow, reforming the academic culture means challenging deeply ingrained notions of institutional prestige and status.[54] When universities raid one another's faculties, it has been said, they do not do it because they seek cutting-edge classroom teachers.[55]

Not only do narrowly drawn faculty reward systems stress research over undergraduate teaching, they also seem to emphasize mere quantity over the quality of whatever research and scholarly work is actually done.[56] As many researchers have noted, there is little, if any, evidence to show that the quality of scientific research done by faculty, as indicated by citations to the articles published or the standing of the journals in which the articles appear, for example, affects much of anything. Time in rank and the sheer number of publications produced constitute the two most important factors determining promotion rates.[57] The inevitable outcome of the failure to discriminate between quality and quantity, of course, is an ever-increasing accumulation of "gunpoint" scholarship.[58] A key to the psychological dynamic involved is the rhetoric most commonly employed in academic circles, where the talk is not about quality but simply about research "output" and scholarly "production."[59] What is all the more remarkable about the sheer volume of writing produced is that when queried, a majority of published professors confess quite candidly that the act of writing is not something they particularly enjoy or necessarily find intrinsically rewarding.[60]

Ernest Boyer's 1990 study, *Scholarship Reconsidered: Priorities of the Professoriate,* found that 67 percent of all liberal arts faculty reported that they had never published a book; 38 percent had never published in a professional journal; and 49 percent were not engaged in research that was expected to lead to publication. These findings, widely commented upon, have led some observers to conclude that while undue emphasis on grant-writing, research, and publishing is chiefly a problem in large universities, the same is not true of smaller colleges. In fact, this may once have been the case. However, the situation now seems to be changing rapidly. Pressures on faculty to publish and present papers at professional conferences have been especially strong at the most competitive universities, perhaps the top four dozen or so, but the publish-or-perish imperative is being felt more and more within the ranks of the remaining two or three thousand institutions of higher learning in the country.[61] The power of the most prestigious universities to inspire imitation from lesser schools, it must be said, ought not to be underestimated. Increasingly, smaller colleges and universities whose faculty reward structures traditionally were not much affected by the research and publishing ethos have now begun moving in the same direction.

Recent surveys suggest that research- and scholarship-oriented reward systems for faculty are fast becoming the norm throughout academe; and if present trends continue, they seem destined within the next few years to become enshrined in nearly all types of four-year institutions, across all disciplines. Irrespective of the professed mission of the institution or its disciplinary focus, it now appears, those who do publish already tend to be paid more than those of their colleagues who do not, even in many small colleges. Those faculty members who publish the most are the ones most handsomely rewarded. Generating so-called institutional cost overhead from the grants that sometimes support the research that leads to publications is, of course, a decided plus factor as well. (Teaching, on the other hand, tends to be a neutral or even a negative factor in determining salaries.) Hence, as more than a few analysts have concluded, American academe may be moving toward a single faculty reward structure, a system designed to maximize published scholarship and to minimize the time and effort faculty spend on instruction.[62]

Faculty members respond to rewards. "Research and publication as a precondition of promotion through our vertical rank structure," observes E. Margaret Fulton, "has worked to replace the genuinely educated professor with the educational entrepreneur, the academic gamesperson."[63] Paul Von Blum, writing in *Stillborn Education: A Critique of the American Research University* (1986), terms it "one of the most brutal ironies" of contemporary university life that developing a reputation as an excellent teacher rather than researcher is "professionally disadvantageous and dangerous."[64]

But what of the claim that teaching and research are mutually reinforcing and tend to enrich one another? As it turns out, the evidence is mixed. The preponderance of empirical data garnered from scores of studies conducted over the past two or three decades, however, indicates quite persuasively that claims about creative linkages between academic research, publication, and teaching have little, if any, overall basis in fact.[65] Research productivity and teaching seem to be mostly unrelated—all of which is to say that there is scant evidence to support the view that being very good at research is a good predictor of pedagogical expertise and effectiveness in the classroom, or visa versa.

Some faculty members who are judged to be first-rate classroom teachers are also distinguished and prolific scholars.[66] But many are not. Contrariwise, some researchers who bring in substantial grant support and do outstanding work also enjoy reputations as good teachers. Again, some do not. Sometimes the cutting-edge research in which a professor is engaged enlivens and inspires his or her teaching. Just as often, there is little or no connection between a particular scholarly undertaking and the teaching being done. The inescapable irony, then, is that those who insist upon the idea of a close interrelationship between teaching and research or grant-writing and who rely on the connection as the basis for decisions about hiring, tenure, salary raises, and promotion ultimately must rest their case not on proven fact but on unconfirmed intuition. It is an article of faith, what one contributor to the debate characterizes as "a reflex defense of the academic status quo," rather than an informed conclusion based on the best available results of creditable research.[67]

Even if academic grantsmanship and research did not detract from the importance placed on student instruction, there might be possible cause for celebration in the fact that university scholars are so productive. Undeniably, much good work is done in all fields, both in terms of basic inquiry as well as in applied research in certain disciplines that yields tangible benefits to society. Unfortunately, it is difficult to defend the vast majority of research publications generated as important and original contributions to knowledge, so vital and important that their existence justifies the apparent neglect of undergraduate teaching in favor of the activities that produce them.[68]

More than a few members of the professoriate itself will be the first to admit as much. Research, they concede, seems in many cases to have become an end in itself, without much in the way of real-world referents or public resonance. On closer inspection, a great deal of what is turned out is seen as yielding little in the way of benefit to anyone or anything. Most of it does not push back the frontiers of basic knowledge and fails to contribute anything of significance to the general populace or any particular segment thereof—with the possible exception of those external agencies that help underwrite or subsidize its costs. When academics are asked informally about what proportion of the literature produced annually in any given discipline they would judge to be truly significant, the percentage figures most frequently cited rarely rise above 5 or 10 percent.

Co-opted, forced into becoming accomplices to a system that obliges them to engage in activities for which they have little liking or aptitude, to seek funding for and to conduct studies few others besides their close circle of peers and professional colleagues are apt to read or consult, and to write even when they have little to say, faculty members themselves will sometimes admit the whole enterprise has become an absurdly inflated boondoggle, an undertaking of dubious worth, carried on in many cases at public expense and without much utility, cultural or intellectual. In Page Smith's phrase, most of it is "busywork on a vast, almost incomprehensible scale." What the research is most likely to produce, as he puts it, is a corpus of literature "as broad as the ocean and as shallow as a pond."[69]

Typically dressed up in ponderous and nearly incomprehensible argot, overly specialized beyond any legitimate disciplinary need, and consisting for the most part of microscopic analyses of narrowly drawn topics far removed from issues of larger public import, faculty publications in the social sciences and humanities in particular, in one critic's words, amount to little more than a "weak gruel of dead abstractions occasionally seasoned with obscure pomposities."[70] Moreover, because large sweeping theories in general are suspect, because academic culture distrusts those who dare to venture outside the bounds of their own accredited fields of expertise, and because popularization of almost any type is frowned upon, prudence dictates that professors become intellectual and scholastic miniaturists of sorts, speaking to and for the exclusive benefit of others like themselves within the academic cloister. Among outsiders who try to decipher them, faculty publications provide ample confirming testimony for the charge.

CHALLENGING THE
FACULTY REWARD SYSTEM

Why do so few academics question or challenge a system that tends to denigrate teaching and overemphasize scholarly publication as the basis of the faculty reward structure? Why, for that matter, is it not considered strange in academic circles to speak of research *opportunities* and, in the same breath, to talk about teaching *loads?*[71] Again, why is it that professors will complain about the effort given over to teaching when it allows less time for pursuing their "own" work? (Whose work then, it might be asked, is classroom instruction?) Why is it that despite widespread support for and appreciation of the importance of teaching, the bias explicit in the current system exhibits so much persistence and staying power? And why is it, despite numerous suggestions for reform advanced in recent years, that so many colleges and universities seem to be drifting off in a direction exactly opposite from that supported by the public at large and a considerable segment of the American professoriate itself?[72]

At one level, part of the answer probably inheres in the reluctance of individual academics to question a system in which they have acquired—or are earnestly seeking to acquire—a vested interest. Considering how difficult it is to secure an appointment at a good school in certain fields, once employed, an ambitious young assistant professor is unlikely to believe he or she has any choice in the matter of publishing—and perhaps correctly so. Challenging the main criterion upon which future tenure, salary increments, or promotions depend is not a prescription for long-term career success. To criticize established norms, to wonder openly about the propriety of a system that insists that each new initiate demonstrate scholarly prowess in a public forum, to subject research and scholarship to peer review is to risk being branded irresponsible, threatened, or incompetent. Fear of ridicule and failure is often a powerful reinforcer working to keep people in line.

The professional socialization to which the neophyte scholar is subjected is likely to be quite irresistible. Rare is the individual willing or able to withstand peer pressure, to risk the displeasure or disdain of colleagues. In an all-encompassing environment that stresses achievement, that selectively rewards certain types of accomplishments and downplays or ignores others, and that constantly reinforces the message that building up a résumé with a record of scholarly papers presented and research studies published will have a direct bearing on continuing employment, dissenting voices are not likely to be heard. Any faint suggestion that publications are the equivalent of the emperor's new clothes—widely admired though few can see anything there at all—is not apt to be taken seriously.[73]

Obviously, too, money has much to do with the lack of any fundamental challenge to the system. In those fields where externally funded research is the norm, and regular operating budgets depend heavily on supplementary funding from outside sources, few institutions are prepared to discourage their faculties from seeking grants. Indeed, the efforts of academic bureaucrats are much more likely to be aimed at *increasing* the level of grant-writing activity faculty engage in. At most doctoral degree–granting institutions, as a case in point, providing support for any significant number of graduate research assistants without so-called soft monies would be nearly impossible. Faculty have their own vested interests to protect—entire academic empires (specialized institutes, research centers, and the like) have been built on the entrepreneurial spirit of those skilled in grantsmanship. At some schools, sad to say, in some departments and disciplines a faculty member's annual salary raise is actually tied more or less directly to the total dollar amount of external grant monies he or she has brought in within any given year.

The sheer strength of the systemic imperative to publish or perish makes it easy to ignore still other salient considerations. So deeply ingrained are the rituals of academic initiation into the professoriate, it is difficult not to regard the rite of publishing as a symbolic affirmation of a colleague's professional commitment and to esteem it accordingly. Practically everyone is assigned to teach a fixed number of classes and encouraged to accept certain committee assignments. This much is assumed and more or less taken for granted. But the appearance in print of an article or research paper is an impressive reification—and tangible confirmation—of a person's scholarship in a way that teaching is not. Precisely because it serves so unmistakably as a symbolic marker of academic competence and merit, a publication cannot be readily dismissed (leaving aside the question about how many people will ever read it). But means and ends tend to become confused: Authors value their published work not so much because it contributes something of significance to the world of scholarship but because its very existence helps to advance their academic careers.

At another level, the single best explanation for the emphasis currently placed on published scholarship is just that a journal article, a monograph, a book, or a book chapter serves so effectively as a performance indicator. Not only can publications be counted, they can be reviewed by colleagues for purposes extending from the scoring of grant applications to decisions about promotion or tenure. As sociologist Gordon Fellman of Brandeis University rightly observes, the same principle applies to external constituencies. "Legislators and foundations who fund universities and faculty are often bewildered by the very difficult task of assessing what professors and universities do," he notes. "In a society enamored of numbers and supposed objectivity, and in a business culture that takes numbers more seriously than anything else at all, the pressure for quantitative measurements like numbers of publications is immense.... The inordinate attention to publication may suggest implicitly then . . . exasperation in not being able to evaluate teaching" in quite the same fashion.[74] Because the canon of objectivity (or some reasonable facsimile thereof) seems to demand something more tangible than estimations of teaching ability, the dollar amount of grants faculty members have attracted and how much they have published offer good surrogates for measurable productivity.

It does seem valid to observe, by way of contrast, that methods of assessing teaching in ways that discriminate clearly between acceptable and outstanding or superlative instruction are lacking. No one, it appears, is entirely satisfied with the evaluation procedures currently put forth, ranging from student course evaluations and questionnaires to faculty peer reviews of classroom performance, not even when used judiciously in combination with one another. Hence, if the foregoing analysis is substantially correct, in a cultural milieu that greatly values quantitative metrics, it is not to be expected that classroom teaching would receive as much attention as research and scholarship.

The apparent lack of attention paid to instruction often escapes notice, though its omission should be obvious. Oddly enough, little concern is shown for helping graduate students develop teaching skills early on while they are still in training as future professors. Research skills are emphasized heavily, teaching typically is not. Seminars on collegiate pedagogy, workshops devoted to classroom assessment and evaluation techniques, conferences on test construction, provision for supervised internships before graduate teaching assistants are given full responsibility for their own classes—these are still novel ideas in academe. Yet workshops devoted to helping faculty develop their grant-writing skills have been around for decades. Rhetoric aside, institutional behavior serves to expose the real priorities involved when it comes to deciding which faculty activities are most important.

There is a story frequently recounted in academic circles, probably apocryphal, about a prestigious teaching award once offered at a major institution. Nominations of candidates were solicited campuswide. The recipient, it was announced, would receive a plaque, a substantial check—and as a bonus, a reduction in his or her teaching assignment for the year. Unfortunately, the irony involved might escape those faculty in any given institution who are forever complaining that teaching "loads" are already too high compared with assignments elsewhere and ought to be reduced forthwith. Something is awry in the contemporary academy when a faculty member's prestige is often gauged by how *few* classes he or she is assigned to teach.

The relative unimportance ascribed to teaching surfaces in many other ways as well. Despite impressive evidence to the contrary, for example, it is simply assumed that anyone sufficiently well informed to earn a doctorate in a given subject automatically grasps how best to impart knowledge to others. In some instances, of course, there are naturally gifted teachers with an immediate and intuitive feel for how to proceed. For the great majority, however, learning how to teach is a hit-or-miss proposition, a matter of unguided experimentation and trial and error. And, of course, most college professors want to believe they are good teachers. Yet many are not, and there are few around prepared to disabuse them of their illusions. Nor usually are there mentors charged with helping new teachers improve. Hence it is not surprising that colleges and universities tolerate so much bad or indifferent teaching. What is remarkable under present circumstances is that so many very good teachers are to be found in college classrooms.

Naturally, it is the students who pay the price for the commonplace neglect of teaching as an intellectual challenge and object of reflection in its own right.[75] Students may complain about poor teaching and misdirected priorities; they may lodge protests against certain professors who think of teaching as drudgery and are not in the least hesitant about letting their students know how they feel. They may feel outraged that they must compete with other imperatives for a professor's time, attention, and assistance. But it usually is of little avail, because faculty members understand the importance of playing the game. As they are well aware, the action is in the library or the laboratory, not the classroom. Hence, to agree with Stanford University's Donald Kennedy that "It is time for us to reaffirm that education—that is, teaching in all its forms—is the primary task" of higher education today is certainly commendable.[76] The declaration has almost a heroic ring to it. But to the degree that acting on that reaffirmation would pose a frontal challenge to the dominant mores and professional norms of the academy, the task will not be an easy one.[77]

SCHOLARSHIP RECONSIDERED

More than any other single work of recent vintage, a 1990 Special Report by the Carnegie Foundation entitled *Scholarship Reconsidered: Priorities of the Professoriate,* is credited with having brought the teaching-versus-research issue to the forefront of public consciousness. Ernest Boyer's suggestion that academic scholarship should be redefined and its meaning broadened to include other activities besides traditional research attracted attention quickly. Within two years the report had attained the status of something close to a best-seller in academic circles.

"We believe the time has come to move beyond the tired old 'teaching versus research' debate and give the familiar and honorable term 'scholarship' a broader, more capacious meaning, one that brings legitimacy to the full scope of academic work," Boyer announced.[78] Scholarship, he explained, means engaging in original research. But the work of the scholar also means "looking for connections, building bridges between theory and practice, and communicating one's knowledge effectively to students." Basing his argument on a model of scholarly work first proposed by Eugene R. Rice, vice-president of Antioch College, Boyer claimed the work of the professoriate ought to be thought of as having four separate yet overlapping functions: discovery, integration, application, and teaching, each of them valid and important in its own right.

Briefly, the scholarship of "discovery" reflects the model of original research long prized within colleges and universities. Closely related is the scholarship of "integration," the act of drawing connections across different disciplines, placing specialties in some larger context, reinterpreting data in new and revealing ways, exploring boundaries, reworking knowledge topographies, interpreting multidisciplinary work, and discerning new meanings in what has previously been discovered. These first two kinds of scholarship, as Boyer describes them—discovery and integration of knowledge—reflect the investigative and synthesizing traditions of academic life. The third element, the "application" of knowledge, has as its focus engagement with consequential problems and issues, with the utility of what is known. Fourth, there is the scholarship of "teaching," involving the work of connecting a teacher's understanding with a student's learning. "What we urgently need today," Boyer declares, "is a more inclusive view of what it means to be a scholar—a recognition that knowledge is acquired through research, through synthesis, through practice, and through teaching."[79]

Whether this or some similar specification of legitimate scholarly activities and functions can prove helpful in broadening the faculty reward system remains to be seen. Indications today are that at least some few institutions, stung by public criticism, are beginning to think afresh their own research paradigms and have announced plans to revamp their faculty reward structures along the lines suggested by Rice and Boyer. Additionally, a handful of comprehensive university campuses—those whose graduate programs are more circumscribed than those at major research institutions, but that have been inclined to emulate the norms of elite schools—are now questioning whether their research emphasis has been misplaced.[80] Rewarding professors for activities related to teaching, and not just the discovery of new knowledge, traditionally the only kind of scholarship that counts for promotion, may represent a step in the right direction.

Sometimes also it is suggested that there should be multiple "tracks" along which a professor's career could proceed. Thus, for example, for those who would prefer to invest heavily in research and consider teaching more of a chore than anything else, research appointments would be most appropriate. Those preferring to be evaluated primarily or exclusively on the basis of their teaching would be allowed to do so, serving under the terms of an instructional appointment. The chief merit of the proposal, or so it is claimed, is that it would recognize real differences in ability, interest, and career focus rather than lumping all members of the faculty together on the same basis. (One possible objection is that the scheme would give rise inevitably to a two-tiered system, with research appointments the more prestigious and remunerative of the two.) If successful, having two parallel, separate career tracks would serve to honor both teaching and research, without insisting that everyone should be equally adept at both or to the same degree.

Less often cited as a potential solution is a faculty reward system more responsive to the *changing* profile of activities in which a professor is most likely to engage over time. From a developmental perspective, it might make sense to allow criteria governing salary increments and promotions to change over an extended period, corresponding to the natural inclination of academics to engage in different professional activities at various points in their respective careers. Younger faculty might wish to concentrate at first on teaching, then move toward the establishment and pursuit of a research agenda in subsequent years, followed by more energy and attention focused on professional service, outreach, student advisement, and the like later on. (It is unclear, however, whether the literature on faculty development offers sufficient guidance and direction for designing any such reward system.) More important and worth preserving would be the underlying principle of allowing faculty members to negotiate the precise mix of teaching, research, and service involvements governing their performance assessments at any given point in time. At the very least, alternatives to the narrow procrustean system now most commonly in place are urgently needed.

SHIFTING PRIORITIES
AND NEW IMPERATIVES

The question of what else may be needed to reshape today's academic culture in colleges and universities is itself likely to provoke continuing debate in the years ahead. What seems virtually certain, at any rate, is that circumstances now prevailing cannot be expected to endure indefinitely. Many state legislatures already have served notice that they intend to reassess the concept of tenure in publicly assisted institutions, with a view toward its possible abolishment. If it begins to look as if academics cannot or will not put their own houses in order, it is equally likely that lawmakers may pass legislation mandating changes in the faculty reward structure in order to give greater prominence to teaching.

Meanwhile, the economics of publishing are such that hard-copy journals and academic serials may soon become a thing of the past. So-called electronic journals ("cyber-journals") already exist in profusion, and their numbers are growing. Subsisting only in the peculiar netherworld of cyberspace, taking on conventional hard-copy form only when downloaded off a computer net, they offer the best hope of continuing to supply viable outlets for faculty writing on the scale now prevailing. Whether soft-copy publishing can serve as a credible and satisfactory substitute for the more traditional placements for academic research, in effect successfully challenging the mystique of the printed word, still seems uncertain.

Finally, although the general public may be willing to support the notion of a select few research universities where undergraduate teaching is not a top priority, it appears unlikely that the tendency of other schools to take on the same system of priorities will be allowed to continue indefinitely without challenge. There are simply too many prospective students and their parents who value institutions of higher learning not for their outreach and service functions and still less for their research mission but for the teaching they are capable of supplying. Rightly or wrongly, as prudent consumers, they will expect and demand nothing less than the highest-quality instructional programs possible.

VI.

ACADEMIC ACCOUNTABILITY: WHAT IS TO BE DONE?

AN EROSION OF PUBLIC CONFIDENCE

In 1985 a National Assessment of Educational Progress (NAEP) examined literacy levels among a large national sample of twenty-one- to twenty-five-year olds. It was found that roughly half of the young adults surveyed *who had graduated from college with bachelor's degrees* could not perform such simple intellectual tasks as summarizing the content of a newspaper article, calculating a 10 percent tip for lunch, or interpreting a bus schedule.[1] Findings such as these ought to be troubling, even though, of course, it is generally true that colleges and universities do not set out to develop proficiency in deciphering bus schedules or figuring luncheon tips. As a rule, these are not the specific skills that higher learning tries to foster. But presumably colleges occasionally do demand of students that they read, write, perform simple mathematical calculations, and make the effort to think reflectively and critically. Such requirements surely ought to produce college graduates who can perform tasks at a level one might otherwise expect from high school students.

The NAEP findings were not exceptional. On the contrary, they were consistent with almost every recent attempt before and since to inventory the intellectual performance levels of college students across the country. Time and time again, it is revealed that a certain number of today's graduates are not much more than minimally literate to all intents and purposes. Reading and writing abilities among a small albeit significant minority of former collegians remain poor. These people tend for the most part to be woefully deficient in basic knowledge across the disciplines and seem to possess little intellectual curiosity or appreciation for the life of ideas. Even as adults, a much larger percentage of college graduates lack rudimentary awareness of, or much interest in, current events and public affairs. The chronic complaint from employers in business and industry is that about one in every six to eight collegiate degree holders they hire are missing basic literacy competencies and cannot perform even at a secondary-school level. To put it bluntly, the baccalaureate degree conferred by American colleges and universities is no longer a reliable or universal guarantee of even basic literacy. The public therefore should not be blamed for its growing skepticism about what is occurring—or, rather, what is not happening—on the nation's campuses.

Fundamental literacy and numeracy skills presumably ought to have been acquired well before high school graduation. The temptation runs strong to blame elementary and secondary educators for having failed to help students develop the skills they should need—but apparently are not required to have—for college. On the other hand, as is often noted, college entrance standards exert a powerful influence upon the exit standards of secondary education. And from the 1960s on, when institutions of higher learning hastened to embrace open admission policies, the effect on the lower schools was devastating. In effect, institutions of so-called higher learning sent out a message that college-bound youngsters did not need to worry overmuch about acquiring computational and writing skills. They probably were going to get admitted upon graduation from high school anyway, no matter how ill-prepared they might be.[2]

The consequence for postsecondary education has been more disastrous still. With the exception of a few dozen institutions retaining selective admission standards, most colleges and universities today confront if not hordes, then certainly substantial numbers, of poorly prepared entering students. The best and brightest students seeking admission are as capable and academically competent as ever. The problem in collegiate admission lies not with top-flight entrants but with the unconscionably high percentage of mediocre or poor students gaining admittance alongside their more proficient peers. Reportedly, in the late 1980s two out of every five freshmen were showing up on public campuses in Florida and Georgia in need of remedial instruction, as did nearly half of the entering freshmen under twenty-one years of age in Tennessee.

In New Jersey, one-third of those accepted for admission to the state's publicly assisted colleges were found deficient in verbal and computational skills; and just 15 percent could solve elementary algebra problems. The pattern in literally scores of states throughout the country has been much the same. Remedial instruction (euphemistically called "developmental education"), sometimes bearing college credit and hence contributing to the satisfaction of degree requirements, has mushroomed on campuses, soaking up resources and energies that should be expended on genuine college-level teaching and learning.[3]

Opinion polls indicate that public feelings about higher education in the main are positive. But they further reflect what can only be described as an attitude of profound ambivalence.[4] Higher learning is still greatly valued, especially for its assumed economic benefits. A college education is believed to confer a decided advantage when it comes to obtaining a better-paying job; and a diploma is still considered both desirable and worth pursuing in today's economy. At the same time, no great prestige attaches to the baccalaureate degree. It is accepted nowadays almost as a commonplace that the bachelor's degree serves as little more than a minimal credential, much as a high school diploma did in years past. Hence, coupled with favorable opinions are suspicions about declining academic standards.

When queried, members of the general public evince a great deal of skepticism and confusion about conditions in colleges and universities. Faculty are thought to have too much autonomy and too few classes to teach. Widely reported abuses take their toll: instances of university-based research data having been falsified, media reports of faculty members accused of sexually harassing students, revelations of the stratospheric compensation paid chief academic executives relative to salaries earned by ordinary faculty (in Arkansas in 1995, for example, it was revealed that several of the highest-paid employees on the public payroll worked as administrators at the state's major university), high student loan default rates at many schools, and big-time college athletic scandals that seem to surface with almost predictable regularity.[5] Questions are raised as to whether campus athletes are being held to the same standards as are all other students; it is widely suspected they are not. That college sports tend to skew priorities in favor of mass entertainment—and revenues—over academics also is widely suspected or assumed. Critics of higher education also point to rampant program duplication, citing examples where institutional expansion obviously has advanced beyond demonstrated need. Others complain that not nearly enough is being done to hold down costs.

What the public allegedly wants from higher education is educational quality, institutional efficiency, reinforcement of fundamental societal values, and a fair price tag.[6] Yet as one writer phrases it, at a time "when society expects virtually all of its major enterprises to boost their per-unit outputs or lower their unit costs, those within the ivied walls somehow deem themselves immune."[7] Typical are demands that institutions of higher learning do more to reduce administrative overhead (a budget item that is growing, on average, at more than twice the rate of all instructional expenditures combined). Schools are urged to utilize or refurbish existing physical facilities instead of continuing to erect new ones (getting over their "edifice complex," as someone once quipped). Personnel and other resources, it is said, should be put to maximal use. "Rising tuition, declining productivity, dubious practices, and slipshod quality have grown so pervasive in academe," one declaration has it, "that public pressure is mounting for government officials to take some sort of action. If higher education, left to govern itself, develops as many flaws and eccentricities as the public now perceives, perhaps its autonomy *should* be curbed."[8]

Unhappily, just at a time when institutions of higher learning are under growing political pressure for reform and demands are being made for closer public agency oversight of colleges and universities, they find themselves facing yet another financial crisis of major proportions. Asked to do more and to do it better, they now have fewer and fewer resources with which to do it. Since the late 1980s, competition for public resources has become more acute at every level—federal, state, and local—and the near-inevitable outcome has been a marked slowdown (adjusted for inflation) in the growth of funding for higher education. Continuing a trend begun in the mid-1970s, public higher education's share of state budgets, for instance, has not only continued to decline, but the downturn is more pronounced now than ever before in recent memory.

Hard-pressed to make ends meet, academic institutions have elected to shift an ever-expanding portion of costs over to students and their families. Tuition and fees have skyrocketed in consequence, more than doubling at public colleges and universities within the span of a single decade. Over the last ten years or so, the tuition bill at independent colleges and universities has nearly tripled. According to most projections, prospects for real increases in state or federal outlays for higher education at any point in the near future seem extremely unlikely. While specific situations differ greatly from state to state, the so-called financial crunch affecting higher education overall is not expected to get better any time soon. Indeed, it may have worsened considerably by the century's end.

Colleges and universities so far have responded in time-honored fashion: by deferring capital maintenance and improvements, retaining and keeping equipment in service for longer periods of time, scaling back new projects, hiring more part-time and fewer full-time faculty, freezing salaries, limiting or cutting back on library holdings and new acquisitions, increasing class sizes, and reducing the number of course sections offered. If these traditional measures prove insufficient to moderate further tuition increases and to keep expenses down, the general consensus among policymakers is that more drastic cost-containment initiatives will need to be attempted, some of them (in the case of publicly assisted institutions) imposed from without.[9]

All the while, according to some observers, a good portion of the professoriate simply does not "get it" (to employ a popular colloquialism). Psychologist Catherine Chambliss of Ursinus College in Pennsylvania wryly notes, "There surely is evidence of rampant denial on campuses today. Rather than face the challenges squarely, many professors effect a hasty retreat to ivory towers, insisting that things haven't really changed and business-as-usual will suffice." Faculty members continue to grumble about tight budgets, assuming that the administration is somehow to blame or is withholding resources for its own inscrutable and unknowable purposes. Talk of fiscal crisis is discounted as a manipulative ploy on the part of deans and other leaders to stifle dissent and keep things placid.[10]

Some professors, Chambliss observes, deflect their frustration and anxiety in near-classic displays of psychological displacement. Absorbed in territorial skirmishes with colleagues, faculty members expend their energies waging interdepartmental and interdivisional battles over scarce resources rather than working together to find ways of utilizing more effectively what is available. External edicts demanding productivity and hard results fail to accomplish their intended purposes, she argues, if only because faculty members rarely respond well to orders and resent being told what to do. "We take umbrage at even relatively minor encroachments on our substantial freedom. The more faculty are pushed from above, the more they invest their impressive intellectual talents in reactance and bolstering their opposition to new demands."[11]

The sobering truth, she concludes, is that "tough times call for campus cooperation and collaboration more than ever, and many institutions trapped by wastefully draining infighting and destructive competition from within simply won't make it." In her considered opinion, faculty "need to be shaken up a bit, in order to move from the lazy posture of denial. And they need to be helped to steer clear of displaced hostility and projected suspiciousness. They need to be given the chance to arrive at their own conclusion that [reform] is a necessity, rather than an option."[12]

THE ACCOUNTABILITY IMPERATIVE

Higher education conventionally has associated academic quality with resource "consumption," that is, with the amount of resources it has been able to attract and spend. In the past, a college or university whose enrollments and budget were growing was thus considered productive. Quality was attested to by the addition of prestigious research and graduate programs. Accountability was thought of mainly in terms of financial stewardship, by how well and in how much detail an academic institution could document how revenues were spent as functions of, for example, faculty-student ratios, numbers of academic credit hours generated, instructional programs sustained, and total numbers of degrees awarded.

More recently, new quality assurance efforts have been launched that extend well beyond issues of resource utilization. Many focus instead on student learning outcomes. The hard fact of the matter, alleges Maryland's secretary of higher education, is that conventional indices of institutional functioning have not fulfilled their intended purpose of demonstrating a "return" on what is "invested" in higher education. Quite bluntly, most colleges and universities have neither been asked—nor have they succeeded in showing—whether student learning actually has occurred.[13]

By the late 1980s a basic shift in thinking was well under way. Fully two-thirds of all states had requirements on the books that public institutions of higher learning give evidence they were actually producing desired outcomes for students. The typical mandate (enunciated but not always rigorously or uniformly enforced) was that each publicly assisted college or university should generate an explicit statement of those results or outcomes the institution expected to produce, supply documentation for the measures or indices to be employed in assessment, and then provide a clear indication of the extent to which the school was, in fact, obtaining the outcomes it had set out for itself as goals.[14]

The reaction from most colleges and universities throughout the 1980s and continuing into the 1990s produced an inconsistent mix of responses, old and new. To date, scant success appears to have been registered in demonstrating whether students have acquired higher-level cognitive skills and specific skill competencies while completing a baccalaureate degree program. Nor have so-called value-added approaches (learning increments defined in terms of the differential between academic performance tested for at the time of initial admission and upon graduation) won widespread acceptance. Easier by far to document as indicators of institutional performance have been graduation rates and pass rates of graduates on national or state licensing or certification examinations in such fields as teaching and nursing. Other measures fall back on such conventional indices as instructional cost per credit hour generated, faculty-student enrollment ratios, and the like.

The trend among public policymakers today by and large, however, is to move away from reliance on enrollment-driven funding and to attempt to tie budgetary support to an institution's ability to document results. The metaphor for academic accountability most often invoked combines the notion of an institution of higher learning as a production unit, a factory perhaps, together with that of the college or university as a corporate enterprise engaged in retail sales. The school as a business "produces" knowledge, which it then offers for sale. Competing with other sellers in a particular "market," the college or university establishes a "marketing" plan intended to confer a competitive edge for attracting prospective buyers, namely, students. For their part, students as tuition-paying "customers" are said to be making an "investment" in the education sought, hoping for an adequate "return" on that investment. (Implied, but not always stated explicitly, is the presumption that in higher education as in any other purchasing transaction, the customer is always right.)

Coupled with the theme of customer satisfaction is criticism of higher education for its alleged unresponsiveness, its seeming aloofness toward those who seek its services. College and university leaders, runs the complaint, must listen more closely, must respond more fully to what their constituencies profess to want from institutions of higher learning. Recent years have thus witnessed the growing popularity among academic planners of quality assurance systems originally devised for corporate business and industry such as Total Quality Management (TQM) and Continuous Quality Improvement (CQI), systems now proposed for use in colleges and universities. Dedication to servicing clients' needs has become a watchword in academic circles as a hallmark of quality, responsiveness, and hence accountability.

Many administrative leaders, no less than faculty, find the whole notion behind the metaphor of higher education as a business involving buying and selling utterly repugnant. Some go so far as to oppose any effort to assess students' skills and knowledge whatsoever, claiming that the most important learning colleges and universities endeavor to impart is least susceptible to precise measurement. "Many in higher education recoil at the word 'customer.' They believe that education has a higher purpose than selling products like detergent or garage door openers," one group of researchers has recently observed with vast understatement. "Nevertheless," they add, "we prefer and use the word . . . because we believe that it is an important reminder that higher education is in business to serve others, not to perpetuate itself or to make self-interested choices. . . . We believe that the purpose for organizations resides outside the organization."[15] As proponents of assessment are fond of emphasizing, "Assessment is a feasible art. And assessment bears clear benefits. Those campuses where comprehensive systems for measuring student learning and outcomes are now in place report improvements in curricula, instruction, collegiality, student advisement, retention, placement rates, and certification exam scores. Most important, it appears that students are in fact learning more."[16]

Interestingly, not all educators share misgivings over quality assurance measures and the accountability imperative, some going so far even as to offer "money-back guarantees" on diplomas conferred. Rejecting the suggestion that knowledge is an intangible commodity that can neither be sold nor bartered away, several hundred community colleges currently promise their students that if they fail to find jobs within six months following graduation, or if employers find their skills deficient, graduates may return to campus for supplemental course work free of charge. "Higher education has never been accountable before," Rockland Community College president Neal Raisman was quoted in 1995 as having declared. "We tell the public, 'Give us money, and we will guarantee you nothing.' I would never buy a toaster like that!"[17]

Particularly among two-year schools, the idea of appending "warranties" to diplomas is spreading, in Illinois, Nebraska, Michigan,

Texas, New Jersey, and elsewhere. One four-year liberal arts college—St. John Fisher in Rochester, New York—even offers students up to $5,000 cash in the event they fail to secure employment within half a year after graduation. "An education that works," boasts its brochure, "We guarantee it." Critics are appalled, wondering how far the marketing will go. "What's the guarantee for a theology major? Salvation?" asks Bard College president Leon Botstein. "This trivializes education. It places a minimum standard, not a maximum one, on excellence."[18]

The major sticking point so far as many academics are concerned, once again, is the assumption (widely shared by accountability proponents) that learning is all of a piece, that at least in principle there is little or no difference between assessing skill proficiency by means of some test performance, on the one hand, and, on the other, ascertaining that the student, for example, has a critical appreciation for the role of the scribal class in the political economy of the earliest Sumero-Akkadian autarchies, grasps the nature of the "dogmatic slumber" from which Kant reportedly awoke upon reading Hume, or understands how Karl Marx appropriated Hegelian metaphysics in developing the theory of dialectical materialism. If the metrics of assessment are the same in all cases, critics of outcomes evaluation have no legitimate grounds for objecting. But if it turns out that so-called higher levels and orders of learning by their very nature cannot be tested for adequately in a straightforward performative way, often-reiterated charges that the mania for outcomes assessment represents a reductive sort of intellectual "minimalism" in higher education gains credibility.

RATIONAL STRATEGIC PLANNING

Given the collective hegemony of public institutions of higher learning in America today, most private colleges and a majority of private-sector universities (excepting the most prestigious among them) are basically in a reactive mode. That is, they are forced to respond to opportunities where public institutions are not fulfilling a need or where they can compete successfully with publicly-assisted schools by offering high-quality programs at a competitive cost, or by targeting a special clientele. For a majority of today's students, "going to college" means attending a public institution of higher education. Insofar as publicly assisted schools are concerned, to the extent that much of their funding and some of their programming hinges on the actions of a state coordinating board, responsibility for academic reform in the name of public accountability must begin not with individual colleges and universities but with state-wide agencies and state legislatures.[19]

The extent to which individual schools' operations are coordinated through some centralized state agency differs considerably from state to state. How closely a college's units are monitored and scrutinized, and how difficult or easy it may be to eliminate or add courses or degree programs, depends greatly on the state governance and oversight system under which the public college or university functions. No matter how prominently strategic planning figures in the life of an individual campus, decisions about priorities and programs, about future resource allocations, and about staffing and development are rendered within the larger context of some type of state coordinating system.[20]

Often overlooked in discussions about alleged academic inefficiency and unwarranted program duplication within any given state is the point that responsibility for the much-lamented proliferation of parallel degree programs does not rest solely with the respective governing boards of the state's several academic institutions. Rather, it traces back to the state's own department of education, coordinating board, or equivalent agency. And, of course, behind the state's higher education bureaucracy stands the state legislature itself.

In terms of actual program development or discontinuance, very little rational strategic on a statewide basis is ever accomplished. The process more nearly resembles the political horse-trading typical of any politicized undertaking, where expansion at one institution is matched by the creation of new programs at another. Localism is a potent force; and rare is the state legislator willing to stand up to the demands of constituents for the establishment or expansion of a public college in his or her district. The truth is, if states now find themselves burdened with more colleges and universities than they can afford to support adequately, with too many identical programs serving the same needs and competing with one another for students, and with academic offerings for which there are not enough takers, the fault rests squarely with legislators themselves. In some states, for instance, despite a pronounced oversupply of prospective teachers in certain fields, literally dozens of teacher preparation programs are kept open. A particular state may find itself supporting far more preparatory programs than are needed, collectively producing far more graduates than the marketplace can ever reasonably be expected to absorb. By the same token, when a state university has multiple campuses, it is virtually a foregone conclusion that each campus will compete fiercely for resources just as if it were a separate and autonomous institution in its own right. Once again, market conditions relative to programs offered are given scant consideration.

Despite duplication and wastefulness, it is neither realistic nor fair to expect individual colleges and universities by themselves to surrender programs voluntarily, of their own accord. The burden of deciding what shall be shut down and what retained must fall to those responsible for having authorized the offerings in the first place. More broadly still, somehow the political will and courage must be mustered to resist popular demands that the state support a college or university within easy commuting distance of each and every one of the state's citizens. Expectations that the student will have ready access to a full and comprehensive range of degree programs, in every field, at every institution, regardless of what is offered elsewhere within the state's boundaries, must be deflated. (The best response to those who piously invoke the land grant ideal as an excuse for unlimited growth and universal access is to point out that, historically speaking, the thinking behind the original Morrill Acts falls well short of providing an adequate warrant for either.)

The task of identifying the best among several similar programs and singling them out as "centers of excellence" worthy of public support is, politically speaking, a difficult and perilous undertaking. So too is the challenge of deflecting or adjudicating among the competing demands of state institutions for new programs and graduate degrees, each school bent on furthering its own growth and expansion. Yet unless or until external agencies prove themselves equal to the challenge, allegations about needless duplication and repeated charges of inefficiency from lawmakers and others will continue to sound more than a little hypocritical.

The underlying objective of statewide planning in higher education is easier to articulate than it is to achieve or enforce. Basically, what is needed is political consensus in support of the notion that, ideally, *public colleges and universities should function as elements of an ecologically balanced, interdependent whole.* That is, barring some radical change in the social environment of which they are a part, efforts should be made to reaffirm the identity, mission, and functions of each type of institution and, further, to insist that the institutions involved live within their respective niches.

Two-year community colleges, for example, should strive to be the best local institutions they are capable of becoming. They ought not to be supported in their efforts to compete directly with four-year institutions or to transform themselves into baccalaureate-level colleges. Most probably, their efforts should be concentrated on community development and outreach, on adult learning, and on high-quality vocational preparation. Currently fashionable attempts to bring them in within the protective embrace of far-flung state systems of higher education and make them "feeders" to the universities are unlikely to do either much good.

Four-year public colleges, historically speaking, have been notorious for aspiring to shed their identities as purely local or regional baccalaureate-level institutions. Aided and abetted by state politicians, their goal almost always has been to become full-fledged universities, an objective they achieve by securing the state's authorization to add on graduate-level programs and degrees. The result in many cases has been a proliferation of advanced programs and graduate degrees, many of questionable quality, extending far beyond any demonstrable societal need.

Meanwhile, institutions, ever responsive to the status and prestige hierarchy common to academe, have sought to further their own comparable ambitions to become research-oriented doctoral universities. Over and over again the result has been the same: a political unwillingness or financial inability on the state's part to provide adequate and appropriate funding for the one, two, or three doctoral-level institutions it is already charged with supporting. In brief, though there is much that individual colleges and universities can do by way of cost-cutting, logically the first precarious steps toward fiscal reform must be taken by state legislators and their respective coordinating governance agencies.

FACULTY GOVERNANCE AND ACADEMIC FREEDOM

In the best of times, efforts aimed at keeping the management and administration of colleges and universities open, flexible, and efficient would be highly desirable and worthwhile. In today's economic and social policy environment, where demands for accountability are being sounded louder than ever, those efforts have become essential.[21] The literature on management and governance has expanded enormously in recent years, much of it marked by discussions about authority and power and the distribution of the two most appropriate to the optimal functioning of the academy. Often invoked is talk of "flatter" and leaner organizations, of "grass-roots" decision making, of "ad-hocratic" management and bureaucratic "deconstruction," of structural reconfiguration and radical streamlining. On the other hand, as one senator once reportedly commented, "Higher education is a thousand years of tradition wrapped in a hundred years of bureaucracy." Organizational change on a scale matching the rhetoric of systemic reform, of "down-sizing" and "right-sizing," may be long in coming.

Oversimplifying greatly, one major theme to emerge from a profusion of association reports, institutional self-studies, and position papers put out in recent years is that the specific role of the faculty in academic governance differs tremendously, depending on the type of institution involved. Questions of power, authority, influence, autonomy, and participation, unfortunately, are not always carefully distinguished from one another in governance discussions. Moreover, there appears to be continuing uncertainty about the extent to which faculty members actually want to participate in certain aspects of institutional decision making. Some faculty seek to be engaged in the actual shaping of policy. Others prefer to distance themselves from the running of the college or university, preferring instead just to have opportunities to challenge policies as the need arises.

Some faculty place a very high value on their own personal autonomy and do not wish to become involved directly in the work of various academic committees charged with setting or implementing policy. Others eschew participation in the belief that it leads neither to real influence or to power. Still others prefer informal influence to formal participation.[22] What is clear—again from a faculty perspective—is that collaborative and "participatory" governance is most widely regarded as an ideal. So long as faculty are afforded ample opportunities for consultation and participation in management decisions; so long as communication with administrative leaders is open, honest, and timely; and assuming the management of the institution is conducted in a fair and evenhanded fashion, most faculty members reportedly prefer not to be burdened with responsibility for overseeing operations on a day-to-day basis.

In any event, the structural peculiarity of the academy as an institution is that decision-making processes that most directly affect how a college or university carries out its mission typically occur at the lowest level of the system. It happens within individual academic departments led by heads or chairs. Deans of individual schools or colleges within a university, for example, may encourage or withhold support for certain academic initiatives, but their role is more nearly one of coordinating and articulating decisions made by the various departments over which they exercise managerial oversight.

The responsibility of middle-echelon administrators, in turn, is mainly one of orchestrating policies, procedures, and resource allocations that affect all of the schools or colleges comprising the whole, together with the coordination of ancillary support functions, ranging from physical plant management and institutional development (that is, fund-raising) to student activities and services. (What central administrators above the level of deans, including vice-provosts, provosts, vice-chancellors, chancellors, and university presidents, do for a living remains forever a mystery to most working faculty.) Thus, power and authority governing how resources and services are distributed flow downward, while authority and influence over academic matters tend to percolate upward. The basic logic of it all, if there is one, is as old as the university model itself.

First-rate institutions enjoy a strong faculty presence in governance matters at all levels. This of course is as it should be. Unlike businesses perhaps, historical experience rather clearly demonstrates that academic institutions cannot be led effectively by autocratic bureaucrats, perched atop a power pyramid, intent upon top-down management and control. Accordingly, faculty members want and expect complete and open access to budget development. They profess to want meaningful involvement in establishing and evaluating the institution's mission, goals, and objectives. They expect to have a say in matters pertaining to their own professional growth and renewal, not to mention control over policies and procedures governing the recruitment, hiring, or firing of colleagues. Faculty want a say in decisions affecting salaries and promotions. Above all, they demand— and within the broadest limits possible are entitled to have—authority over curricula and classroom-related matters.[23]

Yet, in another sense it needs to be said that faculty members *cannot* have it every which way. That is, they cannot demand accountability for goal-setting, resource allocations, and the establishing of institutional priorities from ranking administrators while at the same time expecting those same managerial leaders to leave the faculty to its own preoccupations when it comes to responding to accountability demands issuing from external constituencies. For good or for ill, if faculty truly control the fortunes of a college or university, while administrators only guide and direct its operations, faculty must share responsibility for keeping the institution accountable to those upon whom the academic enterprise depends for its very existence. Evidence that faculty bodies are fully prepared to accept that responsibility is not especially reassuring.

More often than not, the strength and vitality of the faculty voice in governance are directly tied to academic freedom. The American Association of University Professors maintains a "censured list" of institutions whose administrations have been found in violation of accepted principles of academic freedom. Rarely nowadays—with very few notable exceptions—is a major, prestigious college or university included on the list. More typically identified as culprits are smaller, less well-known institutions, places where the power of the faculty is weak and ineffectual. They tend to be places where the administration, free of faculty-imposed constraints, has been free to behave in an arbitrary or dictatorial fashion judged inimical to academic freedom.

As the decade of the 1990s draws to a close, however, vigilance against piecemeal efforts to chip away at academic freedoms may turn out to be more rather than less important than formerly. Colleges and universities of all institutions within society have a long tradition of being the most open to original and controversial thought; and academic liberty has been regarded as the very bedrock of what universities are about. Lately, though, issues involving free speech on campus have shifted, though apparently subtly enough not to arouse the ire of such official bodies as the American Association of University Professors. This time around the threat is posed from within the ranks of students and faculty members themselves more than it is by know-nothing administrators or intolerant trustees. Today, it can be argued, academic freedom is not significantly endangered by attempts to suppress demagogues who stand on soapboxes—or before classroom lecterns—spouting heresy or attempting to insinuate subversive thoughts into tender young minds. The threat derives more from patterns of intimidation against those who have violated someone else's canons of political acceptability. The public at large mistakenly tends to dismiss campus controversy over "political correctness" as a kind of straining at gnats. Unfortunately, the dangers to free speech and equity on campus are as real and substantial as ever.

Some few years ago a professor at the University of Minnesota sued the institution, claiming she had failed to secure a tenure-track appointment because of her gender. Instead of defending itself, the university reportedly settled out of court without admitting discrimination and then announced a new policy in future of giving hiring preference to women. Also in Minnesota, an entire academic department was confronted with "sexual harassment" charges brought— anonymously—by four students. The alleged offenses included disagreeing with a student about the role of a female character in a story, assigning reading lists to which the students objected, and the awarding of low grades. At Virginia Polytech a popular professor who happened to use ribald and perhaps inappropriate humor in his lectures was driven to resign after a very small number of students declared his humor offensive. (The overwhelming majority of students in the class reportedly found nothing to object to about his lecturing.) If and whenever these incidents begin to form a repeated pattern on a campus, there is cause for alarm.

The merits of the specific cases cited aside, academic freedom is threatened when the notion somehow gains credibility that everyone has an innate and unalienable "right" not to be offended by anyone else and that the mere fact that someone claims to be offended constitutes proof that someone else did something deserving sanctions.[24] If faculty do not assume responsibility for fostering a campus environment within which free speech is tolerated, even grossly offensive speech, it seems unlikely that outsiders will be willing to lend the cause of academic freedom strong support either. And at the risk of mentioning the obvious, an institution divided against itself, its members even disagreeing with one another over the rules of discourse, cannot respond effectively to external demands that it remain accountable for its practices.

With shared authority and influence in governance comes shared responsibility. For present purposes, it is vital to stress the point that whereas the work of curriculum and program development, for example, does not take place in a social vacuum, and that decisions about instruction are formatively influenced by forces and factors outside the halls of ivy, primary responsibility for academic choices as such rests ultimately with members of the academic profession. Faculty, after all, are the experts. Hence, if curricular redesign on a scale rarely before attempted is essential in today's climate of accountability, it is chiefly to members of the professoriate in colleges and universities that the public must look for intellectual and moral leadership.

COHERENCE IN THE CURRICULUM

All things considered, it may well prove to be history's verdict that any coherent and comprehensive program of liberal studies as the center-piece of undergraduate education is no longer possible. It is entirely conceivable, in other words, that vocational or so-called professional education is so well entrenched at the baccalaureate level and enjoys such strong popular support that general learning of a traditional sort will survive in colleges and universities only as a kind of afterthought, a vestigial appendage to the business of supplying students with discrete skills for employment. Some would say it has already happened, except possibly in the case of a small handful of private liberal arts colleges.

Consistent with the ideology of the multiversity, what the public appears to want more than anything else from higher education of all types and at all levels is, simply, direct job training. Moreover, there is much to suggest that in recent years advocates of accountability in higher education have tended to make common cause with vocation-alists, insisting that graduates' job placement rates ought to be made to serve as a major index of institutional quality and responsiveness to public need. The resulting "synergy" tends to generate its own mo-mentum, posing a political dynamic capable of virtually overwhelm-ing anyone who would offer caveats. For whatever reasons, in any event, it is plain that those who would dissent from the wholesale vocationalization of collegiate curricula today rightly sense they have been placed on the defensive.

If the idea of general or liberal education is to survive, colleges and universities will need to face up to the short-term risk of resisting public demands for an almost infinite array of discrete, relatively low-level vocational preparatory programs at the bachelor's level of the type now commonly found on the nation's campuses. Naturally, substituting an unorganized assortment of separate liberal arts courses, spread out among departments and weighted to ensure that each unit gets its share of students to teach, will hardly suffice either.[25] The first order of business then will be for faculty and campus administrators to launch a concerted effort aimed at restoring academic coherence and integrity to the undergraduate liberal arts degree. And of course it will not happen—at least, no one can feel confident it will happen—so long as the illusion is harbored that the baccalaureate-degree program in nearly anything resembling its present configuration, consisting of not much more than an accidental array or lengthy menu of disconnected and largely

unrelated courses, poses either an attractive or viable alternative to
professional programs bearing the promise of future employment.

On most campuses, the faculty has held itself back from any
collective effort to identify and make explicit the skills, knowledge, and
values or dispositions that ought to be the hallmarks of a good education,
elements that do not always arrange themselves neatly according to the
discipline-specific boundaries now reified by the ways academic institutions are organized. As a direct result, it is often said, the college
curriculum has degenerated into a kind of grab bag, organized, if at all,
by distribution requirements. Practically nowhere is there any real core;
and in the absence of a consensus on what should be learned, it has been
much easier to let students make most of their own choices.[26]

Confirming evidence is not hard to find. In 1989, for example, the
National Endowment for the Humanities reported that it was possible to
graduate from 77 percent of the nation's colleges without a student's
ever having been obliged to study a foreign language; from 45 percent
of all institutions of higher learning without having completed a single
course in American or English literature; from 41 percent without
studying mathematics; and from 38 percent without ever having taken
even one history course.[27] Neither the public nor the professoriate itself
reacted to the Endowment's revelations with cries of outrage and
dismay. Still less did they provoke hasty efforts to redress matters. There
was only deafening silence.

Given the state of disarray into which liberal learning has fallen
in recent decades, interposing a comprehensive and uniform set of
faculty-designed examinations for students to complete midway
through the junior year might make very good sense indeed. Not only
would the provision force faculty members to think through anew the
question of what ought to be tested for and by what procedures (oral
interrogations and essay-writing assignments as well as machine-
scored testing) and accordingly encourage a more systematic approach
to curriculum development, publicizing the results of examinations
completed prior to a student's selection of a major concentration of
studies ought to earn approbation from accountability enthusiasts as
well. Together with more stringent grading and an integrative capstone
experience to enrich the academic major or concentration, more than
enough data should be generated to allow institutions to ascertain how
much student learning has taken place.

Regardless of how liberal arts education fares in the future, members of the professoriate also will need to face up to the problem of

curricular "creep"—or by default allow less-qualified outsiders to address it. The well-known tendency for collegiate curricula to grow and expand as new courses appear and old ones subdivide cannot be allowed to continue indefinitely. Or so it would seem, given the budgetary constraints most institutions are increasingly forced to observe. It is always easier to create a new course than it is to eliminate an old one, less painful to grow by accretion than to acknowledge rational boundary conditions through a process of substitution and replacement.

Adjusting to limits will be painful. As the Commission for Educational Quality of the Southern Regional Education Board wisely observes in one of its recent reports, "As in every walk of life, the most difficult decisions involve deciding what good things not to do."[28] The issue basically is not one of doing more with less. It has become one of determining how to do fewer things better.

INSTRUCTIONAL INNOVATION

Part and parcel of the movement for greater accountability in higher education is the demand for renewed attention to matters of pedagogy—not simply that more attention should be paid to teaching per se, but that efforts should be made to improve the quality of learning that goes on. Not everything that must be learned, for example, need be taught. Many institutions are already moving away from a teaching model that has insisted traditionally that everyone learns at the same lock-step pace and in the same way. Recognizing that some important learning occurs outside the classroom, with or without benefit of the structure of a formal course, some colleges and universities have long experimented with offering credit by examination in selected subject areas. There is little new about these approaches; they more nearly represent a return to the once-common practice of allowing students to "sit" for examinations whenever they felt sufficiently well prepared. Together with independent study and guided tutorials, satisfying requirements by examination poses a welcome expansion of the array of learning procedures more and more colleges and universities are now willing to recognize and endorse.

Other new teaching methodologies await further exploration. Electronic technologies incorporating satellite teleconferencing and distance learning from remote sites, interactive video, hypertext, virtual reality simulation, holographics, computer networking, self-paced computer-based instruction, and other applications of automated information storage and retrieval systems offer considerable promise for the future, provided they can be made more cost-effective and are utilized judiciously, with due regard for the human element essential to meaningful learning. The ideal always (possibly excepting narrowly drawn skill classes and courses where the material is purely factual and exceedingly cut-and-dried) is to find new ways of reproducing some modern equivalent of Mark Hopkins on one end of the log and a student on the other. The challenge, so to speak, is to re-create a setting akin to that of Rousseau's fictional Émile conversing with his personal mentor, some psychological environment parallel to the Athenian *agora* where a latter-day Socrates and his disciples engage in dialogue and debate. If digital technology can help bring it about, and do so without rendering instruction more impersonal and detached, its advent can only be welcomed with enthusiasm.

At a time when transparencies on overhead projectors or static displays on LCD panels represent cutting-edge technology so far as most real-world college classrooms are concerned, however, the real potential of the so-called electronic classroom may not become apparent any time soon. More worrisome and problematic by far is the widespread belief, encouraged by more than a few self-styled, highly publicized media gurus, that electronic technologies in future will serve to "extend" the teaching capacity of faculty members and thereby help keep costs down.

Why hire six different Shakespeare scholars, it is asked rhetorically, when the lectures of one outstanding teacher can be beamed via television to student audiences on scores of campuses? Why should half a dozen or more schools duplicate one another's foreign language offerings when it is possible for students geographically distant from one another to "tune in" on instruction from a single site? Why not let each school specialize in one or two language programs and share its instruction with those enrolled elsewhere? For that matter, why should students gather together physically, at the same time and in the same place, for a class, when the means are at hand for them all to receive instruction from a common source, but at times and places of their own individual choosing?

It is vital to remember that previous experiments with mediated instruction extending back over the past three decades have enjoyed mixed success at best. As a particular case in point, students always have complained about televised lectures, finding them boring, impersonal, and alienating. Nevertheless, cautionary lessons of the past notwithstanding, much is still being made now of the potential for using instructional television, e-mail dialoging, and computer-based, self-contained "learning modules" that students can access from their home work stations at their own convenience. Skeptics may be forgiven their hesitation if they do not rush to embrace the latest electronic "delivery systems" uncritically. If the practical consequence of their use is to accentuate the tendency for knowledge to be looked upon as a prepackaged commodity conveyed through "canned" instruction, it is difficult to feel enthusiastic about what may lie ahead. And if the coming Brave New World of instructional technology renders a live transaction between teacher and learner obsolete or less important, educators will have little reason to cheer its arrival. Undoubtedly mediation has much to offer in the long run. The challenge will be to find ways of utilizing it wisely, without isolating and dehumanizing teachers and learners alike, and in the service of defensible academic objectives.

EXTERNAL ACCREDITATION

Traditionally, accreditation of degree programs and discipline-based academic units or by outside bodies or external agencies has been considered a major index of institutional quality and therefore accountability. Accreditation has been thought of as an integral part of the self-regulatory mechanism colleges and universities use to maintain quality control, thus affording protection for the public interest.

In its loosest and most informal sense, members of a particular administrative unit assume exclusive responsibility for documenting programmatic compliance with the published standards of a relevant professional association or academic society. There the matter rests. More formal and elaborate by far is the process by which a program unit, department, school, or college assembles and submits a comprehensive "self-study" or preliminary report, preparatory to an actual visit to the campus by a review team of faculty peers appointed from other institutions. Upon the team's arrival, members interrogate students, staff, faculty, and administrators associated with the program or unit in question. Finally, the team draws up its own report, consisting of recommendations for improvements and a final judgment as to whether the program or department meets the accrediting body's standards and criteria. Programs in the field of psychology, for example, seek a stamp of approval from the American Psychological Association (APA). Other academic disciplines have their own specialized accrediting agencies and standards to which each is supposed to hold itself accountable.

There are several variants. Sometimes program standards derive not from a national association but from a regional or state body. Otherwise, the procedures are the same: an internal assessment, followed by a campus visitation, concluding with an external judgment as to whether a program is to be accredited, wholly or in part, and for what period of time. Professional schools (as distinct from individual academic disciplines) in nursing, education, law, and others have their own accrediting bodies. In the case of teacher education, for example, in addition to state norms or standards with which all programs are expected to comply, the National Council for the Accreditation of Teacher Education (NACTE) functions as a type of imprimatur, supplying its own detailed and extensive list of requirements to which individual programs must conform. Finally, there are regional and national bodies whose accreditation procedures are directed toward institutions as unitary wholes, rather than to any particular subunit thereof.

On the surface, the logic of impartial and disinterested external review appear both congruent with and supportive of the impetus toward institutional accountability. The reality is somewhat different. First, it needs to be pointed out, external accreditation can be a very expensive proposition: Each program or department is likely to spend hundreds of dollars annually maintaining its affiliation with a particular accrediting association and thousands more when it comes up for formal review. Collectively, the cost of maintaining accredited programs throughout a university requires a major resource expenditure.

Second, accreditation standards tend to be lengthy and complex. Compliance is costly in light of standards that make it nearly impossible to eliminate redundancy across programs, particularly when a great number of specific courses are mandated for inclusion in any given program. Barriers are created to efforts by institutions of higher learning when they try to share courses across disciplines or to impose limits on the total number of credit hours required for a bachelor's degree.[29] Accreditation standards more than anything else have been responsible over the last few years for driving up the total number of credit hours needed to complete the undergraduate degree.

Third, accreditation sometimes has less to do with genuine academic quality and more with prestige, status, and standing. Accreditation is a useful student recruitment tool, especially at the graduate level, because prospective degree candidates in certain fields at least show strong preferences toward a fully accredited program compared with one that is not. In some instances future employment prospects and licensure depend on graduation from an accredited graduate or undergraduate degree program. Less clear is whether accreditation always confirms the quality assurances claimed for it. Mere compliance with standards— numbers and paper qualifications of faculty, faculty-student ratios, specific courses—may not necessarily ensure the level of quality to which accreditation is supposed to attest.

Finally, despite its appearance of impartiality and objectivity, the accreditation process itself is often incestuous—that is, the faculty members in a given program not only have a vested interest in maintaining accreditation for their own unit, but through their professional or academic associations, may themselves as individuals have contributed directly or indirectly to the drafting or revision of the same standards with which they now seek to conform. The problem is least pronounced at the national level; it can sometimes figure as a real factor at regional and state levels. Needless to add, faculty are only too happy to appeal to "standards" when pressing their case for the addition of new faculty, more courses, or support facilities mandated by an accrediting body.

The best solution may be to retain and strengthen accreditation at the postbaccalaureate level wherever possible, utilizing external agencies to buttress the quality of graduate professional studies where it can be shown to be cost-effective. But the entire cumbersome apparatus as it applies to undergraduate programming needs to be abandoned. The better alternative to current practice is for each college or university to assume responsibility for its own bachelor's-level offerings, so that the whole is not controlled as the mere sum of its parts. Curriculum development must be approached as a unitary, undertaking, involving all interested parties working toward common goals. Piecemeal accreditation of the individual components of a total program seems neither necessary nor, in today's climate, especially useful.

ACADEMIC STANDARDS REVISITED

Conspicuous by its absence in most discussions of accountability is the counterpart to student learning outcomes at or near the completion of an undergraduate degree—namely, stipulating the academic proficiencies required of entering students. In this respect the asymmetrical character of most debate is clearly revealed. It is only to be expected perhaps that an influential segment of the public at large would stoutly resist any suggestion that access to public higher education should be more limited or restricted than is now the case. Open admission, or something close to it, has achieved the status of a sacred populist cow. Next to cost, the public reportedly worries more about access than anything else in higher education. Yet logically, if colleges and universities are to be held accountable to a fixed of outcome measures, it seems only fair that they should have some say in determining standards for admission as well. By the same token, it should be added, granting institutions of higher learning the prerogative could turn out to be a mixed blessing, since it would oblige them to give hard thought to the question of what should be considered prerequisite for student success in a coherent course of studies. More than a few faculties might be extremely reluctant to engage the task.

To date scant attention has been paid to problems and issues involving the transition from secondary school to college.[30] Here some historical background is useful. In the colonial era, for example, when the typical college curriculum was thoroughly classical, there seemed to be little need for college entrance requirements in anything except Greek and Latin. By the early 1800s, as collegiate curricula were gradually broadened and became more inclusive of modern subjects, proficiency was demanded in additional subjects—first geography, history, and English, later grammar, composition, and literature. After the Civil War, further requirements in the sciences and modern foreign languages were added. But because colleges differed considerably among in terms of what was required for admission, secondary schools found it nearly impossible to anticipate how best to prepare their future graduates for college. The discontinuity between secondary and higher education grew more troublesome and obvious with each passing decade. By the 1880s, most observers felt it had become a veritable chasm.

Some educational reformers felt that colleges should use their entrance requirements to force secondary schools to meet higher scholastic standards. Others felt just as strongly that collegiate standards should be adapted to the existing levels of preparatory schools. Either way, the gap between collegiate and lower education needed to be bridged. In due course a number of colleges hit upon the solution of establishing "preparatory departments," charged with bringing students up to standard. Few were satisfied with what still seemed to be a stopgap measure, particularly when the strong temptation was to extend college credit for work completed at the preparatory level. Nonetheless, preparatory programs proved durable, some continuing in existence well into the early twentieth century.

Attempts to achieve a better articulation of secondary school and college assumed many different forms throughout the latter third of the nineteenth century. For want of any obvious alternative, some institutions resigned themselves to granting admission to students who had obtained a secondary-level diploma or certificate, no matter how deficient their preparatory training. Others accepted large numbers of so-called conditioned students on a probationary basis, hoping to help bring them up in conformity with regular standards as they progressed in their collegiate studies—an ambition, it must be observed, which was rarely realized.

Yet another practice begun by institutions of higher learning (the University of Michigan was reportedly the first) was to send faculty representatives out to visit and inspect individual high schools periodically. The expectation was that faculty would help to improve lower-school academic standards and assist secondary teachers in preparing some of their charges for college admission. In embryonic form, the beginnings of high school accreditation may be traced back to this custom of faculty oversight over selected schools. Although the system worked within the boundaries of a single state, it failed to meet the needs of students who wished to attend an out-of-state college. Eventually, regional associations were formed to serve accreditation purposes on a larger scale.

A second innovation intended to remedy the problem of chaotic college entrance requirements assumed the form of uniform examinations. The "Regents" examination in New York were the first to appear in the late 1870s; by the 1890s testing was under way under the auspices of the newly formed College Entrance Examination Board. Despite initial hesitancy, with the passage of time more and more colleges and universities began abandoning their own independent entrance examinations in favor of those administered by the College Board.

A third effort to build a bridge between secondary schools and colleges took yet another direction: attempting to introduce greater uniformity in the specific courses required for college admission. Although the movement was not initially successful, indirectly it gave rise to a more enduring solution, the development of academic "counts" or "points" or "credits" for specific types of courses successfully passed, which in turn evolved as "units" as defined by the Carnegie Foundation for the Advancement of Teaching. Carnegie units greatly facilitated the standardization of college entrance requirements, allowing comparisons of courses completed to determine students' eligibility for admission to a college or university. When admission officers, for a variety of reasons, subsequently began relying more on standardized academic aptitude and achievement tests for decisions about admission, the use of Carnegie unit tallies or profiles showed a marked decline.

Strangely enough, and despite a long history of involvement by colleges and universities in the work of lower-school reform, any suggestion that today's faculties share a vested interest in the quality of preparation shown by entering college students is likely to draw blank stares. The work of high schools is widely held to be something separate and apart from what happens on college campuses. Liberal arts faculty especially evince little interest in becoming involved with elementary and secondary schools. Presumably they feel they have enough to do in their own professional homes, or that responsibility for anything having to do with the lower schools rests with teacher-educators.

All the same, the seeming lack of recognition among leaders in higher education that what does or does not transpire in the country's high schools has a direct bearing on the quality and level of preparedness shown by students admitted into colleges and universities is surprising. It is almost as if the belief prevails that each year's crop of entering college freshmen is created ex nihilo, that whatever has transpired before students miraculously appear on the academy's doorstep is somehow irrelevant to their subsequent college careers.

Meanwhile, there is general recognition that academic standards in all but the best of the nation's high schools leave a great deal to be desired. Not much agreement is to be found on what remedies will be required, or whether the ills that plague many secondary schools are inherently insoluble. Suggestions that a curriculum should be set in place that begins in the earliest grades by teaching children history and literature, mathematics and science, music and foreign languages are periodically put forth and as regularly ignored or fatally compromised. So, too, are demands that a more exacting core curriculum be established in high schools. As in other industrialized countries, runs one argument, American youths should be required to enroll for meaningful courses and achieve good grades as the precondition for being allowed to progress through the system.

The custom of allowing students to pass onward through successive grade levels without much regard for actual scholastic accomplishment, a kind of uncontrolled institutional peristalsis, it is said, must be brought to a halt. What results from the cumulative inadequacies of an educational system where standards are lacking is even more painfully obvious at the high school level than at the collegiate level. Each year at graduation, poorly educated students emerge unprepared either for skilled employment or for genuine college-level work. And they march forth out into the world bearing diplomas that in all too many instances signify very little, if anything, in the way of authentic academic achievement.

One way that colleges and universities can help spur school reform is to establish clear and explicit standards for college admission. The opportunity for higher education to define in advance what it is that entering freshmen should know and be able to do ought not to be missed. As Rita Kramer, author of *Ed School Follies* (1991), insists, "More exacting college and university entrance requirements would necessitate higher standards for high schools in order to meet them, and eventually for elementary schools, which would have to provide literacy and numeracy, in order to prepare for high school."[31] Colleges and universities, in any event, may have little choice in the matter as high schools also come to rely more and more on outcomes measures and performance tests for their own prospective graduates. Institutions of higher learning may well be forced to adapt and realign their own entrance criteria and requirements, particularly those selective schools that have long relied on SAT or ACT scores, high school class standing, or course units completed in deciding whom to admit.

Provided some reasonable and appropriate phase-in period were allowed, colleges and universities have a chance to develop and maintain standards that clearly define what skills and knowledge graduating twelfth-graders ought to possess if they hope to gain collegiate admittance. There is at least some historical evidence to indicate that when schools do require more stringent standards for college entrance, high school students begin to take more challenging and demanding academic courses. They will expend the extra effort needed to conform to the criteria colleges have established.[32] The point to be emphasized is that institutions of higher learning will be far better positioned to hold themselves accountable for the quality of education they afford students when they assume greater responsibility for determining the basis upon which those same learners are admitted in the first place. Outcome-based assessment cuts both ways: if postsecondary schools need to be able to document "output" relative to some independent set of academic achievement standards, they must likewise exercise some amount of discretion in controlling learner "input" too.

TEACHER PREPARATION

There are several reasons why including some brief mention of teacher education within a broader discussion of accountability in higher education is both helpful and necessary. Teacher preparation programs, often criticized and much-maligned (some 1,200 to 1,250 of them in all), flourish almost eutrophically in most colleges and universities; and they attract substantial numbers of students, whether those enrolled actually have declared themselves as education majors or end up obtaining degrees in professional education. Indeed, without the presence of large numbers of teachers-in-training on their campuses, many smaller colleges might be forced to close their doors. The future of teacher education presumably has a bearing on the quality of tomorrow's teachers and thus, one must suppose, figures as one important factor among several in determining the caliber of education students receive from the elementary grades onward. Ultimately, the academic competence or proficiency of the next generation of college students is affected. Hence, teacher education affords an important link between higher and lower learning. In the final analysis, how well or how poorly prospective teachers are prepared for their careers may be said to represent a major indicator of higher education's accountability to the lower schools, institutions on which higher learning itself ultimately depends.

A frequent complaint heard is that teacher education programs place too great an emphasis on pedagogical techniques and methodological studies, that they pay insufficient attention to grounding prospective teachers in the subject matter they intend to teach.[33] Typically, as one critic asserts, schools, colleges, and departments of education on campuses across the country are producing "experts in methods of teaching with nothing to apply those methods to. Their technique is abundant, their knowledge practically nonexistent." Instead of history, literature, mathematics, and the sciences, teacher candidates allegedly are set to studying instructional strategies, "soft" educational psychology, and pedagogical philosophy. Accordingly, it is not to be wondered at that in many high schools, teaching in the substantive disciplines reputedly has given way to courses in filmmaking, driver education, and marriage and family living. "Neither possessing nor respecting knowledge themselves," Rita Kramer asks, "how can teachers imbue their students with any enthusiasm for it? Nowhere in America today is intellectual life deader than in our schools—unless it is in our schools of education."[34]

It turns out that in this one respect at least, the indictment is somewhat overdrawn. Close analysis of how most teacher preparation programs are organized would indicate that those seeking licensure or certification as teachers in fact *are* required to complete a substantial number of liberal arts or other noneducation courses, just as are their peers majoring in other disciplines. Whereas the range varies greatly from school to school, contrary to what some critics have claimed, secondary education students usually are obliged to satisfy all or nearly all requirements of a major in the subject they intend to teach. Or, alternatively, someone majoring in a given discipline also completes courses need for teacher licensure.

Professional education courses, sometimes including student teaching and practica or guided classroom observations, account on average for no more than about twenty-eight or thirty credit hours, or roughly one-fourth of the total hours needed for a bachelor's degree. Among elementary and early childhood education majors, or those concentrating in special education, professional education course requirements are likely to be more extensive, amounting to upward of 35 or 40 percent of the total credit hours required.

Many observers argue even these slightly more modest totals are still too high. At the same time, some critics will concede that providing *some* didactic instruction for prospective classroom teachers is necessary—in curriculum development, basic teaching methodologies, legal issues, student assessment, classroom management, learning theory, diagnosing and remediating learning disorders, and so forth—though perhaps nothing more extensive than could be fitted comfortably into a single semester or its equivalent. "Everything [teacher candidates] need to know about how to teach," avows Rita Kramer, "could be learned by intelligent people in a single summer of well-planned instruction."[35]

Quite possibly, she suggests, the training of teachers of the very young, where nurturing capacity is important, should be separated off from the preparation of those intending to work with older students, where mastery of subject-matter content is more important. People preparing themselves to work in child-care centers or to teach in the primary grades might best be served during their undergraduate training by absorbing as much knowledge as possible about child development and learning. Otherwise, all prospective teachers should complete a meaningful liberal arts degree in an academic subject (or, better yet, an integrative combination of disciplines) and then follow up with a period of supervised teaching.

Some critics of teacher education today are prepared to go so far as to urge the disbanding of schools and departments of education altogether. The undergraduate major in secondary education or in curriculum and instruction (not to mention the five-year and fifth-year graduate certification programs in education now gaining in fashion), it is said, should be abolished. Substantive training in subject matter allegedly can and should be entrusted to disciplinary specialists, not to self-styled experts in curriculum and instruction. Methodology should be integrated with the subject itself as the main focus, not the techniques for imparting the knowledge to others. And what *cannot* be taught about teaching, or so it is argued, can *only* be learned in context, in the field, under the close surveillance of a supervisor and other experienced classroom teachers. Only if tomorrow's teachers are broadly educated and rooted in knowledge of the liberal disciplines will prospects for improving elementary and secondary education improve.

Abolishing teacher preparation units would carry several serious drawbacks, however. The most obvious, usually overlooked by detractors of teacher education programs, is that subject-matter experts on campuses do not necessarily have a developed interest in pedagogical issues and concerns. Nor do they all possess the ability to convey to others how their respective specialties are best taught to learners below the college level. Intimate knowledge of a field may be necessary, but it is nowhere near being a sufficient condition for helping others to teach the subject matter of that field competently. (The poor quality of teaching done by college professors who are otherwise experts in their fields should offer relevant testimony in this respect.) In any case, most professors are so far removed from the realities of today's elementary or high school classrooms, it is difficult to imagine that very many of them would know how to function effectively in a teaching role outside of higher education. Working in an elementary or secondary school today, after all, is an entirely different matter from teaching in a college or university. The task is much harder in the former case, the challenges to success much greater.

By themselves, clinical, on-site apprenticeships are unlikely to help improve the quality of teaching done in the lower schools (though, naturally, they may help new entrants into the field to achieve entry-level proficiency in classroom management and instruction). The fact of the matter is, most novice teachers teach as they themselves have been taught or as they observe others around them teaching. Somehow, if improvements are to occur, ways must be found to help entering teachers to work, as it were, "against the grain" when necessary; to innovate and depart from established routines as opportunities allow; to seek new and better alternatives to traditional practice. (The problem is partly one of lack of attention to pedagogy; more important still as constraints on improvement are the horrendous conditions under which lower-school teachers often work—including impossibly large classes, heavy teaching assignments, and intractable student discipline problems.) That conventional teacher training programs have not been notably successful in promoting instructional excellence may be beside the point if the alternatives proposed are unlikely to fare much better.

On balance, even allowing for some truth to charges that some—but not necessarily all—education courses lack substantive content or intellectual rigor, teacher education programs probably are not the abysmal failures harsh critics represent them to be, any more than they are the resounding successes teacher educators claim for them. The plight of teacher preparation in academia—beset by charges of anti-intellectualism, of substituting process for content, of separating theory from practice, of their seeming remoteness from the realities of today's schools—well illustrates the problem of undergraduate professional training generally in American higher education. It is probably true that teacher candidates are burdened with far too many courses of dubious utility and vacuous content. But much the same could be said in equal measure of preparatory programs for other professions and occupations as well—fashion merchandising, public relations and affairs, recreation and park administration, law enforcement, community development, and countless other fields dignified by having achieved the status of place-holders in the academy.

Students' intellectual and career needs differ. Still, there are ample grounds for arguing that *all* future professionals would be better served in the long run by having them absorb themselves in the more generic and fundamental forms of knowledge represented by the liberal arts, assuming, of course, that they are coherently conceptualized and effectively taught. Future social workers arguably need more solid work in psychology, political science, and sociology than the requirements of their major typically allow; narrowly trained engineering majors presumably could benefit from the leavening provided by broader exposure to the social sciences, fine arts, and humanities; journalists-in-training need to acquire a broad liberal arts background perhaps as much as do prospective teachers; librarians should come to love books before they learn how to catalog and store them; and so on.

The only real difference is that the shortcomings and inadequacies of campus-based teacher preparation are more visible and, possibly, more difficult to overlook or ignore.

In some final accounting, academic responsibility—in the sense of serving society's best and highest interests—will remain little more than a rhetorical slogan invoked as occasion demands until some greater semblance of order and intelligibility in the undergraduate experience as a whole is regained. At the very least, part and parcel of the task of restoring integrity and coherence to the bachelor's degree will require rethinking the issue of what knowledge college students most need to acquire regardless of their future careers, what instruction should occupy their first three years or so on campus. On one point at least there is little room for doubt. Whatever learning might be gleaned from courses bearing such titles as "Foundations of Sports Management in the Secondary School" or "Principles and Processes of Papier-Mâché Construction in the Elementary Classroom" can be safely excluded from consideration.

FACULTY PERFORMANCE AUDITING

Discussions of accountability in higher education at the macrocosmic level focus on institutional performance. The question is about how the college or university (or a constituent school, college, or department) as a collective entity pursues its mission and otherwise fulfills its professional, academic, and societal obligations. On a more microcosmic level, the question at issue is the quality of an individual's job performance and how to assess it. Evaluating the workings of an institution is a complex task; evaluating the work of individuals within it is not much easier. As Larry Braskamp and John Ory, two authors of a recent reference on faculty evaluation, remark, though faculty performance always has been difficult to describe and judge, there is increasing public pressure on academics to demonstrate personal and professional accountability as well.[36] Colleges and universities increasingly are being asked by state agencies, alumni, donors, foundations, legislatures, and the public at large to explain how faculty members spend their time, to account for their activities, and to give some demonstration of how well or how poorly they perform their duties.

The word "assess," it has been pointed out, derives from the Latin *assidere,* meaning "to sit beside."[37] There is a fitting air of ambiguity about this etymological derivation, suggesting as it does either a companion or an overseer, a colleague with whom one may collaborate in performing a task, or, alternatively, someone looking over one's shoulder, observing and passing judgment on how well the task is performed. Unfortunately for those who prefer to stress the more benign or nonpunitive connotation, the term's lineage actually traces back most directly to matters of *tax* assessment, or to *sitting beside a judge,* or one who renders a verdict of some sort. To conduct an "assessment" or evaluation means, almost inevitably, passing judgment, making a determination of the merit of some activity.

Putting the best face on it, proponents of faculty assessment emphasize the very real and potentially valuable side benefits to be derived from assessing faculty performance more rigorously and systematically than has been customary in the past. The very process, it is sometimes argued, serves to focus attention on criteria and evidence needed for making reliable judgments about faculty competence. Faculty evaluation requires that the range and diversity of what faculty members do is clearly identified. It stimulates faculty to consider more carefully what standards are applicable in judging how well they conduct their professional activities. Finally, the assessment process allegedly encourages the gathering of better evidence upon which informed judgments can be made.

The claim invoked by assessment apologists almost as a ritualized incantation is that the primary purpose of evaluating faculty performance is actually "formative," that is, its intent is to assist faculty members to become more self-aware about their work and to encourage efforts toward improving performance. Few are deceived. The *most* important—but still largely defensible—reasons for elaborate faculty performance evaluation procedures are twofold. First, a more thorough auditing allows a college or university to supply an accounting of faculty activities for the benefit of outsiders. The results of comprehensive assessment permit the school to identify more approximately what it is faculty do, roughly how much time they spend doing it, and how their efforts are distributed across a broad range of possible responsibilities. Faculty evaluation is aimed at yielding some indication of how well those employed by the institution fulfill their duties and functions.

Second, faculty assessment is intended to generate data for making comparative judgments between and among faculty members, to provide a basis for individual decisions about contract renewal, the granting of tenure, promotions, and salary adjustments. Rhetoric alleging otherwise aside, faculty performance judgments first and foremost are "summative" in nature.

Judging faculty "productivity" so far as securing research grants is concerned is a relatively straightforward matter of tallying up monies awarded, coupled perhaps with a judgment about the standing of the funding agencies involved. (A multimillion-dollar grant from the National Science Foundation to refine neutrino detection presumably would carry more weight than a small stipend from the local community horticulture club to help advance ways of combating peony or rhododendron blight.) If training grants and service contracts are judged important, the same principle applies: The measure of productivity is the number and amount of contracts received. Obviously, too, whether the terms of the grant or contract have been carried out figures in as a consideration.

Published or presented research is somewhat more problematic. Traditionally, the single most common approach has been purely quantitative. How many papers were generated within a given period of time? Attempts to introduce qualitative elements are familiar enough. Was the paper delivered at a national conference and was it peer-reviewed prior to acceptance? Was the research published, and if so, did it appear in a reputable or prestigious journal? Did a publication reflect original research, or was it solely exegetical or interpretive of others' work? Was the book (preferably) a scholarly treatise published by an academic press or was it a commercially produced "pedagogical" text in the field?

Still other criteria for assessing scholarship have been suggested. One entirely unobjectionable set of standards recently advanced stipulates that a scholar's work should be judged on the basis of the extent to which it reflects a thorough knowledge of the field, has a well-defined objective, employs appropriate methods and procedures, uses resources effectively, communicates clearly, and offers important or significant results.[38]

Complicating matters are basic dissimilarities between scientific research and scholarship in the humanities or fine arts. Issues go well beyond matters of utility or tangible results, and include questions about how to assess work done in the performing arts, the significance assigned to the commercial potential of research findings, how to distribute credit for work completed by multiple authors, alternative interpretations of what constitutes legitimate research (perhaps along the lines suggested by Ernest Boyer and others), and so on. Few assessment proponents are yet able to offer much specific guidance in such matters, except to urge that the overall assessment of a person's work should be "broad and rich and varied," and ought to include self-evaluations, peer reviews, and, where appropriate, student opinions.[39]

As recognition grows that teaching, no less than research, should be assessed, increasing attention is being given to ways of evaluating instructional quality.[40] Student course evaluations have been most often relied on, though it is now suggested more and more frequently that some form of faculty peer review would be equally useful. But the very notion of peer review makes some faculty members nervous, immediately conjuring up images of intrusive classroom visitations by judgmental colleagues. Traditionally, teaching has been considered a private activity; and some faculty members find the prospect of evaluators sitting in on a lecture intimidating.[41] Classroom observation, however, is not the only method of conducting a peer review. Alternatives might involve the submission of a videotape for later viewing, or assembling and submitting a teaching portfolio containing copies of course syllabi, tests, class handouts, and other relevant documentation.[42]

The fact that much of what an academic does involves solitary pursuits conducted in isolation from others oftentimes can make the assessment task difficult.[43] But even the more "public" activities of student advisement, consulting, and professional service serve to introduce complications in assessing faculty performance. "Internal service" as an assessment rubric or category is apt to encompass everything from advising students and directing theses and doctoral dissertations to serving on various committees at any institutional level. Assessment criteria in these areas are both ambiguous and difficult to apply rigorously.

The sheer range of external professional service activities faculty members are likely to engage in makes qualitative judgments equally hard to come by. Depending on his or her field of expertise and interests, for example, a faculty member might be found consulting and lending technical assistance to business and industry, working with governmental and community service agencies, serving as an expert witness for legislative hearings, collaborating with schools and civic organizations, sitting on committees of professional and academic societies and associations, administering summer arts programs, editing newsletters or journals—the list of possibilities goes on and on.

Inevitably perhaps, the complexity of the task of trying to render faculty members accountable for their activities in some objective format gives rise to documentation procedures that are as tedious as they are complex. The ever-increasing record keeping and paperwork involved, faculty are wont to complain, is almost enough to drive them to their knees in despair. As efforts to refine evaluation increase, so also do the length and detail of the assessment instruments required. Significantly, whether faculty productivity studies actually enhance the quality of work accomplished remains open to question and dispute. Whether great mounds of data generated through the process conduce to more precise comparisons and thus more equitable personnel decisions is likewise uncertain.

If faculty performance auditing genuinely advances the cause of accountability, it most likely does so only indirectly, and in ways rarely recognized or acknowledged. The real virtue of the assessment process, perhaps, is not that it identifies more precisely what it is faculty do or even how well they do it. Rather, its contribution lies in serving to highlight critical features of the work environment within which faculty activities take place. If the institution professes to value teaching as much as research, for example, and proposes to reward the former as well as the latter, it becomes important to enhance a supportive teaching culture within the unit, to devise specific ways of reinforcing the message that instructional excellence is not only valued but will be rewarded. Conversely, what needs to be avoided is the situation cynical faculty most often cite: The institution claims to honor teaching, but when it comes time to award a salary increase, only the year's publications count.

"Good citizenship" and collegiality are sometimes cited as attributes faculty colleagues especially prize in one another. But if those qualities affect peer performance reviews—that is, if they figure in tenure and promotion decisions—it is all the more important to scrutinize the institution's culture in order to identify factors within it that hinder or promote just those habitual characteristics. If productive interaction among colleagues is the goal, it becomes important to ascertain whether faculty competition is encouraged at the expense of cooperation. When collaborative endeavors are said to be deserving of reward, it is vital to identify whatever factors might work to isolate faculty members from one another and draw them apart, thereby making shared ventures unlikely.

Once again, if a generalized attitude of concern and solicitude toward students is valued by the faculty unit, it is important to devise ways of minimizing interfering distractions and to free up more time for faculty to devote to students. Minimally, the institution cannot properly claim to value a faculty member for having a strong student orientation, on the one hand, and then fail to reward or acknowledge that individual because he or she pays too much attention to students, on the other. In short, *what the act of assessment properly conducted can accomplish is to underscore the importance of keeping the reward system and the actual work environment fully congruent with one another.* The aim should be to encourage a closer articulation or linkage between the evaluative performance criteria that dominate faculty assessments with those specific activities faculty are most strongly encouraged by the surrounding environment to pursue.

ACCOUNTABILITY AND SOCIAL RESPONSIBILITY

The accountability movement in American higher education is likely to be a prominent force in academe for years to come. In its least sophisticated manifestations, it is a social and cultural force serving chiefly to encourage the much-criticized practice of "bean counting." Phrasing the same point a little differently, the most primitive form of assessment yields little more than simpleminded quantitative judgments about institutional and individual performances of great internal complexity. The tacit assumption throughout is that somehow the *qualitative* value of someone's work performance is exhausted by a specification of all of its *quantitative* features.

Academics will tolerate this kind of assessment measurement as an unavoidable irritant they must contend with in exchange for whatever academic autonomy and freedom society affords them in their work. As a matter of fact, they usually have no choice in the matter. What they will refuse to do—and rightly so—is to take its rites and rituals seriously. Even today, the inclination of many faculty members is to treat institutional and individual evaluation as an empty charade, a hollow exercise devoid of meaning. Among its staunchest opponents, the entire accountability movement is perceived to be an imposition lacking legitimacy. Less extreme (and to some extent well justified) is the claim that in the final analysis—literally—only so much can be weighed and measured. Ultimately, *the efficacy and quality of faculty work involve imponderables not reducible to any meaningful quantification.* To suppose otherwise is to give credence to a fiction utterly at odds with the complex reality of academic life.

The questions with which the search for both institutional and individual accountability begins are entirely understandable. It seems to make sense to demand of a social institution such as a college or university that it at least try to give evidence for its effectiveness in achieving certain ends. The parallel requirement that faculty members make a good-faith effort to render an accounting of their performance also seems justifiable. What is not defensible or warranted is the expectation that responses to questions posed about how academics and their institutions function can be any more specific or precise than the character and complexity of the academic enterprise allow.

VII.

A CONCLUDING POSTSCRIPT

Higher education in the United States in the closing years of the twentieth century has become a gargantuan enterprise, currently encompassing schooling at the postsecondary level for about 14.5 million or more students, attending close to 4,000 different institutions, employing upward of 900,000 or more faculty members and staff, at an estimated cost approaching $175 billion yearly.[1] Yet, paradoxically, at a time when more and more people are attending colleges and universities, and academic credentials are being pursued on a scale virtually without historical precedent, there is near-universal acknowledgment that these are troubled times for the academy. Indicative of the current climate are revelations that, according to opinion polls, the public's confidence in higher education, while still basically positive, has dropped nearly 60 percent over the past three decades.[2]

The century's last decade or so has proven itself to be an exceedingly unstable era for higher education, marked as it has been by rising tuition costs, diminished financial aid, a soft job market for college graduates, a high rate of white-collar unemployment, and a constant effort on the part of academic institutions to garner essential resources while cutting costs. Colleges and universities routinely struggle to make ends meet, simultaneously attempting to respond to volatile demographic changes—fluctuations in traditional student cohorts, periodic enrollment declines punctuated unexpectedly by periodic and temporary enrollment upswings, an emergence of new constituencies, and a seeming oversupply of graduates.[3]

Fiscal shortfalls in recent years have been especially severe among public colleges and universities (collectively enrolling nearly four-fifths of all students), although private sector institutions have experienced similar problems. Reduced legislative appropriations in many states, coupled with lower federal outlays for student scholarships and loan programs, have caused most public academic institutions to undergo successive rounds of budget cuts. Whereas enrollments among traditional and graduate students showed a modest increase overall at the decade's midpoint, fully one-fifth of all four-year schools saw enrollment declines relative to the levels achieved in the late 1980s and in the early 1990s. Where real growth occurred, much of it was accounted for by larger numbers of part-time and older students enrolling. Transfers between schools are increasingly common, as are students attending school on a part-time basis; and the length of time needed for the average undergraduate to complete the bachelor's degree is now closer to five years than to the traditional four-year period of yesteryear.

Economic exigency has translated into an "affordability" crisis for many potential college-goers. Costs incurred by colleges and universities for operations, equipment, and facilities clearly have begun to exceed the tuition that many students can afford to pay; in fact, an ever-increasing percentage reportedly need full financial support in order to attend at all. During the 1980s, for example, the median tuition at public and private colleges and universities increased at annual rates of about 5 and 6 percent, respectively, over the Consumer Price Index (CPI). By the mid-1990s, the cost per student in public universities was increasing approximately 3 percent above the CPI, at a time when state appropriations were increasing at an annual rate of less than half a percent. Hence revenues from higher student demand were failing to offset increasing expenses, resulting in financial retrenchment at all but a fortunate few institutions.

Facing severe budget deficits, academic leaders in recent years have resorted to curtailing or eliminating faculty positions and academic programs lacking high demand. When new faculty are hired, the trend has been toward recruiting entry-level candidates for full-time positions and hiring lower-cost part-time faculty wherever possible. Fiscal problems have served to accelerate the movement to assess higher education outcomes, including the work of individual faculty members. To some extent, colleges and universities have begun to heed calls from policymakers for measures aimed at enhancing the quality of undergraduate education, improving instruction, and appraising faculty productivity.

But just as often, as many have commented, in today's environment "institutions give equal or greater weight to implementing sophisticated marketing techniques that increase the yield of paying 'customers.' These 'consumerist' strategies emphasize extracurricular activities and other amenities, not academic rigor. Faculty members are encouraged or pressured to eschew professional norms for utilitarianism—treating their students as *consumers* to be won over by wit and charm, as much as by pedagogy and expertise."[4]

Hard times have tended to lend urgency to calls for reform, some of them well intended, some not. Faculty workloads, for example, are being scrutinized more closely than ever, usually with a view toward increasing teaching assignments while reducing professorial autonomy. Assessment analyses have grown more sophisticated, or at least more complex, fastening on the minutiae of faculty workweek length and numbers of hours devoted to teaching, research, advising, service, and administration. Meanwhile, scathing indictments of academic tenure, counterbalanced by impassioned defenses of the institution, seem more frequent than ever.[5] Nor has faculty job security alone been singled out for attention. Virtually all aspects of academic life have come under review, and to a degree almost unimaginable just a few short years ago. Much of the debate taking place within the academy— the sheer fact that it exists—must be reckoned a healthy exercise in critical self-examination.

Whether all of the scrutiny higher education seems to be undergoing will prove productive and useful in terms of producing specific and tangible results, however, remains to be seen. On one side, the results could be negative if external constituencies try to intervene in ways that serve to deprive colleges and universities of their traditional autonomy in matters of teaching, curriculum development, and research. On the other, if closer public surveillance galvanizes the professoriate to bestir itself and to seize the initiative in helping to effect needed changes, the outcome could be extremely beneficial.

One encouraging harbinger is to be found in indications of an emergent consensus on behalf of the idea that questions of basic institutional *purpose* must frame the reform agenda in higher education for the years ahead. Ernest Boyer, writing in the late 1980s, observed, "Scrambling for students and driven by marketplace demands, many undergraduate colleges have lost their sense of mission. They are confused about their mission and how to impart shared values on which the vitality of both higher education and society depend. The disciplines have fragmented themselves into smaller and smaller pieces, and under-graduates find it difficult to see patterns in their courses or to relate what they learn to life."[6] Growing awareness of confusion over purposes may be an essential first step toward dispelling some of the ambiguity and uncertainty surrounding academic goals.

Clear and consistent institutional objectives, a clear definition of what the academic institution is about, declares Arthur Chickering of George Mason University, is "critically important" in higher education today. Much more attention must be paid, he asserts, to the question of what the undergraduate degree means in today's world; and that meaning must be stated more explicitly in terms of the ways students are intended to be affected and changed as a result of completing a degree program.[7]

As Chickering puts it, institutional objectives must be taken seriously. They need to become part of the "working knowledge" of all parties involved; and when they are, in multiple ways they can help create more "educationally powerful" environments. In the first place, policies, programs, and practices take on greater internal coherence and consistency when there are shared undergirding purposes, objectives, and values. Second, clear objectives can assist students in clarifying their own reasons for coming to the institution and their own purposes while they are there. The result should be improved self-selectivity, improved retention, and increased degree completion rates. Third, shared institutional value commitments can of themselves become objects of analysis, discussion, debate, challenge, and modification.[8] Students learn through the process of making institutional purposes explicit; ideally, they can become more conscious and flexible in integrating such objectives as part of their own experience.

Charles Karelis, director of the Fund for the Improvement of Postsecondary Education, argues for those who believe that the social meanings attached to the bachelor's degree are so broad and so divergent in today's society that it would be nearly impossible to capture them in some inclusive and explicit formulation.[9] Chickering and many others would disagree. All colleges and universities, he avows, irrespective of their particular mission and particular clientele, should seek to identify and teach for the core competencies and human characteristics required for successful careers, responsible citizenship, and a good life.[10] In principle, identifying the knowledge, skills, and dispositions students need most in order to increase their prospects of living rich, useful, and productive lives in the early twenty-first century ought not to lie beyond human imagination and ingenuity.

One measure of how far colleges and universities have to go is vividly illustrated by how college catalogs describe degree programs—with lists of required or recommended courses and numbers of credit hours demanded. Rarely if ever are explanations supplied of the meaning or purpose of any particular degree program, and still less often are there specifications of what students are intended to know or appreciate or be aware of or have the ability to do as a result of having pursued any particular program. Nor are such explanations something faculty seem comfortable discussing with students. The external machinery of degree programs is featured prominently; the purposes the machinery serves—or is supposed to serve—are hardly mentioned at all.

The American professoriate, it is to be hoped, will resist adamantly any externally imposed definitions and expectations as an infringement on academic freedom, most particularly if they turn out to be crabbed, narrowly conceived, and limiting of human potential. A uniform and codified set of competencies presumed applicable to all would be both unwise and inherently unworkable. Nor, of course, is it to be expected that the full meaning and purpose of the undergraduate experience can ever be exhausted by some simplistic specification of skill development and reductive performance competencies. But to suppose that even in theory the task of restoring integrity to the curriculum and conferring some specific meaning to the baccalaureate degree at individual institutions exceeds the bounds of possibility does a grave disservice to those already engaged in the effort.[11] Moreover, appreciation is growing for the fact that many colleges and universities *do* have the capacity to transform themselves, to redefine themselves as authentic "learning communities," if and when they summon the will to attempt the process.[12]

Institutions of higher learning, notes Donald Stewart, president of the College Board, always have served the private end of personal economic achievement. Historically, colleges and universities have needed to be responsive to short-term outcomes and students' immediate demands for so-called practical learning.[13] But his fear is that the tendency to emphasize short-term results has grown so pronounced within academe as to hinder the capacity of academic leaders to imagine or assign any larger or more generous significance to higher learning.

Higher education must continue to pose for itself questions about its purpose and agenda, particularly the meaning of the baccalaureate degree. The most urgent need, he argues, is to invent "systemic means for surveying higher education's contributions to public discourse, to the generation of multiple perspectives, to a resistance to presentism, to creative imaginations and perceptive feelings, and to renewed application of the intellectual life to our daunting social challenges."[14] The point is well taken. Without some larger vision, some sense for the multiple purposes higher learning can and should serve, the alternative is likely to be simply more of the same—a popular but increasingly dysfunctional system of higher education, one ultimately ill-suited to meeting the challenges of the century ahead.

NOTES

Preface

1. See Stephen H. Balch, "Political Correctness or Public Choice?" *Educational Record* 73 (Winter, 1992): 21.
2. Note the discussion in Thomas Toch, "Raising Our Academic Sights," *College Board Review* 162 (Winter, 1991-92): 22-27, 37.
3. Jaroslav Pelikan, *The Idea of the University, A Reexamination* (New Haven, CT: Yale University Press, 1992), p. 12.
4. Cited in Eric Ashby, "The University Ideal: A View from Britain," in Clark Kerr et al., *The University in America* (Santa Barbara, CA: Center for the Study of Democratic Institutions, 1967), pp. 29-30.

Chapter I

1. See Kevin J. Dougherty, *The Contradictory College* (Albany, NY: State University of New York Press, 1994), pp. 5-7; and Billie Wright Dziech and William R. Vilter, eds., *Prisoners of Elitism: The Community College's Struggle for Stature* (San Francisco: Jossey-Bass, 1992).
2. William Zumeta, "State Policies and Private Higher Education," *Journal of Higher Education* 63 (July/August, 1992): 363-417.
3. Consult David S. Guthrie, "Mapping the Terrain of Church-Related Colleges and Universities," *New Directions for Higher Education* 79 (Fall, 1992): 3-27; and Kenneth W. Shipps, "Church-Related Colleges and Academies," *New Directions for Higher Education* 79 (Fall, 1992): 29-54.
4. Henry G. Badger, "Higher Education Statistics: 1870-1952," *Higher Education* 11 (September, 1954): 10-15; and Toby Oxtoby et al., "Enrollment and Graduation Trends from Grade School to Ph.D., 1899-1973," *School and Society* 76 (1955): 225-231.
5. Carnegie Foundation for the Advancement of Teaching, *A Statistical Portrait of Higher Education* (Berkeley, CA: Carnegie Commission on Higher Education, 1972), p. 41.
6. National Center for Education Statistics, *Projections of Education Statistics to 2003* (Washington, D.C.: U.S. Department of Education, Office of Educational

Research and Improvement, 1992), p. xiii; Chronicle of Higher Education, eds., *Almanac of Higher Education 1994* (Chicago: University of Chicago Press, 1994), p. 76. Totals reported in the *Chronicle of Higher Education Almanac 41* (September 1, 1994), p. 1, vary slightly from figures reported elsewhere.

7. National Center for Education Statistics, p. xiii.

8. National Center for Education Statistics, p. xii; and Chronicle of Higher Education, eds., p. 42.

9. See Raymond Walters, *Four Decades of U.S. Collegiate Enrollments* (New York: Society for the Advancement of Education, 1960); and Calvin B. T. Lee, *The Campus Scene, 1900-1979* (New York: David McKay, 1970), pp. 75ff.

10. Clark Kerr et al., *Troubled Times for American Higher Education* (Albany: State University of New York Press, 1994), p. 118.

11. See Charles J. Anderson, *A Fact Book on Higher Education* (New York: Macmillan, 1989), pp. 5-9, 133-145; and Thomas D. Snyder et al., *Digest of Educational Statistics 1993* (Washington, D.C.: National Center for Educational Statistics, October, 1993), pp. 172-223.

12. Raymond Walters, "Statistics of Attendance in American Universities and Colleges, 1949," *School and Society* 70 (December, 1949): 392; Educational Policies Commission, *Higher Education in a Decade of Decision* (Washington, D.C.: National Education Association, 1957), pp. 4-5, 31-32; Charles J. Anderson, *Fact Book on Higher Education* (Washington, D.C.: American Council on Education, 1968), p. 809; and Martin Trow, "American Higher Education: Past, Present, and Future," *Educational Researcher* 15 (April, 1988): 13-15.

13. Carnegie Foundation, p. 43.

14. Kerr et al., pp. 118-119; and Chronicle of Higher Education, eds., p. 44.

15. "Fact File: Projections of College Enrollment, Degrees, and High-School Graduates, 1993 to 2004," *Chronicle of Higher Education* (January 19, 1994): A34.

16. National Center for Education Statistics, p. xi.

17. Chronicle of Higher Education, eds., p. xi.

18. Marjorie O. Chandler and M. C. Rice, *Opening Fall Enrollment in Higher Education,* 1967 (Washington, D.C.: United States Office of Education, 1967), pp. 52-134; and "White, Negro Undergraduates at Colleges," *Chronicle of Higher Education* (April 22, 1968): 3-4.

19. S. Arbeiter, "Black Enrollments: The Case of the Missing Students," *Change* 19 (May/June, 1987): 14-19; R. Allen, "Black Colleges v. White Colleges," *Change* 19 (May/June, 1987): 28-31; N. Joyce Payne, "The Role of Black Colleges in an Expanding Economy," *Educational Record* 68 (Fall, 1987/Winter, 1988): 104-106.

20. Kerr et al., p. 118.

21. "Number of Minority Students in Colleges Rose by 9% from 1990 to 1991, U.S. Reports," *Chronicle of Higher Education* 39 (January 20, 1993): A30.

22. Chronicle of Higher Education, eds., p. 58.

23. Kerr et al., p. 119.

24. "Plus Ça Change: The Annual Report on the Economic Status of the Profession, 1993-94," *Academe* 80 (March-April, 1994): 26.

25.   See James Michael Brodie, "Whatever Happened to the Job Boom?" *Academe* 81 (January/February, 1995): 12.

Chapter II

1.   R. S. Peters, "Education as Initiation," in Reginald D. Archambault, ed., *Philosophical Analysis and Education* (New York: Humanities Press, 1965), pp. 92-93.

2.   The point is adapted from A. Phillips Griffiths, "A Deduction of Universities," in Archambault, ed., pp. 187-189.

3.   See Elaine El-Khawas, Deborah J. Carter, and Cecilia A. Ottinger, compilers, *1988 Community College Fact Book* (New York: Macmillan, 1988), pp. 7-8.

4.   Figures cited are supplied in Kevin J. Dougherty, *The Contradictory College* (Albany, NY: State University Press of New York, 1994), p. 3.

5.   Consult Leslie Koltai, "Community Colleges: Making Winners Out of Ordinary People," in Arthur Levine, ed., *Higher Learning in America, 1980-2000* (Baltimore: Johns Hopkins Press, 1993), p. 100.

6.   This practice is long-standing. See Eric Ashby, *Any Person, Any Study* (New York: McGraw-Hill, 1971), pp. 9-13.

7.   See Norton W. Grubb, "The Decline of Community College Transfer Rates: Evidence from National Longitudinal Surveys," *Journal of Higher Education* 62 (March/April, 1991): 194-217; and United States Bureau of the Census, *School Enrollment—Social and Economic Characteristics of Students: October, 1991, Current Population Reports,* Series P-20, No. 469 (Washington, D.C.: U.S. Government Printing Office, 1993): 61.

8.   Koltai, pp. 100-102.

9.   The analysis follows Dougherty, chaps 1 and 15. See also Terry O'Banion, "Teaching and Learning: A Mandate for the Nineties," *Community College Journal* 64 (February-March, 1944): 20-25; John Walsh, "It's Off to Work We Go: Why Education Must Be Re-Engineered, " *Community College Journal* 64 (December-January, 1993-94): 34-37; Marlene Griffith and Ann Connor, *Democracy's Open Door: The Community College in America's Future* (Portsmouth, NH: Heinemann, 1994); Allen A. Witt et al., *America's Community Colleges: The First Century* (Washington, D.C.: American Association of Community Colleges, 1994); and George A. Baker et al., eds., *A Handbook on the Community College in America: Its History, Mission, and Management* (Westport, CT: Greenwood Press, 1994).

10.   Dougherty, p. 8.

11.   Ibid., pp. 263-272.

12.   Quoted in Mark H. Curtis, "Crisis and Opportunity: The Founding of AAC," in *Enhancing, Promoting, Extending Liberal Education: AAC at Seventy-Five* (Washington, D.C.: Association of American Colleges, 1988), p. 5.

13.   Carnegie Foundation for the Advancement of Teaching, *Carnegie Foundation Technical Report: A Classification of Institutions of Higher Education*

(Princeton, NJ: Carnegie Foundation for the Advancement of Teaching, 1987), pp. 3-5.

14. See, for example, David W. Breneman, "Are We Losing Our Liberal Arts Colleges?" *AAHE Bulletin* 43 (October, 1990): 3-6.

15. Paul Woodring, *The Higher Learning in America: A Reassessment* (New York: McGraw-Hill, 1968), p. 11.

16. See Allan O. Pfnister, "The American Liberal Arts College in the Eighties: Dinosaur or Phoenix?" in *National Institute of Education/American Association of Higher Education, Contexts for Learning: The Major Sectors of American Higher Education* (Washington, D.C.: U.S. Government Printing Office, 1985), p. 35.

17. Quoted in Page Smith, *Killing the Spirit, Higher Education in America* (New York: Penguin, 1991), pp. 42-43.

18. Ibid., pp. 37-38, 41.

19. E. K. Rand, "Bring Back the Liberal Arts," *Atlantic Monthly* 171 (June, 1943): 80. See also Willis Rudy, *The Evolving Liberal Arts Curriculum: A Historical Review of Basic Themes* (New York: Bureau of Publications, Teachers College, Columbia University, 1960), p. 1.

20. Quoted from Frederick Rudolph, *The American College and University: A History* (New York: Alfred Knopf, 1962), p. 12.

21. Alpheus S. Packard, "The Substance of Two Reports of the Faculty of Amherst College to the Board of Trustees, with the Doings of the Board Thereon," *North American Review* 28 (April, 1829): 300.

22. Carl Becker, *Cornell University* (Ithaca, NY: Cornell University Press, 1943), pp. 19-20.

23. Rudolph, pp. 25-26.

24. Cited in Lawrence R. Veysey, *The Emergence of the American University* (Chicago: University of Chicago Press, 1965), p. 24.

25. Quoted in Rudolph, pp. 133-134.

26. Woodring, p. 15.

27. Quoted in Rudolph, p. 220.

28. Ibid, p. 240.

29. Henry P. Tappan, *University Education* (New York: Putnam's, 1851), pp. 15-16.

30. Charles Eliot Norton, "The Intellectual Life of America," *New Princeton Review* 6 (1888): 323.

31. W. A. Merrill, "The Practical Value of a Liberal Education," *Education* 10 (March, 1890): 441.

32. Alexander Meiklejohn, "College Education and the Moral Ideal," *Education* 28 (May, 1908): 558.

33. See A. Lawrence Lowell, *At War with Academic Traditions in America* (Cambridge, MA: Harvard University Press, 1934), pp. 5-7, 40-41.

34. Consult Samuel Schuman, "A Life in the Liberal Arts," *Liberal Education* 79 (Spring, 1993): 32-37; Edward P. St. John, "The Transformation of Private Liberal Arts Colleges," *Review of Higher Education* 15 (Fall, 1991): 83-106; and Henry H. Crimmel, *The Liberal Arts College and the Ideal of Liberal*

Education: The Case for Radical Reform (Lanham, MD: University Press of America, 1993).

35. See, for example, Robert Zemsky et al., "On Reversing the Ratchet," *Change* 25 (May-June, 1993): 56-62; and Joseph A. Merante and Richard C. Ireland, "The Competitive Edge, Why Some Small Colleges Succeed," *College Board Review* 169 (Fall, 1993): 8-13, 28-29.

36. See Woodring, p. 16; and Veysey, p. 58.

37. An excellent analysis is supplied in Conrad Cherry, "Boundaries and Frontiers for the Study of Religion: The Heritage of the Age of the University," *Journal of the American Academy of Religion* 57 (Winter 1989): 807-827.

38. Quoted in Allan Nevins, *The State Universities and Democracy* (Urbana, IL: University of Illinois Press, 1962), p. 35.

39. Quoted in Veysey, pp. 61, 122.

40. Quoted in W. H. Cowley and Don Williams, *International and Historical Roots of American Higher Education* (New York: Garland, 1991), p. 131.

41. Jonas Viles et al., *The University of Missouri: A Centennial History* (Columbia: University of Missouri Press, 1939), p. 108.

42. Tappan, p. 50.

43. Cited in Richard Hofstadter and W. Smith, *American Higher Education: A Documentary History* (Chicago: University of Chicago Press, 1961), p. 478.

44. Quoted in Smith, p. 63.

45. See Veysey, p. 63.

46. Useful references for this development include Earle D. Ross, *Democracy's College: The Land-Grant Movement in the Formative Stage* (Ames: Iowa State College Press, 1942); Ross, "Contributions of Land-Grant Colleges and Universities to Higher Education," in William W. Brickman and Stanley Lehrer, eds., *A Century of Higher Education: Classical Citadel to Collegiate Colossus* (New York: Society for the Advancement of Education, 1962), pp. 94-109; and James L. Morrill, *The Ongoing State University* (Minneapolis: University of Minnesota Press, 1960).

47. Cited in Christopher J. Lucas, *American Higher Education: A History* (New York: St. Martin's Press, 1994), p. 153.

46. Quoted in Smith, p. 63.

49. Ibid., p. 57.

50. Quoted in Hofstadter and Smith, p. 602.

51. Veysey, pp. 123, 151.

52. Cherry, p. 814.

53. Hofstadter and Smith, p. 493.

54. Note the excellent discussion in John Higham, "The Matrix of Specialization," in Alexandra Oleson and John Voss, eds., *The Organization of Knowledge in Modern America, 1860-1920* (Baltimore: Johns Hopkins University Press, 1979), pp. 3-18.

55. Both quotations appear in Veysey, p. 198.

56. See Cherry, p. 817; and Lucas, pp. 191-194.

57. Karl Jaspers, *The Idea of the University,* ed. Karl Deutsch (London: Peter Owen, 1960), pp. 53-54.

58. Quoted in Woodring, p. 22.

59. Jaroslav Pelikan, *The Idea of the University: A Reexamination* (New Haven, CT.: Yale University Press, 1992), p. 9.

60. Quoted from J. M. Cameron, *On the Idea of a University* (Toronto: St. Michael's College, University of Toronto Press, 1978), p. 15.

61. Newman, *The Idea of the University* (I.v.ii; I.v.iv), quoted from Pelikan, pp. 33-34.

62. Newman (I.vii.i.), quoted from Pelikan, p. 71.

63. Quoted from Cameron, p. 145.

64. Thorstein Veblen, *The Higher Learning in America* (Stanford, CA: Academic Reprints, 1954; originally published by B.W. Huebsch, 1918), p. 17.

65. Ibid., pp. 18, 22, 23, 59.

66. Ibid., pp. 26-27.

67. Ibid., p. 43.

68. Ibid., pp. 32, 33, 39.

69. Robert Maynard Hutchins, "The Issues," in Clark Kerr et al., *The University in America* (Santa Barbara, CA: Center for the Study of Democratic Institutions, 1967), p. 5.

70. Ibid., p. 5.

71. Quoted in Pelikan, p. 104.

72. Hutchins, "The Issues," p. 5.

73. Robert Maynard Hutchins, *The Higher Learning in America* (New Haven, CT: Yale University Press, 1962), pp. xiii-xiv.

74. Hutchins, "The Issues," p. 7.

75. See Hutchins, *The Higher Learning in America,* pp. 4-12.

76. Ibid., p. 36; Hutchins, "The Issues," p. 7.

77. Hutchins, *The Higher Learning in America,* p. 47.

78. Ibid., pp. 66-67.

79. Robert Maynard Hutchins, *The Learning Society* (New York: Frederick A. Praeger, 1969), pp. 108-109.

80. Clark Kerr, *The Uses of the University* (New York: Harper Torchbooks, 1963), p. vi.

81. Ibid., p. 1.

82. Ibid., pp. 8-9, 6.

83. Ibid., p. 17.

84. Kerr, "Toward the More Perfect University," in Kerr et al., *The University in America,* p. 10.

85. Kerr, *The Uses of the University,* pp. 18, 45, 49.

86. Cameron Fincher, "The Idea of the University in the 21st Century: An American Perspective," *British Journal of Educational Studies* 41 (March, 1993): 28-29.

87. See, for example, Ira Harkavy and John Puckett, "Universities and the Inner Cities," *Planning for Higher Education* 20 (Summer, 1992): 27-33.

88. See Charles Sykes, *Profscam: Professors and the Demise of Higher Education* (Washington, D.C.: Regnery Gateway, 1988); and Sykes, *The Hollow Men: Politics and Corruption in Higher Education* (Washington, D.C.: Regnery Gateway, 1990).

89. Smith, pp. 7, 20, 179, 197-198.

90. Harkavy and Puckett, pp. 27, 33.

91. See Ernest Lynton, *Making the Case for Professional Service* (Washington, D.C.: American Association for Higher Education, 1995).

92. Cited in *Campus Compact, The Project for Public and Community Service* (Denver: Education Commission of the States, 1995): 5.

93. Eric Ashby, "The University Ideal: A View from Britain," in Kerr et al., *The University in America,* p. 33.

Chapter III

1. Stephen H. Balch, "Political Correctness or Public Choice?" *Educational Record* 73 (Winter, 1992): 21.

2. John S. Brubacher, *Bases for Policy in Higher Education* (New York: McGraw-Hill, 1965), p. 2.

3. See Brand Blanshard, "Democracy and Distinction in American Education," in Sterling M. McMurrin, ed., *On the Meaning of the University* (Salt Lake City: University of Utah Press, 1976), p. 29.

4. Frederick Rudolph, *The American College and University* (New York: Vintage, 1962), p. 282.

5. Ibid., p. 289.

6. Ibid., p. 260.

7. Laurence R. Veysey, *The Emergence of the American University* (Chicago: University of Chicago Press, 1965), p. 237.

8. Ibid., p. 357.

9. Ibid., p. 272.

10. See W. T. Foster, "Our Democratic American Colleges," *Nation* 88 (1909): 325; and Foster, "The Gentleman's Grade," *Educational Review* 33 (1907): 386-392.

11. Veysey, pp. 100,143, 211.

12. Henry Rosovsky, *The University: An Owner's Manual* (New York: W.W. Norton & Company, 1990), p. 61.

13. Robert Solomon and Jon Solomon, *Up the University: Re-Creating Higher Education in America* (Reading, MA: Addison-Wesley, 1993), p. 77.

14. Eric Ashby, "Reconciliation of Tradition and Modernity in Universities," in McMurrin, pp. 19-20.

15. Solomon and Solomon, p. 78.

16. See Gail A. Kluepfel, "Developing Successful Retention Programs: An Interview with Michael Hovland," *Journal of Developmental Education* 17 (Spring, 1974): 28-33.

17. William A. Henry, "In Defense of Elitism," *Time* (August 29, 1994): 65; excerpted from Henry, *In Defense of Elitism* (New York: Doubleday, 1994).

18. The treatment and examples are adapted from Brubacher, pp. 2-13.

19. Abraham Flexner, *Universities: English, German, American* (Fair Lawn, NJ: Oxford University Press, 1930), p. 338.

20. Quoted in Brubacher, p. 8.

21. Ibid., pp. 9-10.

22. Henry Seidel Canby, *Alma Mater* (New York: Farrar, Straus & Giroux, 1936), pp. 80-81.

23. Quoted in Robert M. Hutchins, "The Issues," in Clark Kerr et al., *The University in America* (Santa Barbara, CA.: Center for the Study of Democratic Institutions, 1967), p. 6.

24. Peter Schrag, "Open Admissions to What," in Philip Rever, ed., *Open Admissions and Equal Access* (Iowa City, IA: American College Testing Program, 1971), pp. 49ff.

25. Henry, *In Defense of Elitism,* p. 63.

26. Ibid., p. 63.

27. Ibid., p. 64.

28. Ibid., p. 64.

29. W. Timothy Weaver, "Educated Beyond Our Intelligence," *Journal of Education* 168 (1986): 56-57.

30. Consult T. R. McConnell, "Surfeit or Dearth of Highly Educated People?" in McMurrin, pp. 63-80.

31. W. Timothy Weaver, *The Contest for Educational Resources* (Lexington, MA.: Lexington/D.C. Heath, 1982).

32. Henry, *In Defense of Elitism,* p. 65.

33. Blanshard, p. 36.

34. Henry, *In Defense of Elitism,* p. 65.

35. John Leo, "A University's Sad Decline," *U.S. News & World Report* (August 15, 1994): 20.

36. W. A. Kaplan, "The College and the Students," in *The Law of Higher Education* (San Francisco: Jossey-Bass, 1990), pp. 229-252.

37. Weaver, "Educated Beyond Our Intelligence," p. 53.

38. Ibid., pp. 53-54.

39. Ibid., pp. 56-57.

40. Henry, *In Defense of Elitism,* p. 65. Consult also Jerry R. Wilder and James R. Somers, Jr., "A Recurring Dilemma: Open vs. Selective Admissions," *Contemporary Education* 55 (Fall, 1953): 9-12; Carnegie Council on Policy Studies in Higher Education, *Selective Admissions in Higher Education* (San Francisco: Jossey-Bass, 1977); W. L. Morse, "Who Should Decide Who Goes to College?" in Rever, ed., pp. 5-16; and W. W. Willingham and H. M. Breland, "The Status of Selective Admissions," in Carnegie Council, pp. 69-74.

41. Blanshard, p. 48. The length to which higher education is urged to go in keeping students in college is discussed in Mary K. Kinnick, "Student Retention: Moving from Numbers to Action," *Research in Higher Education* 34 (February, 1993): 55-69.

42. For a summary of relevant research findings, consult Ernest T. Pascarella and Patrick T. Terenzini, *How College Affects Students* (San Francisco: Jossey-Bass, 1991), pp. 286-290.

43. Ibid., pp. 558-559, 560.

44. Ibid., p. 563.

45. Thomas Verner Smith, *The American Philosophy of Equality* (Chicago: University of Chicago Press, 1927), pp. 308-309.

46. Balch, p. 24. See William T. Yates, "Equity Management: Affirmative Action for the 21st Century," *Change* 25 (March-April, 1993): 40-43; Beth Dietz-Uhler and Audrey J. Murrell, "Resistance to Affirmative Action: A Test of Four Explanatory Models," *Journal of College Student Development* 34 (September, 1993): 352-357; and Theodore Cross, "Suppose There Was No Affirmative Action at the Most Prestigious Colleges and Graduate Schools," *Journal of Blacks in Higher Education* 3 (Spring, 1994): 44-51.

47. Dinesh D'Souza, *Illiberal Education: The Politics of Race and Sex on Campus* (New York: Vintage, 1992), p. 186.

48. Ibid., p. 251.

49. See Richard Kahlenberg, "Class, Not Race," *New Republic* 212 (April 3, 1995): 21-27.

50. D'Souza, p. 253. The contrary position is well argued for by Dana Y. Takagi, "We Should Not Make Class a Proxy for Race," *Chronicle of Higher Education* (May 5, 1995): A52.

51. The example is adapted from Kahlenberg, p. 24.

52. Ibid., p. 25.

53. Henry, *In Defense of Elitism*, p. 65.

Chapter IV

1. J. M. Cameron, *On the Idea of a University* (Toronto: St. Michael's College, University of Toronto Press, 1978), p. 44; and W. B. Carnochan, *The Battleground of the Curriculum* (Stanford, CA: Stanford University Press, 1993), pp. 3-4.

2. Benjamin R. Barber, *An Aristocracy of Everyone, The Politics of Education and the Future of America* (New York: Ballantine, 1992), pp. 8-9.

3. Carnochan, pp. 6-7.

4. See Frederick Rudolph, *Curriculum: A History of the American Undergraduate Course of Study Since 1636* (San Francisco: Jossey-Bass, 1977).

5. See David Andrew Weaver, ed., *Builders of American Universities: Inaugural Addresses* (Alton, IL.: Shurtleff Press, 1950), pp. 16, 23ff.; the text also is reproduced in Charles W. Eliot, *Educational Reform* (Englewood Cliffs, NJ: Prentice-Hall, 1898), p. 1.

6. Eliot, in Weaver, p. 24.

7. On the changes introduced at Harvard, and the reactions that ensued, see LeBaron R. Briggs, "President Eliot, as Seen by a Disciple," *Atlantic Monthly* 144 (November, 1929): 597; R. M. Wenley, "The Classics and the Elective System," *School Review* 18 (October, 1910): 518; Andrew F. West, "Must the Classics Go?" *North American Review* 138 (February, 1884): 152-159; James

McCosh, *New Departure in College Education* (New York: Scribner, 1885), especially pp. 4ff.; Noah Porter, *The American College and the American Public,* 2nd ed. (New Haven, CT: C. C. Chatfield, 1870), pp. 15-16; and Richard R. Bowker, "The College of Today," *Princeton Review* 13 (January, 1884): 93.

8.   McCosh, pp. 4, 12, 22.

9.   Quoted in Thomas Woody, *History of Women's Education in the United States,* vol. 2 (Lancaster, PA: Science Press, 1929), p. 220.

10.   Porter, p. 103.

11.   Andrew West, *A Review of President Eliot's Report on Elective Studies* (New York: J. K. Lees, 1886), p. 14.

12.   Quoted in Carnochan, p. 17.

13.   Quoted ibid., p. 18.

14.   Porter, pp. 35-36.

15.   See Hazen C. Carpenter, "Emerson, Eliot, and the Elective System," *New England Quarterly* 24 (March, 1951): 13-34; D. E. Phillips, "The Elective System in American Education," *Pedagogical Seminary* 8 (June, 1901): 210-212; Charles F. Adams, Jr., *A College Fetish* (Boston: Lee and Shepard, 1883), pp. 18ff; William S. Gray, *Provision for the Individual in College Education* (Chicago: University of Chicago Press, 1932), pp. 14ff.; and George W. Pierson, "The Elective System and the Difficulties of College Planning, 1870-1940," *Journal of General Education* 4 (April, 1950): 165.

16.   David Starr Jordan, *The Voice of the Scholar* (San Francisco: Paul Elder, 1903), p. 58.

17.   An instructive reference is Russell Thomas, *The Search for a Common Learning: General Education, 1800-1960* (New York: McGraw-Hill, 1962).

18.   John Dewey, *The Educational Situation* (Chicago: University of Chicago Press, 1902), pp. 85-86.

19.   Frederick Rudolph, *The American College and University: A History* (New York: Vintage, 1955), p. 455.

20.   Note the review in Hoyt Trowbridge, "Forty Years of General Education," *Journal of General Education* 11 (July, 1958): 161-169.

21.   Alexander Meiklejohn, "The Unity of the Curriculum," *New Republic* 32 (October 25, 1922): 2-3.

22.   See Chauncey S. Boucher, *The Chicago College Plan* (Chicago: University of Chicago Press, 1935); and Reuben Frodin, *The Idea and Practice of General Education* (Chicago: University of Chicago Press, 1951), pp. 87-122.

23.   See David Boroff, "St. John's College: Four Years with the Great Books," *Saturday Review* 46 (March 23, 1963): 58-61; and Christopher Jencks and David Riesman, *The Academic Revolution* (New York: Doubleday, 1968), pp. 494 ff.

24.   Donald P. Cottrell, "General Education in Experimental Liberal Arts Colleges," in Guy Montrose Whipple, ed., *General Education in the American College,* Part II, *The Thirty-Eighth Yearbook of the National Society for the Study of Education* (Bloomington, IL: Public School Publishing Company, 1939), pp. 206-207. See also F. R. Leavis, "Great Books and a Liberal Education," *Commentary* 16 (September, 1953): 224-232.

25. Quoted in Gerald Grant and David Riesman, "St. John's and the Great Books," *Change* 6 (May, 1974): 30.

26. Ernest L. Boyer and Arthur Levine, "A Quest for Common Learning," *Change* 13 April, 1981): 30.

27. Alvin C. Eurich, "A Renewed Emphasis Upon General Education," in Whipple, ed., p. 6.

28. Report of the Harvard Committee, *General Education in a Free Society* (Cambridge, MA: Harvard University Press, 1945), pp. 4, 39.

29. Ibid., pp. 40, 51, 64, 93, 145.

30. Gresham Riley, "The Reform of General Education," *Liberal Education* 66 (Fall, 1980): 299.

31. Horace M. Kallen, *The Education of Free Men* (New York: Farrar, Straus & Giroux, 1949), pp. 88-89, 316-318.

32. Ibid., p. 317.

33. See T. R. McConnell, "General Education: An Analysis," in Nelson B. Henry, ed., *General Education, The Fifty-First Yearbook of the National Society for the Study of Education,* Part I (Chicago: University of Chicago Press, 1952), pp. 4-13; Horace T. Morse, "Liberal and General Education: A Problem of Differentiation," in James G. Rice, ed., *General Education, Current Ideas and Concerns* (Washington, D.C.: Association for Higher Education, National Education Association, 1964), pp. 7-12; and Horace T. Morse, "Liberal and General Education—Partisans or Partners?" *Junior College Journal* 24 (March, 1954): 395-399.

34. Daniel Bell, *The Reforming of General Education* (New York: Columbia University Press, 1966).

35. Wayne C. Booth, ed., *The Knowledge Most Worth Having* (Chicago: University of Chicago Press, 1967), pp. 2-3, 7-8, 21.

36. Richard McKeon, "The Battle of the Books," in Booth, ed., pp. 21-23, 170-172, 194-195.

37. Ibid., p. 183.

38. Boyer and Levine, p. 30. See also the fuller exposition in Ernest L. Boyer and Arthur Levine, *A Quest for Common Learning* (New York: Carnegie Foundations for the Advancement of Teaching, 1981).

39. Willis D. Weatherford, "Commission on Liberal Learning," *Liberal Education* 57 (March, 1971): 37.

40. Carnegie Foundation for the Advancement of Teaching, *Missions of the College Curriculum* (San Francisco: Jossey-Bass, 1977), p. 11.

41. Robert Paul Wolff, *The Ideal of the University* (Boston: Beacon Press, 1969); Brand Blanshard, *The Uses of a Liberal Education* (LaSalle, IL.: Open Court, 1973); Christopher Jencks and David Riesman, *The Academic Revolution* (Chicago: University of Chicago Press, 1977).

42. Refer to Robert H. Chambers, "Educating for Perspective—A Proposal," *Change* 13 (September, 1981): 46; and Barry O'Connell, "Where Does Harvard Lead Us," *Change* 10 (September, 1978): 38.

43. Edward Joseph Shoben, Jr., "The Liberal Arts And Contemporary Society: The 1970's," *Liberal Education* 56 (March, 1970): 28-38.

44. Ibid., pp. 30-31.

45. Frank R. Harrison, "The Pervasive Peanut," *Modern Age* 23 (Winter, 1979): 78.

46. Herbert I. London, "The Politics of the Core Curriculum," *Change* 10 (September, 1978): 11.

47. Chambers, p. 48.

48. Samuel Lubell, "The Fragmentation of Knowledge," in Sidney Hook et al., eds., The *Idea of a Modern University* (Buffalo, NY: Prometheus, 1974), pp. 93, 94.

49. Cited in Jürgen Herbst, "The Liberal Arts: Overcoming the Legacy of the Nineteenth Century," *Liberal Education* 66 (Spring, 1980): 24-25; and subsequently rephrased in Henry Rosovsky, *The University: An Owner's Manual* (New York: W. W. Norton, 1990), pp. 105-107ff.

50. See Stephen J. Makler and Robert J. Munnelly, "Harvard in the 1980's: A Question of Adaptability," *Educational Leadership* 37 (January, 1980): 304-306.

51. Quoted in ibid., p. 305.

52. See Alie Abel, "Liberal Learning: A Tradition with a Future," *Liberal Education* 64 (May, 1978): 117; and Chambers, p. 49.

53. Quoted and discussed in Kenneth R. R. Gros Louis, "General Education: Rethinking the Assumptions," *Change* 13 (September, 1981): 35ff.

54. Jerry Gaff, "Reconstituting General Education: Lessons from Project GEM," *Change* 13 (September, 1981): 53. See also Gaff, "General Education for a Contemporary Context," in *New Models for General Education, Current Issues in Higher Education* No. 4 (Washington, D.C.: American Association for Higher Education, 1980), pp. 1-5.

55. Theodore D. Lockwood, "A Skeptical Look at the General Education Movement," *Forum for Liberal Education* (November, 1978): 1-2.

56. Examples included William J. Bennett, *To Reclaim a Legacy: A Report on the Humanities in Higher Education* (Washington, D.C.: National Endowment for the Humanities, 1984); Arthur Levine, *Handbook on Undergraduate Curriculum* (San Francisco: Jossey-Bass, 1978); Gary Miller, *The Meaning of General Education* (New York: Teachers College Press, 1988); Study Group on the Conditions of Excellence in American Higher Education, *Involvement in Learning: Realizing the Potential of American Higher Education* (Washington, D.C.: National Institute of Education, 1984); Lynne Cheney, *50 Hours: A Core Curriculum for College Students* (Washington, D.C.: National Endowment for the Humanities, 1989); E. D. Hirsch, Jr., *Cultural Literacy: What Every American Needs to Know* (New York: Random House, 1987); Allan Bloom, *The Closing of the American Mind: How Higher Education Has Failed Democracy and Impoverished the Souls of Today's Students* (New York: Simon and Schuster, 1987); Association of American Colleges, *Integrity in the College Curriculum* (Washington, D.C.: Association of American Colleges, 1985); Association of American Colleges, *New Vitality in General Education* (Washington, D.C.: Association of American Colleges, 1988); and Association of American Colleges, *The Challenge of Connecting Learning* (Washington, D.C.: Association of American Colleges, 1990).

57. See C. Wegener, *Liberal Education and the Modern University* (Chicago: University of Chicago Press, 1978); Michael Simpson, "The Case for the Liberal Arts," *Liberal Education* 66 (Fall, 1980): 315-319; and David G. Winter et al., *A New Case for the Liberal Arts* (San Francisco: Jossey-Bass, 1981).

58. Quoted in Gros Louis, p. 34.

59. Paul L. Dressel, "Liberal Education: Developing the Characteristics of a Liberally Educated Person," *Liberal Education* 65 (Fall, 1979): 313-322.

60. Richard A. Fredland, "Beyond Bounded Education," *Change* 13 (September, 1981): 37.

61. Ibid., p. 41.

62. Derek Bok, *Higher Learning* (Cambridge, MA.: Harvard University Press, 1986), p. 40.

63. Linda Ray Pratt, "Liberal Education and the Idea of the Postmodern University," *Academe* (November-December, 1994): 49.

64. Association of American Colleges, *Integrity in the College Curriculum,* pp. 23-24, 27-32.

65. Paul Woodring, *The Higher Learning in America: A Reassessment* (New York: McGraw-Hill, 1968), p. 201-205.

66. Note the discussion in Jan H. Blits, "The Search for Ends: Liberal Education and the Modern University," in Blits, ed., *The American University, Problems, Prospects and Trends* (Buffalo, NY: Prometheus, 1985), p. 92; and in Jacob Klein, "The Idea of Liberal Education," in Willis D. Weatherford, ed., *The Goals of Higher Education* (Cambridge, MA.: Harvard University Press, 1960), p. 35.

67. See Cameron, pp. 13, 15.

68. Pratt, p. 48.

69. Woodring, p. 201.

70. Blits, p. 93.

71. Rudolph H. Weingartner, *Undergraduate Education, Goals and Means* (New York: Macmillan, 1992), p. 2.

72. The analysis here follows Bok, pp. 40-42.

73. Ibid., p. 41.

74. W. B. Carnochan, *The Battleground of the Curriculum* (Stanford, CA: Stanford University Press), p. 117.

75. Note the discussions and polemics gathered together in Paul Berman, ed., *Debating P.C.: The Controversy Over Political Correctness on College Campuses* (New York: Dell Bantam Doubleday, 1992).

76. Hirsch, pp. xiii, 2.

77. Bloom, p. 249.

78. Mortimer R. Kadish, *Toward an Ethic of Higher Education* (Stanford, CA: Stanford University Press, 1991), p. 10.

79. Virginia Smith, "New Dimensions for General Education," in Arthur Levine, ed., *Higher Learning in America, 1980-2000* (Baltimore: Johns Hopkins University Press, 1993), pp. 243-258.

80. Martin Kaplan, "The Wrong Solution to the Right Problem," in James W. Hall, ed., *In Opposition to Core Curriculum, Alternative Models for Undergraduate Education* (Westport, CT: Greenwood Press, 1982), p. 4.

81. For example, consult the analysis supplied in James W. Hall with Barbara L. Kevles, "The Social Imperatives for Curricular Change in Higher Education," in Hall, pp. 13ff.

82. Ibid., p. 13.

83. David S. Saxon, "Science and Liberal Education: What Lies Ahead," in Blits, ed., p. 16.

84. Quoted by Martin Kaplan, "The Most Important Questions," in Hall, ed., p. 187.

85. Ibid., p. 187.

86. Ibid., pp. 190-191.

87. George C. Douglas, *Education Without Impact: How Our Universities Fail the Young* (New York: Birch Lane, 1992), p. 179.

88. William D. Schaefer, *Education Without Compromise: From Chaos to Coherence in Higher Education* (San Francisco: Jossey-Bass, 1990), p. 10.

89. Ibid., pp. 19-20.

90. Note the discussion in Weingartner, pp. 12ff.; in Schaefer, p. 22; and in Rosovsky, *The University: An Owner's Manual*, pp.105-107.

91. Douglas, p. xiii.

92. Patrick T. Terenzini and Ernest T. Pascarella, "Living with Myths, Undergraduate Education in America," *Change* 26 (January/February, 1994): 29, 31.

93. Ibid., p. 31.

94. Ibid., p. 31.

95. Douglas, p. 40.

Chapter V

1. Cameron Fincher, "The University in the 21st Century: An American Perspective," *British Journal of Educational Studies* 41 (March, 1993): 38.

2. See Patrick T. Terenzini and Ernest T. Pascarella, "Living with Myths: Undergraduate Education in America," *Change* 26 (January/February, 1994): 29, 31; and Rudolph H. Weingartner, "Between Cup & Lip, Reconceptualizing Education as Students Learning," *Educational Record* 75 (Winter, 1994): 13-19.

3. Fincher, p. 38.

4. Ibid., p. 39-40.

5. Ted Marchese, "What Our Publics Want, But Think They Don't Get, From a Liberal Arts Education," *AAHE Bulletin* 47 (November, 1994): 8-10.

6. Ibid., p. 8.

7. Ibid., p. 10.

8. Robert Solomon and Jon Solomon, *Up the University: Re-Creating Higher Education in America* (Reading, MA: Addison-Wesley, 1993), p. 3.

9. Raphael Sassower, "On Madness in the Academy," *Journal of Higher Education* 65 (July/August, 1994): 473-485.

10. Ibid., p. 474.

11. Solomon and Solomon, p. 3.

12. See Eugene Arden, "Is Tenure 'Obsolete'? An Opinion and a Survey," *Academe* 81 (January/February 1995): 38.

13. James E. Perley, "Tenure, Academic Freedom, and Governance," *Academe* 81 (January/February, 1995): 44.

14. Henry Rosovsky, *The University: An Owner's Manual* (New York: W. W. Norton, 1990), p. 177.

15. Quoted in Perley, p. 44.

16. Quoted in Paul Nuchims, "A Pastiche of Quotes and Ideas Leading to a Challenge," *Academe* 81 (January/February, 1995): 40.

17. Ibid., p. 40.

18. Rosovsky, pp. 179-180. The standard background reference is Richard Hofstadter and Walter P. Metzger, *The Development of Academic Freedom in the United States* (New York: Columbia University Press, 1955). Also useful is a study sponsored by the Commission on Academic Tenure in Higher Education: William R. Keast and John W. Macy, eds., *Faculty Tenure* (San Francisco: Jossey-Bass, 1973).

19. Keast and Macy, p. 127.

20. Hofstadter and Metzger, p. 395.

21. John S. Brubacher and Willis Rudy, *Higher Education in Transition,* 3rd ed. rev. (New York: Harper & Row, 1976), p. 371.

22. Hofstadter and Metzger, p. 137.

23. Keast and Macy, p. 133.

24. Ibid., p. 133.

25. H. L. Stewart, "Columbia University and the Liberties of the Citizen," *Nation* 105 (October 25, 1917): 452.

26. The full text of the AAUP's 1915 "Report of Committee A on Academic Freedom and Academic Tenure" first appeared in *School and Society* 3 (January 22, 1916): 109-121.

27. J. J. Stevenson, "Academic Unrest and College Control," *Scientific Monthly* 16 (May, 1920): 460.

28. Hofstadter and Metzger, p. 459.

29. Henry S. Canby, *Alma Mater: The Gothic Age of the American College* (New York: Farrar, Straus & Giroux, 1936), p. 153.

30. Page Smith, *Killing the Spirit: Higher Education in America* (New York: Viking Penguin, 1990), p. 115.

31. The full text of the AAUP's *1940 Statement of Principles,* accompanied by interpretive commentary, is supplied in Lester F. Goodchild and Harold S. Wechsler, eds., *ASHE Reader on the History of Higher Education* (Needham Heights, MA: Ginn, 1989), pp. 26-32.

32. Consult Joan Ward Mullaney and Elizabeth March Timberlake, "University Tenure and the Legal System: Procedures, Conflicts, and Resolutions," *Journal of Social Work Education* 30 (Spring/Summer, 1994): 172-184.

33. Ibid., p. 181. See also American Association of University Professors, *Policy Documents and Reports* (Washington, D.C.: American Association of University Professors, 1990), pp. 4ff.

34. Consult R. S. Brown and J. E. Kurland, "Academic Tenure and Academic Freedom," in W. Van Alsyne, ed., *Freedom and Tenure in the Academy* (Durham, NC: Duke University Press, 1993), pp. 325-356.

35. See Rosovsky, p. 181; and Arden, pp. 38-39.

36. Solomon and Solomon, p. 247.

37. Ibid., pp. 244-245.

38. Keast and Macy, p. 5.

39. See Smith, pp. 116-122.

40. Charles J. Sykes, *Profscam: Professors and the Demise of Higher Education* (Washington, D.C.: Regnery Gateway, 1988), p. 137.

41. Solomon and Solomon, p. 246.

42. Benjamin R. Barber, *An Aristocracy of Everyone: The Politics of Education and the Future of America* (New York: Ballantine, 1992), p. 196.

43. Note the discussion in John A. Centra, *Reflective Faculty Evaluation* (San Francisco: Jossey-Bass, 1993), p. 3.

44. See Lynne V. Cheney, *Tyrannical Machines: A Report on Educational Practices Gone Wrong and Our Best Hopes for Setting Them Right* (Washington, D.C.: National Endowment for the Humanities, 1990), p. 51; Bruce Wilshire, *The Moral Collapse of the University* (Albany, NY: State University Press of New York, 1990); Ernest L. Boyer, *Scholarship Reconsidered: Priorities of the Professoriate* (Princeton, NJ: Carnegie Foundation for the Advancement of Teaching, 1990); Derek Bok, "The Improvement of Teaching," *Teachers College Record* 93 (Winter, 1991): 236-251.

45. Jacques Barzun, *Begin Here: The Forgotten Conditions of Teaching and Learning* (Chicago: University of Chicago Press, 1991).

46. See Leslie H. Cocran, *Publish or Perish: The Wrong Issue* (Cape Girardeau, MO: StepUp, 1992), pp. 3-5.

47. Ruth Neumann, "Perceptions of the Teaching-Research Nexus: A Framework for Analysis," *Higher Education* 23 (1992): 159-171.

48. Ian C. Johnson, "Myth Conceptions of Academic Work," *Canadian Journal of Higher Education* 21 (1991): 108-116.

49. Quoted in Robert M. Diamond, "Changing Priorities and the Faculty Reward System," *New Directions for Higher Education* 81 (Spring, 1993): 7.

50. James S. Fairweather, "Faculty Reward Structures: Toward Institutional and Professional Homogenization," *Research in Higher Education* 34 (1993): 603-623.

51. Peter J. Gray, Robert C. Froh, and Robert M. Diamond, *A National Study of Research Universities: On the Balance Between Research and Undergraduate Teaching* (Syracuse, NY: Center for Instructional Development, Syracuse University, March 1992), p. 6. See also Carolyn J. Mooney, "Professors Feel Conflict Between Roles in Teaching and Research," *Chronicle of Higher Education* (May 8, 1991): A15.

52. Ernest Boyer, *College: The Undergraduate Experience in America* (New York: Harper & Row, 1987), p. 6.

53. "Syracuse Wants to Change the Academic Ethos to Place Greater Emphasis on Teaching," *Chronicle of Higher Education* 38 (March 25, 1992): A1, A14-15.

54. Bryan Barnett, "Teaching and Research Are Inescapably Incompatible," *Chronicle of Higher Education* 38 (June 3, 1992): A40.

55. "Syracuse," p. A15.

56. Gray, Froh, and Diamond, p. A15.

57. J. Scott Long, Paul D. Allison, and Robert McGinnis, "Rank Advancement in Academic Careers: Sex Differences and the Effects of Productivity," *American Sociological Review* 58 (October, 1993): 703-722.

58. Carolyn J. Mooney, "In 2 Years, a Million Refereed Articles, 30,000 Books, Chapters, Monographs," *Chronicle of Higher Education* 37 (May 22, 1991): A1, A13, A16.

59. L. Billard, "A Different Path into Print," *Academe* 79 (May-June, 1993): 28-29. See also Edward P. Corbett, "The Shame of the Current Standards for Promotion and Tenure," *Journal of Advanced Composition* 12 (Winter, 1992): 111-116.

60. Mary Kathryn Harrington, "Faculty Writing: Redirection and Renewal," *Innovative Higher Education* 16 (Winter, 1991): 187-196.

61. Gordon Fellman, "On the Fetishism of Publications and the Secrets Thereof," *Academe* 81 (January-February, 1995): 29.

62. Fairweather, p. 621.

63. E. Margaret Fulton, "Historical Commitments in New Times—Teaching and Research: Restructuring and Reorientation," in *The University into the 21st Century: An International Conference on Social and Technological Change* (Victoria, B.C.: University of Victoria, 1985), p. 297.

64. Paul Von Blum, *Stillborn Education: A Critique of the American Research University* (Lanham, MD: University Press of America, 1986), p. 51.

65. See David S. Webster, "Does Research Productivity Enhance Teaching?" *Educational Record* 66 (Fall, 1985): 60-62; and S. D. Neill, "No Significant Relationship Between Research and Teaching, Research Reveals," *University Affairs* 30 (April, 1989): 18.

66. See, for example, Robert A. McCaughey, "But Can They Teach? In Praise of College Professors Who Publish," *Teachers College Record* 95 (Winter, 1993): 242-257.

67. Johnson, p. 112.

68. Ibid., p. 113.

69. Smith, pp. 7, 20, 179, 197-198.

70. See George C. Douglas, *Education Without Impact: How Our Universities Fail the Young* (New York: Birch Lane, 1992), pp. 68-70, 85-89, 93, 95, 100-101.

71. Wilfred Cude, *The Ph.D. Trap* (West Bay, Nova Scotia: Medicine Label Press, 1987), p. 34.

72. Fellman, pp. 28, 30.

73. The analysis follows Fellman, pp. 29-32.

74. Ibid., pp. 28, 32.

75.   Robert M. Diamond, "Instituting Change in the Faculty Reward System," *New Directions for Higher Education* 81 (Spring, 1993): 13-22.

76.   Quoted in Boyer, *Scholarship Reconsidered*, p. 1.

77.   Robert M. Diamond, "The Tough Task of Reforming the Faculty-Rewards System," *Chronicle of Higher Education* 40 (May 11, 1994), pull-out section.

78.   Boyer, *Scholarship Reconsidered*, p. 16.

79.   Ibid., p. 24.

80.   "Syracuse," p. A15.

Chapter VI

1.   Cited in Chester E. Finn, Jr., "Context for Governance, Public Dissatisfaction and Campus Accountability," in Jack H. Schuster, Lynn H. Miller, et al., *Governing Tomorrow's Campuses, Perspectives and Agendas* (New York: American Council on Education/Macmillan, 1989), p. 183.

2.   Ibid., p. 183.

3.   Ibid., p. 184.

4.   Commission for Educational Quality, *Changing States: Higher Education and the Public Good* (Atlanta, GA: Southern Regional Education Board, 1994), p. 15.

5.   Association of Governing Boards of Universities and Colleges, *Ten Public Policy Issues for Higher Education in 1994* (Washington, D.C.: Association of Governing Boards of Universities and Colleges, 1994), pp. 8-9.

6.   Finn, p. 181. For a much broader and detailed interpretation involving governmental policies since World War II toward higher education, consult John W. Sommer, *The Academy in Crisis: The Political Economy of Higher Education* (New Brunswick, NJ: Transaction, 1995).

7.   Ibid., pp. 181-182.

8.   Ibid., p. 180.

9.   Association of Governing Boards, p. 7.

10.   Catherine Chambliss, *Reigniting the Flame: TQM Tactics for Faculty Rejuvenation* (Washington, D.C.: Educational Resources Information Center, ERIC ED 368 276, 1994), p. 2.

11.   Ibid., pp. 2-3.

12.   Ibid., p. 3.

13.   Shaila R. Aery, "Accountability and Assessment in Maryland Higher Education," *Maryland 2000: Journal of the Maryland Association for Institutional Research* (November, 1991): 22-24.

14.   See Craig A. Clagett, "Student Outcomes Performance Accountability Reports: A Prototype," *Maryland 2000: Journal of the Maryland Association for Institutional Research* (November, 1991): 14-21. A quite different perspective is offered by Gabrielle Baldwin, "The Student as Customer: The Discourse of 'Quality' in Higher Education," *Journal for Higher Education Management* 9 (Winter/Spring, 1994): 131-139.

15. Babak Armajami et al., *A Model for the Reinvented Higher Education System: State Policy and College Learning* (Denver, CO: Education Commission of the States, 1994), p. 2.

16. Refer to Peter Ewell, "Assessment: What's It All About," *Change* 17 (November/December, 1985): 35. See also Frederick E. Balderston, *Managing Today's University: Strategies for Viability, Change and Excellence,* 2nd ed. (San Francisco: Jossey-Bass, 1995), pp. 279-301.

17. LynNell Hancock with Claudia Kalb, "Returned for Credit," *Newsweek* (May 22, 1995): 44.

18. Ibid., p. 44.

19. See Kenneth P. Mortimer and T. R. McConnell, *Sharing Authority Effectively, Participation, Interaction, and Discretion* (San Francisco: Jossey-Bass, 1978), pp. 214-240; and Robert Berdahl, "Shared Governance and External Constraints," in Schuster, Miller, et al., pp. 176-179.

20. Consult Philip Kotler and Patrick E. Murphy, "Strategic Planning for Higher Education," in Marvin W. Peterson, ed., *Organization and Governance in Higher Education,* 4th ed. (Needham, MA: ASHE/Ginn, 1991), pp. 239-252.

21. Note the discussions in Barbara Sommer, "Recognizing Academe's Other Faculty," *Planning for Higher Education* 22 (Summer, 1994): 7-10; James E. Sayer, "More Self-Evident Truths for Departmental Governance," *Journal of the Association for Communication Administration* 1 (January, 1994): 47-49; Ernest Boyer et al., *The Academic Profession: An International Perspective, A Special Report* (Ewing, NJ: Carnegie Foundation for the Advancement of Teaching, 1994); Maurice Kogan et al., *Staffing Higher Education: Meeting New Challenges* (Bristol, PA: Project on Policies for Academic Staffing in Higher Education/Kingsley Publishers, 1994); and Ali M. Zargar, *TQM in a Multi-Campus Public University* (Washington, D.C.: Educational Resources Information Center, MF01/PC01, 1994).

22. Note the discussion in A. E. Austin and Z. F. Gamson, "Academic Workplace: New Demands, Heightened Tensions," *Association for the Study of Higher Education Report* No. 10 (1983): 32-35.

23. R. Eugene Rice and Ann E. Austin, "High Faculty Morale, What Exemplary Colleges Do Right," *Change* 20 (March/April, 1988): 51-58. See especially Andrew Halford, *Faculty Morale—Enhancing It in Spite of Diminishing Resources and Challenges* (Washington, D.C.: Educational Resources Information Center, ERIC ED 368 422, February, 1994), p. 5.

24. See Stanley Schmidt, "Deathwatch for Freedom," *Analog* 65 (July, 1995): 8; Robert K. Poch, *Academic Freedom in American Higher Education: Rights, Responsibilities and Limitations* (Washington, D.C.: Office of Educational Research and Improvement/School of Education and Human Development, George Washington University, 1994); and Neil Hamilton, *Zealotry and Academic Freedom* (New Brunswick, NJ: Transaction, 1995).

25. Commission for Educational Quality, p. 20.

26. Finn, p. 184.

27. Cited and discussed in Rita Kramer, *Ed School Follies: The Miseducation of America's Teachers* (New York: Free Press, 1991), p. 216.

28. Commission for Educational Quality, p. 19.

29. Ibid., pp. 19-20.

30. The discussion is adapted and summarized from John S. Brubacher and Willis Rudy, *Higher Education in Transition,* 3rd ed. (New York: Harper & Row, 1976), pp. 241-263.

31. Kramer, p. 212.

32. Commission for Educational Quality, pp. 25-26.

33. See Leon Botstein, "The Price We Must Pay," in Beatrice Gross and Ronald Gross, eds., *The Great School Debate* (New York: Simon & Schuster, 1985), p. 489.

34. Kramer, pp. 212-213.

35. Ibid., p. 214.

36. Larry A. Braskamp and John C. Ory, *Assessing Faculty Work: Enhancing Individual and Institutional Performance* (San Francisco: Jossey-Bass, 1994), p. xiii.

37. Ibid., pp. 12-13.

38. Denise K. Magner, "Report to Focus on Standards for Assessing What Professors Do," *Chronicle of Higher Education* 40 (February 9, 1994): A22.

39. Ibid., p. A22.

40. Note the discussion appearing throughout in Fred Antczak, *Learning and the Public Research University: Twenty-Two Suggestions for Reducing the Tension Between Teaching and Research* (Washington, D.C.: Educational Resources Information Center, MF0 /PC01, 1994). Relevant commentary appears also in David A. Verrier, "Perceptions of Life on the Tenure Track," *Thought and Action* 9 (Winter, 1994): 95-124; and in Judy A. Hughes et al., *Issues Affecting the Professoriate in the 1990s* (Washington, D.C.: Educational Resources Information Center, MF01/PC06, 1994).

41. Interestingly, in a sort of historical inversion, research was once considered a solitary pursuit engaged in by a single scholar locked away in the privacy of the laboratory or library archives. Teaching, on the other hand, was a public affair conducted for the benefit of anyone wishing to attend. Today the reverse seems to be true: Teaching behind closed doors is the norm, whereas research, sometimes involving teams of investigators, is the more public and open undertaking.

42. See Pat Hutchins, "Peer Review of Teaching, New Roles for Faculty," *AAHE Bulletin* 47 (November, 1994): 3-7.

43. Refer to William F. Massy et al., "Overcoming 'Hollowed' Collegiality," *Change* 26 (July/August, 1994): 11-20.

Chapter VII

1. Virginia Smith and Charles Karelis, "Considering the Public Interest, Part I," *Liberal Education* 81 (Spring, 1995): 9.

2. Cited in R. Heydinger and H. Simsek, *A Case Study of Faculty Workload Issues in Arizona* (Denver, CO: State Higher Education Executive Officers, 1992), p. 1.

3. Henry A. Allen, "Workload and Productivity in An Accountability Era," *NEA 1994 Almanac of Higher Education* (Washington, D.C.: National Education Association, 1994), pp. 25-26.

4. Ibid., p. 26.

5. For examples, see Jane L. Jervis, "The Ideal Academy," *Trusteeship* 3 (January/February, 1995): 22-25; and Ernst Benjamin, "Five Misconceptions About Tenure," *Trusteeship* 3 (January/February, 1995): 16-21.

6. Quoted in Arthur Chickering, "Considering the Public Interest, Part II," *Liberal Education* 81 (Spring, 1995): 18.

7. Chickering, p. 17.

8. Ibid., pp. 18-19.

9. Smith and Karelis, p. 10.

10. Chickering, p. 19.

11. See Robert A. Scott and Dorothy Echols Tobe, *The Seven Principles in Action: Improving Undergraduate Education* (Bolton, MA: Anker Publishing, 1995); Jacqueline Didler Maloney, "Elements and Issues in Planning Cross-Disciplinary Clusters from a Faculty Perspective," *Journal of General Education* 43 (1994): 73-80; Peg Downes and William H. Newell, "Overcoming Disciplinary Boundaries," *Liberal Education* 80 (Winter, 1994): 24-26; and Margaret Fieweger, "Strategy for Curricular Change," *Liberal Education* 80 (Winter, 1994): 34-35.

12. Alexander W. Astin, "What Matters in College," *Liberal Education* 79 (Fall, 1993): 4-15; George D. Kuh, "Ethos, Its Influence on Student Learning," *Liberal Education* 79 (Fall, 1993): 22-31; Kuh, "The Other Curriculum: Out-of-Class Experiences Associated with Student Learning and Personal Development," *Journal of Higher Education* 66 (March/April, 1995): 123-155; and Barbara Leigh Smith, "Creating Learning Communities," *Liberal Education* 79 (Fall, 1993): 32-39

13. Donald Stewart, "Considering the Public Interest, Part II," *Liberal Education* 81 (Spring, 1995): 12-17.

14. Ibid., p. 19. See also Daniel J. Brooks, "Evaluating The Center: Global Perspectivism and the Study Of Culture," *Journal of General Education* 44 (1995): 87-107.

SELECTED BIBLIOGRAPHY

Adams, Hazard. *The Academic Tribes.* 2nd ed. Urbana: University of Illinois Press, 1988.

American Association of University Professors. *Policy Documents and Reports.* Washington, D.C.: American Association of University Professors, 1990.

Anderson, Charles J. *A Fact Book on Higher Education.* New York: Macmillan, 1989.

Anderson, Martin. *Impostors in the Temple: American Intellectuals Are Destroying Our Universities and Cheating Our Students of Their Future.* New York: Simon and Schuster, 1992.

Armajami, Babak, et al. *A Model for the Reinvented Higher Education System: State Policy and College Learning.* Denver, CO: Education Commission of the States, 1994.

Ashby, Eric. *Any Person, Any Study.* New York: McGraw-Hill, 1971.

Association of American Colleges. *The Challenge of Connecting Learning.* Washington, D.C.: Association of American Colleges, 1990.

————. *Enhancing, Promoting, Extending Liberal Education: AAC at Seventy-Five.* Washington, D.C.: Association of American Colleges, 1988.

————. *Integrity in the College Curriculum.* Washington, D.C.: Association of American Colleges, 1985.

————. *New Vitality in General Education.* Washington, D.C.: Association of American Colleges, 1988.

Association of Governing Boards of Universities and Colleges. *Ten Public Policy Issues for Higher Education in 1994.* Washington, D.C.: Association of Governing Boards of Universities and Colleges, 1994.

Bagg, Lyman. *Four Years at Yale.* New Haven, CT: C. C. Chatfield, 1918.

Baker, George A., et al., eds. *A Handbook on the Community College in America: Its History, Mission,and Management.* Westport, CT.: Greenwood Press, 1994.

Balderston, Frederick E. *Managing Today's University, Strategies for Viability, Change and Excellence,* 2nd ed. San Francisco: Jossey-Bass, 1995.

Baldridge, J. Victor. *Power and Conflict in the University: Research in the Sociology of Complex Organizations.* New York: John Wiley & Sons, 1971.

Barber, Benjamin R. *An Aristocracy of Everyone, The Politics of Education and the Future of America.* New York: Ballantine, 1992.

Barzun, Jacques. *The American University: How It Runs, Where it is Going.* New York: Harper & Row, 1968.

————. *Begin Here: The Forgotten Conditions of Teaching and Learning.* Chicago: University of Chicago Press, 1991.

————. *The Culture We Deserve.* Middletown, CT: Wesleyan University Press, 1989.

————. *Teacher in America.* Indianapolis, IN: Liberty Press, 1981.

Bell, Daniel. *The Reforming of General Education.* New York: Columbia University Press, 1966.

Bender, Thomas. *Intellect and Public Life: Essays on the Social History of Academic Intellectuals in the United States.* Baltimore: Johns Hopkins University Press, 1993.

Benezet, Louis T. *General Education in the Progressive College.* New York: Teachers College, Columbia University Press, 1943.

Bennett, William J. *To Reclaim a Legacy: A Report on the Humanities in Higher Education.* Washington, D.C.: American Association for Higher Education, 1980.

Berelson, Bernard. *Graduate Education in the United States.* New York: McGraw-Hill, 1960.

Berman, Paul, ed. *Debating P.C.: The Controversy Over Political Correctness on College Campus.* New York: Dell Bantam Doubleday, 1992.

Bess, James L. ed. *Colleges and University Organizations: Insights from the Behavioral Sciences.* New York: New York University Press, 1984.

Blanshard, Brand. *The Uses of a Liberal Education.* LaSalle, IL: Open Court, 1973.

Blau, Peter M. *The Organization of Academic Work.* New York: John Wiley and Sons, 1973.

Blits, Jan H., ed. *The American University, Problems, Prospects and Trends.* Buffalo, NY: Prometheus, 1985.

Bloom, Alan. *Closing of the American Mind: How Higher Education has Failed Democracy and Impoverished the Souls of Today's Students.* New York: Simon and Schuster, 1987.

Bogue, Jesse P. *The Community College.* New York: McGraw-Hill, 1950.

Bok, Derek. *Beyond the Ivory Tower: Social Responsibilities of the Modern University.* Cambridge, MA: Harvard University Press, 1982.

———. *Higher Learning.* Cambridge, MA: Harvard University Press, 1986.

———. *Universities and the Future of America.* Durham. NC: Duke University Press, 1990.

Booth, Wayne C., ed. *The Knowledge Most Worth Having.* Chicago: University of Chicago Press, 1967.

Booth, Wayne. *Mere Rhetoric and the Search for Common Learning.* Washington, D.C.: Carnegie Foundation for the Advancement of Teaching, 1981.

Boucher, Chauncey S. *The Chicago College Plan.* Chicago: University of Chicago Press, 1935.

Bowen, William G., and Julie Ann Sosa. *Prospects for Faculty in the Arts and Sciences.* Princeton, NJ: Princeton University Press, 1989.

Boyer, Ernest L. *Campus Life: In Search of Community.* Princeton, NJ: Carnegie Foundation for the Advancement of Teaching, 1990.

———. *College: The Undergraduate Experience in America.* New York: Harper and Row, 1987.

———. *Scholarship Reconsidered: Priorities of the Professoriate.* Special Report of the Carnegie Foundation for the Advancement of Teaching. Princeton, NJ: Carnegie Foundation, 1990.

Boyer, Ernest, and Fred Hechinger. *Higher Learning in the Nation's Service.* Washington, D.C.: Carnegie Foundation for the Advancement of Teaching, 1981.

Boyer, Ernest, and Arthur Levine. *A Quest for Common Learning: The Aims of General Education*. New York: Carnegie Foundations for the Advancement of Teaching, 1961.

Boyer, Ernest, and Jack H. Schuster. *American Professors: A National Resource Imperiled*. New York: Oxford University Press, 1986.

Boyer, Ernest, et al. *The Academic Profession: An International Perspective, A Special Report*. Ewing, NJ: Carnegie Foundation for the Advancement of Teaching, 1994.

Braskamp, Larry A., and John C. Ory. *Assessing Faculty Work: Enhancing Individual and Institutional Performance*. San Francisco: Jossey-Bass, 1994.

Breneman, David W. *Liberal Arts Colleges: Thriving, Surviving, or Endangered?* Washington, D.C.: Brookings Institution, 1994.

Bromwich, David. *Politics by Other Means: Higher Education and Group Thinking*. New Haven, Conn.: Yale University Press, 1992.

Brubacher, John S. *Bases for Policy in Higher Education*. New York: McGraw-Hill, 1965.

Brubacher, John S., and Willis Rudy. *Higher Education in Transition*, 3rd ed. rev. New York: Harper & Row, 1976.

Burffee, Kenneth A. *Collaborative Learning: Higher Education, Interdependence, and the Authority of Knowledge*. Baltimore, MD: Johns Hopkins University Press, 1993.

Cahn, Stephen M. *The Eclipse of Excellence*. Washington, D.C.: Public Affairs Press, 1973.

Cahn, Stephen M., ed. *Affirmative Action and the University: A Philosophical Inquiry*. Philadelphia: Temple University Press, 1993.

Cameron, J.M. *On the Idea of ta University*. Toronto: St. Michael's College, University of Toronto Press, 1978.

Campus Compact. *The Project for Public and Community Service*. Denver: Education Commission of the States, 1995.

Canby, Henry S. *Alma Mater: The Gothic Age of the American College*. New York: Farrar, Straus & Giroux, 1936.

Carnegie Commission on Higher Education. *Priorities for Action: Final Report of the Carnegie Commission on Higher Education*. New York: McGraw Hill, 1973.

Carnegie Council on Policies Studies in Higher Education. *Selective Admissions in Higher Education*. San Francisco: Jossey-Bass, 1977.

————. *Three Thousand Futures: The Next Twenty Years for Higher Education*. San Francisco: Jossey-Bass, 1980.

Carnegie Foundation for the Advancement of Teaching. *Carnegie Foundation Technical Report: A Classification of Institutions of Higher Education*. Princeton, NJ: Carnegie Foundation for the Advancement of Teaching, 1987.

————. *The Condition of the Professoriate*. Washington, D.C.: Carnegie Foundation for the Advancement of Teaching, 1989.

————. *Missions of the College Curriculum*. San Francisco: Jossey-Bass, 1977.

Carnochan, W.B. *The Battleground of the Curriculum*. Stanford, CA: Stanford University Press, 1993.

Centra, John A. *Reflective Faculty Evaluation*. San Francisco, CA: Jossey-Bass, 1993.

Cheney, Lynne V. *50 Hours: A Core Curriculum for College Students*. Washington, D.C.: National Endowment for the Humanities, 1989.

———. *Humanities in America*. Washington, D.C.: National Endowment for the Humanities, 1988.

———. *Tyrannical Machines: A Report on Educational Practices Gone Wrong and Our Best Hopes for Setting Them Right*. Washington, D.C.: National Endowment for the Humanities, 1990.

Chronicle of Higher Education, eds. *Almanac of Higher Education 1994*. Chicago: University of Chicago Press, 1994.

Clark, Burton. R. *The Academic Life: Small Worlds, Different Worlds*. Lawrenceville, NJ: Princeton University Press, 1987.

———, ed. *The Academic Profession: National, Disciplinary, and Institutional Settings*. Berkeley: University of California Press, 1987.

Cohen, Michael D., and James G. March. *Leadership and Ambiguity: The American College President*. New York: McGraw-Hill, 1974.

Commission for Educational Quality. *Changing States: Higher Education and the Public Good*. Atlanta, GA: Southern Regional Education Board, 1994,.

Cottrell, Donald P. "General Education in Experimental Liberal Arts Colleges," in Guy Montrose Whipple, ed., *General Education in the American College, Part II, The Thirty-Eighth Yearbook of the National Society for the Study of Education*. Bloomington, IL: Public School Publishing Company, 1939, pp. 206-207.

Courts, Patrick L., and Kathleen H. McInerney. *Assessment in Higher Education*. Westport, CT: Praeger, 1993.

Cowley, W. H. and Don Williams. *International and Historical Roots of American Higher Education*. New York: Garland, 1991.

Crimmel, Henry H. *The Liberal Arts College and the Ideal of Liberal Education: The Case for Radical Reform*. Lanham, MD: University Press of America, 1993.

Cude, Wilfred. *The Ph.D. Trap*. West Bay, Nova Scotia: Medicine Label Press, 1987.

Damrosch, David. *We Scholars: Changing the Culture of the University*. Cambridge, MA: Harvard University Press, 1995.

Dewey, John. *The Educational Situation*. Chicago: University of Chicago Press, 1902.

Dickman, Howard, ed., *The Imperiled Academy*. New Brunswick, NJ: Transaction, 1993.

Dougherty, Kevin J. *The Contradictory College*. Albany: State University Press of New York, 1994.

Douglas, George C. *Education Without Impact, How Our Universities Fail the Young*. New York: Birch Lane, 1992.

Douglas, Mary. *How Institutions Think*. Syracuse, NY: Syracuse University Press, 1986.

Dressel, Paul L., and Lewis B. Mayhew. *General Education: Explorations in Evaluation*. Washington, DC: American Council on Education, 1954.

D'Souza, Dinesh. *Illiberal Education: The Politics of Race and Sex on Campus*. New York: Vintage, 1992.

Duffus, Robert L. *Democracy Enters College*. New York: Scribner, 1936.

Dziech, Billie Wright, and William F. Vilter, eds. *Prisoners of Elitism: The Community College's Struggle for Stature*. San Francisco: Jossey-Bass, 1992.

Earnest, Ernest. *Academic Procession: An Informal History of the American College, 1636-1953*. New York: Bobbs, Merrill, 1953.

Eddy, E. D., Jr. *Colleges for Our Land and Time: The Land Grant Idea in Education.* New York: Harper, 1956.

Eells, Walter C. *The Junior College.* Boston: Houghton Mifflin, 1936.

Eliot, Charles W. *Educational Reform.* Englewood Cliffs, NJ: Prentice-Hall, 1898.

Flexner, Abraham. *Universities, English, German, American.* Fair Lawn, NJ: Oxford University Press, 1930.

Foerster, Norman. *The American State University.* Chapel Hill: University of North Carolina Press, 1937.

Fraser, Mowat G. *The College of the Future.* New York: Columbia University Press, 1937.

Fretwell, Elbert K. *Founding Public Junior Colleges.* New York: Teachers College, Columbia University, 1954.

Frodin, Reuben. *The Idea and Practice of General Education.* Chicago: Chicago University Press, 1951.

Gaff, Jerry. "General Education for a Contemporary Context," in American Association for Higher Education, *New Models for General Education, Current Issues in Higher Education* No. 4. Washington, D.C.: American Association for Higher Education, 1980, pp. 1-5.

Getman, Julius. *In the Company of Scholars: The Struggle for the Soul of Higher Education.* Austin: University of Texas Press, 1992.

Goodchild, Lester F., and Harold S. Wechsler, eds. *ASHE Reader on the History of Higher Education.* Needham Heights, MA: Ginn, 1989.

Goodman, Paul. *The Community of Scholars.* New York: Random House, 1952.

Graff, Gerald. *Beyond the Culture Wars: How Teaching the Conflicts Can Revitalize American Education.* New York: W. W. Norton, 1992.

Grant, Gerald, and David Riesman. *The Perpetual Dream: Reform and Experiment in the American College.* Chicago: University of Chicago Press, 1978.

Gray, William S. *Provision for the Individual in College Education.* Chicago: University of Chicago Press, 1932.

Greene, Theodore. *Liberal Education Reconsidered.* New York: Cambridge University Press, 1953.

Habermas, Jürgen. *Knowledge and Human Interests.* Boston: Beacon Press, 1971.

Hall, James W., ed. *In Opposition to Core Curriculum; Alternative Models for Undergraduate Education.* Westport, CT: Greenwood Press, 1982.

Hamilton, Neil. *Zealotry and Academic Freedom.* New Brunswick, NJ: Transaction, 1995.

Harvard University Committee on the Objectives of a General Education in a Free Society. *General Education in a Free Society.* Cambridge, Mass.: Harvard University Press, 1945.

Haskell, Thomas, ed. *The Authority of Experts: Studies in History and Theory.* Bloomington: Indiana University Press, 1984.

Havemann, Ernest, and Patricia Salter West. *They Went to College: The College Graduate in America Today.* New York: Harcourt, Brace, 1952.

Heath, D.H. *Growing Up in College: Liberal Education and Maturity.* San Francisco: Jossey-Bass, 1968.

Henry, David Dodds. *Challenges Past, Challenges Present: An Analysis of American Higher Education Since 1930.* San Francisco: Jossey-Bass, 1975.

Henry, William A. *In Defense of Elitism.* New York: Doubleday, 1994.

Higham, John. "The Matrix of Specialization," in Alexandra Oleson and John Voss, eds., *The Organization of Knowledge in Modern America, 1860-1920.* Baltimore, MD: Johns Hopkins University Press, 1979, pp. 3-18.

Highet, Gilbert. *The Art of Teaching.* New York: Random House, 1954.

Hirsch, E.D., Jr. *Cultural Literacy: What Every American Needs to Know.* New York: Random House, 1987.

Hirsch, E.D., Jr., Joseph F. Kett, and James Trefil. *The Dictionary of Cultural Literacy: What Every American Needs to Know.* Boston: Houghton Mifflin, 1987.

Hoberman, Solomon, and Sidney Mailick. *Professional Education in the United States: Experiential Learning, Issues, and Prospects.* Westport, Conn.: Praeger, 1994.

Hodgkinson, H.L. *Institutions in Transition:A Study of Change in Higher Education.* Berkeley, CA: Carnegie Commission on Higher Education, 1970.

Hofstadter, Richard. *Anti-Intellectualism in American Life.* New York: Alfred A. Knopf, 1963.

Hofstadter, Richard, and C. DeWitt Hardy. *The Development and Scope of Higher Education in the United States.* New York: Columbia University Press, 1952.

Hofstadter, Richard, and Walter P. Metzger. *The Development of Academic Freedom in the United States.* New York: Columbia University Press, 1955.

Hofstader, Richard and W. Smith. *American Higher Education: A Documentary History.* Chicago: University of Chicago Press, 1961.

Hook, Sidney. *Academic Freedom and Academic Anarchy.* New York: Dell, 1969.

———. *Education for Modern Man: A New Perspective.* New York: Alfred A. Knopf, 1963.

Hook, Sidney et al., eds. *The Idea of a Modern University.* Buffalo, NY: Prometheus, 1974.

Horowitz, Helen Lefkowitz. *Campus Life: Undergraduate Culture from the End of the Eighteenth Century to the Present.* Chicago: University of Chicago Press, 1987.

Huber, Richard M. *How Professors Play the Cat Guarding the Cream: Why We're Paying More and Getting Less in Higher Education.* Lanham, MA: University Press of America, 1995.

Hughes, Judy A., et al. *Issues Affecting the Professoriate in the 1990s.* Washington, D.C.: Educational Resources Information Center, MF01/PC06, 1994.

Hutchins, Robert Maynard. *The Higher Learning in America.* New Haven, Conn.: Yale University Press, 1936.

———. *The Learning Society.* New York: Frederick A. Praeger, 1969.

Jacoby, Russell. *The Last Intellectuals: American Culture in the Age of Academe.* New York: Farrar, Straus and Giroux, 1987.

Jarausch, Konrad H., ed. *The Transformation of Higher Learning 1860-1930.* Chicago: University of Chicago Press, 1983.

Jaspers, Karl. *The Idea of the University,* ed. Karl Deutsch. London: Peter Owen, 1960.

Jencks, Christopher, and David Riesman. *The Academic Revolution.* 3d ed. Chicago: University of Chicago Press, 1987.

Johnston, J. S., Jr., et al. *Educating Managers: Executive Effectiveness through Liberal Learning.* San Francisco: Jossey-Bass, 1986.

Jordan, David Starr. *The Voice of the Scholar.* San Francisco: Paul Elder, 1903.

Kadish, Mortimer R. *Toward an Ethic of Higher Education.* Stanford, CA: Stanford University Press, 1991.

Kallen, Horace M. *The Education of Free Men.* New York: Farrar, Straus & Giroux, 1949.

Keast, William R. and John W. Macy, eds. *Faculty Tenure.* San Francisco: Jossey-Bass, 1973.

Kerr, Clark. *The Great Transformation in Higher Education, 1960-1980.* Albany: State University of New York Press, 1991.

————. *The Uses of the University,* 3rd ed. Cambridge, MA: Harvard University Press, 1982.

Kerr, Clark, et al. *The University in America.* Santa Barbara, CA: Center for the Study of Democratic Institutions, 1967.

Kerr, Clark, et al. *Troubled Times for American Higher Education.* Albany: State University of New York Press, 1994.

Kimball, Roger. *Tenured Radicals: How Politics has Corrupted Our Higher Education.* New York: Harper Perennial, 1991.

Kirk, Russell. *Decadence and Renewal in the Higher Learning.* South Bend, IN: Regnery, 1978.

Klitgaard, Robert. *Choosing Elites.* New York: Basic Books, 1985.

Koepplin, Leslie, and David Wilson, eds. *The Future of State Universities.* Elizabeth, NJ: Rutgers University Press, 1986.

Kogan, Maurice et al. *Staffing Higher Education: Meeting New Challenges.* Bristol, PA: Project on Policies for Academic Staffing in Higher Education/Kingsley Publishers, 1994.

Kramer, Rita. *Ed School Follies, the Miseducation of America' s Teachers.* New York: Free Press, 1991.

Lee, Calvin B. T. *The Campus Scene, 1900-1979.* New York: David McKay, 1970.

Levine, Arthur. *Handbook on Undergraduate Curriculum.* San Francisco: Jossey-Bass, 1978.

————. *Why Innovation Fails: The Institutionalization and Termination of Innovation in Higher Education.* Albany: State University of New York Press, 1980.

Levine, Arthur, ed. *Higher Learning in America, 1980-2000.* Baltimore, MD: Johns Hopkins Press, 1993.

Levine, David O. *The American College and the Culture of Aspiration, 1915-1940.* Ithaca, NY: Cornell University press, 1986.

Lewis, Lionel S. *Scaling the Ivory Tower: Merit and Its Limits in Academic Careers.* Baltimore, MD: Johns Hopkins Press, 1975.

Loeb, Paul R. *Generation at the Crossroads: Apathy and Action on the American Campus.* New Brunswick, NJ: Rutgers University press, 1994.

Lowell, A. Lawrence. *At War with Academic Traditions in America.* Cambridge, MD: Harvard University Press, 1934.

Lucas, Christopher J. *American Higher Education: A History.* New York: St. Martin's Press, 1990.

Lynton, Ernest. *Making the Case for Professional Service.* Washington, D.C.: American Association of Higher Education, 1995.

MacIver, Robert M. *Academic Freedom in Our Time.* New York: Columbia University Press, 1955.

Martin, Warren Bryan. *A College of Character.* San Francisco: Jossey-Bass, 1982.

Mayhew, Lewis B. *General Education: A Guide for Colleges.* New York: Harper & Row, 1960.

Mayhew, Lewis B., ed. *General Education: An Account and Appraisal.* New York: Harper and Row, 1960.

McConnell, T.R. "General Education: An Analysis," in Nelson B. Henry, ed. *General Education, the Fifty-First Yearbook of the National Society for the Study of Education, Part I.* Chicago: University of Chicago Press, 1952, pp. 4-13.

McConnell, T.R. et al. *From Elite to Mass to Universal Higher Education.* Berkeley: University of California Center for Research and Development in Higher Education, 1973.

McMurrin, Sterling M., ed. *On the Meaning of the University.* Salt Lake City: University of Utah Press, 1976.

Meiklejohn, Alexander. *The Experimental College.* New York: Harper & Row, 1932.

Metzger, Walter P. *Academic Freedom in the Age of the University.* New York: Columbia University Press, 1955.

Mieczkowski, Bogdan. *The Rat at the Top, Dysfunctional Bureaucracy in Academia.* Lanham, MA: University Press of America, 1995.

Miller, Gary. *The Meaning of General Education.* New York: Teachers College Press, 1988.

Miller, Lynn H., et al. *Governing Tomorrow's Campuses: Perspectives and Agendas.* New York: Macmillan, 1989.

Minnich, Elizabeth, Jean O'Barr, and Rachel Rosenfelds, eds. *Reconstructing the Academy: Women's Education and Women's Studies.* Chicago: University of Chicago Press, 1976.

Mitchell, Richard. *The Graves of Academe.* New York: McGraw-Hill, 1976.

Morrill, James L. *The Ongoing State University.* Minneapolis: University of Minnesota Press, 1960.

Morse, Horace T. "Liberal and General Education: A Problem of Differentiation," in James G. Rice, ed. *General Education, Current Ideas and Concerns.* Washington, D.C.: Association of Higher Education/National Education Association, 1964, pp. 7-12.

Mortimer, Kenneth P., and T. R. McConnell. *Sharing Authority Effectively: Participation, Interaction, and Discretion.* San Francisco: Jossey-Bass, 1978.

National Center for Education Statistics. *Projections of Education Statistics to 2003.* Washington, D.C.: United States Department of Education, Office of Educational Research and Improvement, 1992.

National Education Association, *NEA 1994 Almanac of Higher Education.* Washington, D.C.: National Education Association, 1994.

National Endowment for the Humanities. *A Survey of College Seniors: Knowledge of History and Literature.* Washington, D.C.: National Endowment for the Humanities, 1989.

National Institute of Education/American Association of Higher Education. *Contexts for Learning: The Major Sectors of American Higher Education.* Washington, D.C.: United States Government Printing Office, 1985.

Nevins, Allan. *The State Universities and Democracy.* Urbana: University of Illinois Press, 1962.

Newcomer, Mabel. *A Century of Higher Education for American Women.* New York: Harper & Brothers, 1959.

Niblett, W. R., ed. *Higher Education: Demand and Response*. San Francisco: Jossey-Bass, 1970.

Nisbit, Robert. *The Degradation of the Academic Dogma*. New York: Basic Books, 1971.

Oakeshott, Michael. *The Voice of Liberal Learning*. New Haven, CT: Yale University Press, 1989.

Ortega y Gasset, José. *Mission of the University*. London: Kegan Paul, 1946.

O'Toole, Simon. *Confessions of an American Scholar*. Minneapolis: University Of Minnesota Press, 1970.

Parsons, Talcott, and Gerald M. Platt. *The American University*. Cambridge, MA: Harvard University Press, 1973.

Pascarella, Ernest T., and Patrick T. Terenzini. *How College Affects Students*. San Francisco: Jossey-Bass, 1991.

Pelikan, Jaroslav. *The Idea of the University: A Reexamination*. New Haven, CT: Yale University Press, 1992.

Peterson, Marvin. W., ed. *Organization and Governance in Higher Education*, 4th ed. Needham, MA: ASHE Reader/Ginn Press, 1991.

Poch, Robert K. *Academic Freedom in American Higher Education: Rights, Responsibilities and Limitations*. Washington, D.C.: Office of Educational Research and Improvement/School of Education and Human Development, George Washington University, 1994.

Porter, Noah. *The American College and the American Public*, 2nd ed. New Haven, CT: Chatfield, 1870.

[Professor X]. *This Beats Working for a Living: The Dark Secrets of a College Professor*. New Rochelle, NY: Arlington House, 1973.

Rever, Philip, ed. *Open Admissions and Equal Access*. Iowa City, IA: American College Testing Program, 1971.

Rice, James G., ed. *General Education: Current Ideas and Concerns*. Washington, D.C.: Association for Higher Education/National Education Association, 1964.

Riesman, David. *On Higher Education: The Academic Enterprise in an Era of Rising Student Consumerism*. San Francisco: Jossey-Bass, 1980.

Robbins, Bruce, ed. *Intellectuals: Aesthetics, Politics, Academics*. Minneapolis: University of Minnesota Press, 1990.

——. *Secular Vocations: Intellectuals, Professionalism, Culture*. London: Verso, 1993.

Rosenwig, R.M. *Research Universities and Their Patrons*. Berkeley, CA: University of California Press, 1982.

Rosovsky, Henry. *The University, An Owner's Manual*. New York: W. W. Norton, 1990.

Ross, Earle D. "Contributions of Land-Grant Colleges and Universities to Higher Education," in William W. Brickman and Stanley Lehrer, eds., *A Century of Higher Education: Classical Citadel to Collegiate Colossus*. New York: Society for the Advancement of Education, 1962, pp. 94-109.

——. *Democracy's College: The Land-Grant Movement in the Formative Stages*. Ames: Iowa State College Press, 1942.

Rudolph, Frederick. *The American College and University: A History*. New York: Alfred A. Knopf, 1962.

————. *Curriculum: A History of the American Undergraduate Course of Study Since 1636*. San Francisco: Jossey-Bass, 1977.

Rudy, Willis. *The Evolving Liberal Arts Curriculum: A Historical Review of Basic Themes*. New York: Bureau of Publications, Teachers College, Columbia University, 1960.

Sanford, Nevitt. *The American College: A Psychological and Social Interpretation of Higher Learning*. New York: John Wiley & Sons, 1962.

Schaefer, William D. *Education Without Compromise: From Chaos to Coherence in Higher Education*. San Francisco: Jossey-Bass, 1990.

Schuster, Jack H., and Lynn H. Miller, et al. *Governing Tomorrow's Campuses, Perspectives and Agendas*. New York: American Council on Education/Macmillan, 1989.

Scott, Robert A., and Dorothy Echols Tobe. *The Seven Principles in Action: Improving Undergraduate Education*. Bolton, MA: Anker Publishing, 1995.

Seymour, Daniel. *Once Upon a Campus: Lessons for Improving Quality and Productivity in Higher Education*. Phoenix, AZ: Oryx Press, 1995.

Shaw, Peter. *The War Against Intellect: Episodes in the Decline of Discourse*. Iowa City: University of Iowa Press, 1989.

Sinclair, Upton. *The Goose-step*. Pasadena, CA.: , 1922.

Slossen, Edwin E. *Great American Universities*. New York: Macmillan, 1910.

Smith, Page. *Killing the Spirit, Higher Education in America*. New York: Penguin, 1991.

Smith, Thomas Verner. *The American Philosophy of Equality*. Chicago: University of Chicago Press, 1927.

Snyder, Thomas D., et al. *Digest of Educational Statistics 1993*. Washington, D.C.: National Center for Educational Statistics, October 1993.

Solomon, Robert, and John Solomon. *Up the University, Re-Creating Higher Education in America*. Reading, MA: Addison-Wesley, 1993.

Sommer, John W. *The Academy in Crisis, The Political Economy of Higher Education*. New Brunswick, NJ: Transaction, 1995.

Storr, Richard J. *The Beginnings of Graduate Education in America*. Chicago: University of Chicago Press, 1953.

Study Group on the Conditions of Excellence in American Higher Education. *Involvement in Learning: Realizing the Potential of American Higher Education*. Washington, D.C.: National Institute on Education, 1984.

Sykes, Charles. *The Hollow Men: Politics and Corruption in Higher Education*. Washington, D.C.: Regnery Gateway, 1990.

————. *Profscam: Professors and the Demise of Higher Education*. Washington, D.C.: Regnery Gateway, 1988.

Tappan, Henry P. *University Education*. New York: Putnam's, 1851.

Taylor, Harold. *Students without Teachers*. New York: McGraw-Hill, 1969.

Thelin, John R. *Higher Education and Its Useful Past*. Cambridge, MA: Schenkman, 1982.

Thomas, Russell. *The Search for a Common Learning: General Education, 1800-1960*. New York: McGraw-Hill, 1962.

Tierney, William G. *Building Communities of Difference, Higher Education in the Twenty-First Century*. Westport, CT: Praeger, 1993.

Trilling, Lionel. *Beyond Culture*. New York: Viking Press, 1968.

United States Bureau of the Census. *School Enrollment—Social and Economic Characteristics of Students: October, 1991, Current Population Reports, Series P-20, No. 469.* Washington, D.C.: United States Government Printing Office, 1993.

Van Alsyne, W., ed. *Freedom and Tenure in the Academy.* Durham, NC: Duke University Press, 1993.

Van Doren, Mark. *Liberal Education.* Boston: Beacon Press, 1959.

Veblen, Thorstein. *The Higher Learning in America.* New Haven, CT: Yale University Press, 1962.

Veysey, Laurence R. *The Emergence of the American University.* Chicago: University of Chicago Press, 1965.

Von Blum, Paul. *Stillborn Education: A Critique of the American Research University.* Lanham, MD: University Press of America, 1986.

Walters, Raymond. *Four Decades of U.S. Collegiate Enrollments.* New York: Society for the Advancement of Education, 1960.

Weatherford, Willias D. ed. *The Goals of Higher Education.* Cambridge, MA: Harvard University Press, 1960.

Weaver, David Andrew, ed. *Builders of American Universities: Inaugural Addresses.* Alton, IL: Shurtleff Press, 1950.

Wechsler, Harold S. *The Qualified Student: A History of Selective College Admission in America: Eighth Yearbook of the National Society of Education.* Bloomington, IL: Public School Publishing Company, 1939.

Wegener, C. *Liberal Education and the Modern University.* Chicago: University of Chicago Press, 1978.

Weingartner, Rudolph H. *Undergraduate Education, Means and Goals.* New York: Macmillan, 1992.

West, Andrew. *A Review of President Eliot's Report on Elective Studies.* New York: J.K. Lees, 1886.

Whitehead, Alfred North. *The Aims of Education and Other Essays.* New York: Free Press, 1967.

Wilshire, Bruce. *The Moral Collapse of the University.* Albany: State University Press of New York, 1990.

Wilson, Logan. *American Academics: Then and Now.* New York: Oxford University Press, 1979.

Winter, David G. et al. *A New Case for the Liberal Arts.* San Francisco: Jossey-Bass, 1981.

Witt, Allen A. et al., *America's Community Colleges: The First Century.* Washington, D.C.: American Association of Community Colleges, 1994.

Wolff, Robert Paul. *The Ideal of the University.* Boston: Beacon Press, 1969.

Woodring, Paul. *The Higher Learning in America: A Reassessment.* New York: McGraw-Hill, 1968.

Woody, Thomas. *History of Women's Education in the United States,* 2 vols. Lancaster, PA: Science Press, 1929.

INDEX